INSIGHT GUIDE

PRAGUE

Discovery CHANNEL

APA PUBLICATIONS **L**

Part of the Langenscheidt Publishing Group

ABOUT THIS BOOK

Editorial
Project Editor
Cameron Duffy
Editorial Director
Brian Bell

Distribution

UK & Ireland
GeoCenter International Ltd
The Viables Centre , Harrow Way
Basingstoke, Hants RG22 4BJ
Fax: (44) 1256-817988

United States
Langenscheidt Publishers, Inc.
46–35 54th Road, Maspeth, NY 11378
Fax: (718) 784-0640

Canada
Prologue Inc.
1650 Lionel Bertrand Blvd., Boisbriand
Québec, Canada J7H 1N7
Tel: (450) 434-0306. Fax: (450) 434-2627

Australia & New Zealand
Hema Maps Pty. Ltd.
24 Allgas Street, Slacks Creek 4127
Brisbane, Australia
Tel: (61) 7 3290 0322. Fax: (61) 7 3290 0478

Worldwide
Apa Publications GmbH & Co.
Verlag KG (Singapore branch)
38 Joo Koon Road, Singapore 628990
Tel: (65) 865-1600. Fax: (65) 861-6438

Printing

Insight Print Services (Pte) Ltd
38 Joo Koon Road, Singapore 628990
Tel: (65) 865-1600. Fax: (65) 861-6438

©1999 Apa Publications GmbH & Co.
Verlag KG (Singapore branch)
All Rights Reserved

First Edition 1989
Fifth Edition 1999

CONTACTING THE EDITORS
Although every effort is made to
provide accurate information, we
live in a fast-changing world and
would appreciate it if readers
would call our attention to any
errors or outdated information
that may occur by writing to us:
Insight Guides, P.O. Box 7910,
London SE1 8WE, England.
Fax: (44 171) 403-0290.
insight@apaguide.demon.co.uk

This guidebook combines the interests and enthusiasms of two of the world's best known information providers: Insight Guides, whose titles have set the standard for visual travel guides since 1970, and Discovery Channel, the world's premier source of non-fiction television programming.

Insight Guides editors provide practical advice and general understanding about a destination's history, culture, institutions and people. Discovery Channel and its wide-ranging website, www.discovery.com, help millions of viewers explore their world right from the comfort of their own home and also encourage them to explore it firsthand.

Prague has been at the forefront of Europe since the Middle Ages, when it was the residence of the Holy Roman Emperor. Over the centuries, however, its history has been marked by turmoil and political machinations, the most powerful of which was the stark Communist regime from 1948 to 1989. Emerging from this restrictive way of life, Prague has now found itself Central Europe's favourite city with tourists flocking to take in the preserved architecture and atmosphere that was out of bounds for so long.

How to use this book

The book is structured to guide readers through Prague's sights and culture:

◆ The **History** and **Features** sections, with a yellow colour bar, cover the city's past and culture in lively essays written by specialists.

◆ The main **Places** section, with a blue bar, gives a run-down of all the attractions worth seeing in central Prague and its suburbs. The principal places of interest are cross-referenced by numbers or letters to specially commissioned colour maps.

◆ The **Travel Tips** listings section provides easy-to-find information on such things as transport, hotels, restaurants, sports and shopping. You can locate information quickly by using the index printed on the back cover flap, which is also designed to serve as bookmarks.

◆ The **photographs** are chosen not only to illustrate attractions but also to convey the many moods of Prague and its people.

The contributors

This thoroughly revised edition of *Insight Guide: Prague* has been edited by Insight Guides staffer **Cameron Duffy** and **Zoë Ross**, a freelance editor and writer of travel guides, and builds on the earlier editions, edited by **Joachim Chwaszcza** and **Pam Barrett**.

Martha Lagace, a Prague-based American writer, and a regular contributor to the weekly English-language Prague Post has fully updated and revised the text to convey the rapidly changing face of Prague. She produced new chapters on modern Prague and cultural festivals and fully updated most of the remaining sections. Another American in Prague, **Mimi Fronczak Rogers,** updated the avant-garde architecture, food and pubs and bars chapters and wrote the four pictorial features.

This team retained much of the text of the original contributors, who included **Joachim and Christine Chwaszcza, Eva Meschede, Ota Filip, Vilem Wagner, Johanna von Herzongenberg, Frantisek Kafka** and **Franz Peter Künzel.**

Many of the photographs are the work of **Bodo Bondzio,** who is married to a native of Prague, and **Lesley Player.**

Map Legend

–––– ·· –	International Boundary
⊖	Border Crossing
–·–·–	National Park/Reserve
ⓦ	Metro
✈ ✈	Airport: International/ Regional
🚌	Bus Station
P	Parking
❶	Tourist Information
✉	Post Office
🏰 † ✝	Church/Ruins
†	Monastery
☪	Mosque
✡	Synagogue
🏰 🏚	Castle/Ruins
∴	Archaeological Site
∩	Cave
⒈	Statue/Monument
★	Place of Interest

The main places of interest in the Places section are coordinated by number with a full-colour map (e.g. ❶), and a symbol at the top of every right-hand page tells you where to find the map.

INSIGHT GUIDE
PRAGUE

CONTENTS

A map of Prague is also on the inside front cover. A map of Greater Prague is on the inside back cover.

LILIOVÁ
STARÉ MĚSTO-PRAHA 1

Prague Castle dominates the city

Information panels

Insight on ...

Places

Travel Tips

◆ Full Travel Tips index
   is on page 257

THE HEART OF EUROPE

The exuberance that followed the collapse of communism
was contagious. But can Prague maintain its momentum?

Going to Prague is fun. Wherever you wander in the city, you can sense the spirit of optimism. Of course, you're bound to encounter a certain amount of scepticism about the future: after decades of socialist mismanagement, it is clear that a complete economic recovery is still years away. But despite this, and despite the break-up of the Federal Republic into separate Czech and Slovak states, Prague, the Golden City, is, through all appearances, now regaining its old confidence.

Life on the streets has changed. Since the momentous Velvet Revolution at the end of 1989, the arts, great and small, have once more found their place in the open. Theatre, music, exhibitions, debates – all the things that Prague residents used to long for – are now possible. Not that this is anything new – Czechs, among others, have been leading European culture for much of the modern era. Before 1939 Prague's Cubist movement was second only to Paris .

Hordes of tourists have descended, all eager to see the changes for themselves. Yet despite this invasion, Prague essentially remains a Bohemian city. While its legendary days as a European centre of writers and artists have all but vanished, much of the former ambience has been preserved. There are magical squares, beautifully preserved, with their mysterious play of light and shadow, with music on every corner. And there are narrow streets where it is almost possible to imagine that Rabbi Löw's Golem, the clay monster which came to life, might still be lurking somewhere, out of sight.

Prague is not a fashionable city like Paris or Rome, but there are modern elements, and the new policies have brought about discernible changes. But the charm of the city doesn't rest in elegant shops or newly renovated restaurants. It stems far more from the atmosphere seeping from the narrow alleyways of the Malá Strana, from the Baroque palaces and churches, and of course from Hradčany (Prague Castle), the mighty castle complex that has dominated the city for almost 1,000 years.

Prague's great cultural tradition has worked for centuries to mould this city and its people, and continues to exert a fascination. There is much which is still in poor condition and it will be years before the Czech economy recovers completely from the socialist era. Restored areas such as the Old Town Square and the well-stocked luxury shops on Wenceslas Square, Na Příkopě and Pařížská cannot completely disguise this. But the first decisive steps have been taken. Prague has once again found its place at the heart of Europe.   ❏

PRECEDING PAGES: painting the city; crossing Old Town Square; crowd's attention focused in Old Town Square; façade of the Palais Cernín.
LEFT: band player blowing his trumpet.

Decisive Dates

EARLY HISTORY AND PREMYSLIDS

c. 400 BC A Celtic tribe, the Boii, invade the area and give it the name Bohemia.

AD 400 The Slavs come to the area.

700 A Frankish merchant named Samo establishes the first state in the area.

900 The Přemyslid dynasty rules Bohemia for 500 years and builds the first castle in Prague.

935 Prince Wenceslas is murdered by his brother Boleslav I. He becomes the patron saint of Bohemia.

973 The bishopric of Prague is founded.

1085 Prince Vladislav is proclaimed the first king of Bohemia by Emperor Henry IV.

1158 Vladislav II becomes King Vladislav I; he founds the Strahov Monastery and builds the first stone bridge, the Judith Bridge, across the Vltava.

1173–78 Prince Soběslav II affords equal rights to the German settlers and awards special privileges to German merchants.

1197 Přemsyl Otakar II rules and the privileges of the Bohemian kings are extended by Emperor Frederick II.

1231 Wenceslas I extends and fortifies the Old Town.

1253 Bohemia conquers most of Austria and becomes a major power.

1257 The Malá Strana is granted a town charter.

1278 Přemsyl Otakar II is killed in battle against Rudolf of Habsburg.

1306 Young King Wenceslas II is murdered, ending the Přemyslid dynasty.

THE GOLDEN AGE AND HUSSITE WARS

1310 King John of Luxembourg marries the Přemyslid princess Elizabeth and founds the Luxembourg dynasty. He builds the cathedral.

1344 Prague becomes an archbishopric.

1348 King Charles I (later Emperor Charles IV) founds Prague's university and brings in the city's Golden Age. He also plans the New Town area.

1352 Architect Peter Parler works on St Vitus' Cathedral, and carves Charles IV statue in stone.

1393 King Wenceslas IV has John of Nepomuk thrown into the Vltava from Charles Bridge.

1398 Jan Hus begins preaching about church reforms at the Bethlehem Chapel.

1400 The Electoral Princes depose King Wenceslas.

1409 German professors dispute the teachings of Jan Hus and move to Leipzig to found a new university.

1415 Jan Hus is burned at the stake.

1419 Hussites, led by Jan Želivský, throw members of the King's Council from a window in the New Town Hall (the First Defenestration) and begin Hussite Wars.

1420 At the Battle of Vítkov the Hussites, led by Jan Žižka, repel the armies of Emperor Sigismund.

1420 The Hussites divide into two groups – Utraquists and Taborites.

1433 Hussites compromise with the Catholic Church.

1458 The leader of the Utraquists, George of Poděbrady, becomes king of Bohemia.

1471 The Jagiellon kings of Poland – Vladislav II and Louis – take over the rule of Bohemia.

1526 Louis is killed at the Battle of Mohács in Hungary and the Bohemian throne passes to the Habsburgs, with Ferdinand I.

THE HABSBURGS

1576 Emperor Rudolf II returns Prague to an imperial residence and another Golden Age. The city becomes a centre for artists and scientists.

1609 Rudolf's "Letter of Majesty" grants Bohemian estates freedom of religious worship.

1618 Archduke Ferdinand goes against the "Letter of Majesty". Two governors and their secretary are thrown out of a window in Hradčany (the Second Defenestration) and the Thirty Years' War begins.

1620 At the Battle of White Mountain the Bohemian states are defeated by the Catholic forces; Emperor Ferdinand orders the execution of the leaders of the uprising, and Protestants go into exile.

1680 Bohemian peasants revolt against the feudal government. Baroque art spreads through the city.

GERMAN CONTROL: 1740–1945
1740 In the War of Austrian Succession, armies of Bavaria, Saxony and France capture Prague. Maria Theresa becomes Empress.
1757 Prussian forces attack Prague for seven weeks. Maria Theresa repairs the damage to the city and has Prague Castle extended.
1781 Serfdom is abolished in Bohemia, and Prague's Jewish community, under the rule of Joseph II, are awarded civic rights. They name their area Josefov in honour of the Emperor.
1784 Independent towns of Prague are amalgamated.
1833 The Industrial Revolution comes to Prague and increases the number of Czech workers.
1848 Czechs have been fighting for their right to their own language and culture. A Slavic Congress meets in Prague, led by František Palacký. An uprising of the proletariat is crushed by Austrian forces.
1866 The war between Austria and Prussia ends, and Bohemia withdraws from the German alliance.
1881 The Czech National Theatre opens with a performance of Smetana's *Libuše*. Dvořák and Janáček are two more composers who gain international recognition.
1914 At the start of World War I, Tomáš Garrigue Masaryk goes into exile, but begins to gain support for a united Czechoslovakia.
1918 The Republic of Czechoslovakia is proclaimed on 28 October. Tomaš Garrigue Masaryk becomes the first president, and Edvard Beneš is Foreign Minister.
1935 Edvard Beneš succeeds the ailing Masaryk as the country's president.
1938 The Munich Agreement cedes the Sudetenland to Germany.
1939 Hitler organises his troops to occupy Czechoslovakia, and the Reich Protectorate of Bohemia and Moravia is proclaimed, led by Reinhard Heydrich.
1941 Heydrich is assassinated, and the village of Lidice is obliterated in revenge. The Nazis murder all male inhabitants of the village, deport the women and children, and raze the village to the ground.

COMMUNISM
1945 The Russian Red Army occupies Prague. Sudeten Germans are dispossessed and deported, and more than 240,000 die in the process.

PRECEDING PAGES: the city in 1493, by the River Vltava
LEFT: a portrait of the great reformer, Jan Hus.
RIGHT: Czech President Vaclev Havel, February 1999.

1948 Czechoslovakia becomes a People's Republic. On 7 June Beneš resigns as president and is succeeded by Klement Gottwald. Foreign minister Jan Masaryk, as the only non-Communist, is found dead and suicide is suspected.
1960 The People's Republic becomes the Socialist Republic under a new constitution.
1968 Alexander Dubček becomes Secretary General of the Communist Party and attempts to instigate "Socialism with a human face". Armies from five member states of the Warsaw Pact invade to show their disapproval.
1969 Czechoslovakia becomes a Federal State.
1977 Civil rights group "Charter 77" is founded.

1989 The Velvet Revolution led by mass demonstrations and strikes forces the government to resign. Václav Havel becomes president of the new democratic government, and Communists are banned from participating in government.

THE NEW REPUBLIC
1990 The country changes its name to Czech and Slovak Federal Republic.
1992 Slovakia declares its independence and Havel resigns. Two countries – Slovakia and the Czech Republic – are formed as of 1 Jan 1993.
1993 Václav Havel is re-elected president; the Czech Republic enters a period of commercial boom.
1999 The Czech Republic joins NATO.   ❏

LIBUSE AND THE BOHEMIAN KINGS

From the first romantic and mythical dynasty to the first dukes and kings,
Prague began to develop into a centre of European trade

The foundation of Prague is surrounded by myth. According to legend, Princess Libuše, ruler of a Slavic tribe which had always been led by women, chose a humble ploughman, Přemysl, as her husband. She instructed him to seek out a village on the banks of the Vltava and to found a city there, for which she prophesied great things. According to the legend, Přemysl led a group of followers to the place Libuše described and there founded the Golden City of Prague.

The rise of the Premyslid dynasty

Legend apart, archaeologists confirm that the Prague area has been inhabited since Neolithic times. Celts settled here around 500 BC, Germanic tribes joined them about five centuries later, and Slavs arrived in the 6th century AD. Power struggles were waged for several centuries, and it is probably the emergence of the Přemyslids as the ruling dynasty that engendered the myth of Princess Libuše and the ploughman. The evolution of the city as the political and cultural centre of Bohemia is tied with the rise to power of this dynasty. The battle for supremacy in the Bohemian and Moravian regions between the Slavníkovci and the Přemyslids was won by the latter towards the end of the 9th century. Their rulers moved to a strategic rocky outcrop on the right bank of the Vltava, and built their first stronghold.

Settlements developed in the area below, at first inhabited by people directly supplying the castle, but later by craftsmen. In the early 10th century the Vyšehrad was built, on the same bank of the Vltava (*see page 207–209*), but some distance south of the old castle. The Hradčany was founded later, on an equally commanding left-bank site (*see page 123*). The Přemyslids consolidated a political base as the nucleus of the Bohemian state. Prague quickly became an important centre for trade.

LEFT: a group of figures in the Vyšehrad which portray the Libuše legend.
RIGHT: the bejewelled crown of Bohemia.

Founding of the bishopric

A decisive point in the development of Prague was the success of Boleslav II (967–1035) in obtaining the consent of the Holy Roman Emperor for the founding of a bishopric in AD 973. The first bishop was the monk Adalbert, appointed in AD 982. Adalbert was forced to

flee Prague on several occasions and died in Poland. His relics were seized by Boleslav's successor, Břetislav I (1035–55), and brought back to the city. The plan to use the relics to raise the status of Prague's cathedral failed, but Prague greatly increased in international importance during Břetislav's reign. His greatest achievement was the union of Moravia and Bohemia, although he was forced to recognise his dependence on the German empire.

Břetislav's successor Spytihněv II (1055–61) expelled German merchants from Prague and built St Vitus' basilica. His successor, Duke Vratislav I (1061–92), proved an ally of Henry IV, who made him King of Bohemia.

Market place of Prague

Prague market place is first documented in the late 11th century. It was situated in the area of the Old Town Square (Staroměstské náměstí). In the early 12th century this began to develop into a settlement, becoming known as the Old Town (Staré Město). In the ensuing construction boom, the Romanesque style spread, as the churches dating from this time show.

Soběslav I (1125–40) completed the alterations to the Vyšehrad, begun by Vratsilav II. The Romanesque churches and the castle citadel were completed and the clay walls replaced with stone fortifications. Soběslav also encouraged

the expansion of trade. Under his patronage, the Vyšehrad Cathedral Chapter produced the Vyšehrad Codex, a richly decorated manuscript.

Vladislav II (1140–72), known as Vladislav I after his coronation as King of Bohemia, moved the ruler's residence to Hradčany. He built a royal palace and extended St Vitus'. Strahov Monastery was built in 1140.

King Pšemysl Otakar I (1198–1230) completed the building of the stone Judith Bridge (begun in 1170, in about the same place as today's Charles Bridge), creating a permanent link between the castle and the Old Town. On the opposite bank he also founded the community which is known as Malá Strana, which became the home of skilled workers, carters and fishermen. Bohemia rose to become an important Central European power and Prague an international meeting place. Long-distance trade had been re-routed along the Danube and also through Vienna, but local needs and the trade in luxury goods more than made up for the shortfall.

Extraordinary privilege

By 1230 the Old Town had been given borough status and, in 1231, King Wenceslas I (1230– 53) defended it with a system of walls and fortifications. The building of a city wall was a sign of extraordinary privilege: it protected it from outside attack and bestowed freedom on its citizens, encouraging people to settle here.

The Old Town remained under the jurisdiction of a judge appointed by the king, and was administered by a council. The judge and the councillors were elected by patrician families (nobility and land-owners).

The first guilds arose in the Old Town towards the end of the 13th century. The Jewish quarter was ruled by the king. The Malá Strana was granted the privileges of a city in 1257. Hradčany was next: it developed as the quarter of the aristocracy and clergy, receiving a city charter and walls in 1320. At the beginning of the 14th century, Prague was composed of three towns, each administratively independent and socially and demographically different. In 1300 it is estimated that Prague covered an area of 120 hectares (300 acres), the Old Town occupying 80 hectares (200 acres). ❏

GOOD KING WENCESLAS

One of the early princes of the Přemyslid dynasty was St Wenceslas, the patron saint of Czechoslovakia and the "Good King Wenceslas" of the Christmas carol – although there is little truth to the song and he was never king. He put his duchy under the protection of King Henry the Fowler of Germany, and encouraged German missionaries to come to Bohemia, but was then murdered by his pagan brother Boleslav ("the Cruel") in about AD 935. Boleslav's rule (936–67) saw Bohemia consolidating itself against the German threat. But after the expulsion of the Magyars, it cultivated its connections to the west, extending as far as Rome.

LEFT: statue on tomb of Ottokar I, St Vitus Cathedral.
RIGHT: The Golden Bull, an early manuscript.

ncipit aurea bul
la imperialium con
stitutionum · et pri
mo inuocto adsum
mum creatorem · o

patris
eterni
deus
spes
uni

ca mundi · Qui celi
fabricator ades qui
editor orbis · Tu po
puli memor esto tu
i sic nutris ab alto i
prospice ne gressu
faciat ubi regnat e
ternus · Imperat illi
to leges dictante re
geta · Sed precibus v
tere tui quem dili
gis huius · Cesaris
insignis karoli de
us alme inuicta

Ut ualeat ductore
pio peramena uir
cta · Florentium sy
ne morum sedesq;
ieratas · Ad latices
uitate pios ubi se
mina uite · Diuini

animantur aquis
a fonte supno · Pet
ficata leges spiritus
mundatur ademp
tis · Ut messis que
at esse dei mercesq;
tutur · Maxima re
tenum cumulare i
per uorrea fructus

THE IMPERIAL CAPITAL

The 14th century provided unprecedented prosperity for Prague, led by the visionary Charles IV. But things were soon to change for the worse

From the middle of the 13th century the fortunes of Bohemia and therefore of Prague had been determined by the political and military successes of King Přemysl Otakar II (1253–78). His power, which rested on the vast wealth derived from the silver mines of Bohemia, rose steadily until he reached a position of hegemony in Central Europe. He advanced into Hungary and Slovakia and pushed the frontiers of Bohemia as far as the Adriatic. He won the respect of both the pope and the emperor, but then died at the battle of Dürnkrut fighting Rudolf of Habsburg, who considered the Czech king his greatest rival. The crisis concerning succession was partially alleviated when the claims of King Wenceslas II to the Polish throne were recognised. For a while Henry of Carinthia, Wenceslas II's brother-in-law, ruled, then Rudolf of Habsburg, then Henry again. The Přemyslid dynasty finally died when the young Wenceslas III, the last of the line, was assassinated in 1306 during his Polish campaign.

The times were marked by political power struggles, in which the patrician families of Prague took part, with varied success. The city was besieged, laid waste and plundered several times. In 1310, the Bohemian Estates chose John of Luxembourg (1296–1346) as their new king. The same year he married Elizabeth, the daughter of Wenceslas II, and when he stood with his army at the city walls on 3 December he met no resistance. John was intensely – and expensively – involved in imperial politics and spent most of his time out of the country. Prague castle gradually fell into decay.

Emperor Charles IV

John's son, who would become Charles IV, was born in Prague in 1316 and spent his early years there. But in 1323 he was sent to Paris to the court of his uncle, the king of France, where his education was entrusted to the future Pope Clement VI. Young Charles fell in love with all things French and abandoned his baptismal name of Wenceslas and adopted that of Charlemagne ("Charles the Great"), after his role model and personal patron. He studied at the University of Paris and travelled through

Europe, absorbing the languages and cultures of the various nations. He later married Blanche of Valois, who was equally worldly and cultured.

Charles' early years were marred by a tempestuous relationship with his father, which at one point led him to enter the service of the Doge of Venice and lead an army of mercenaries. But a reconciliation followed, and in 1633, aged 17, he was made governor of Bohemia and Moravia. In spite of his age, Charles had gained experience from his travels and education, and he dedicated himself to bringing prosperity to the country. One of his first acts was to rebuild Prague Castle, remodelling it on buildings he had admired in France.

LEFT: Emperor Charles IV, Prague's most influential ruler, from a votive tablet by Johann Ocko.
RIGHT: bust of Charles IV.

Charles took control of the Bohemian crown lands in 1320, acting for his father who had now gone blind. On John's death in 1346 Charles was elected king of the Germans and, one year later, king of Bohemia. In 1355 he was crowned Holy Roman Emperor. He chose Prague as his permanent residence and set about making the city the political and cultural hub of Central Europe.

Charles University

Prague gained considerably in cultural importance when the university – the first in Central Europe – was built. Charles IV granted the official founding charter on 7 April 1348. The Charles University was intended to draw together scholars from all regions of the empire and had a similar constitution to that of Charles' alma mater, the University of Paris. It was divided into four "nations": Bohemian, Bavarian, Saxon and Polish. These did not represent national groupings, but symbolised the four points of the compass by giving them the name of the nearest neighbour in that direction. Each "nation" had a vote in the university's decision-making, and the posts of rector and chancellor were filled by each "nation" in turn.

To begin with, lectures were held in churches

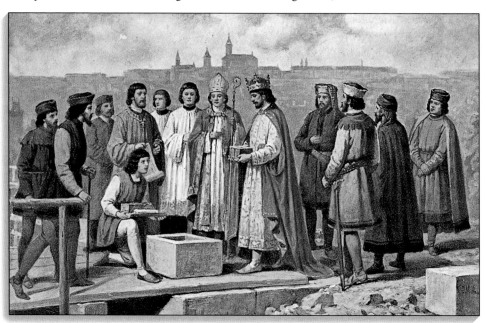

PETER PARLER, THE IMPERIAL ARCHITECT

In 1344, Charles had already managed to use his good relationship with Clement VI to get Prague promoted from a bishopric to an archbishopric. In the same year the building of St Vitus' Cathedral began, on the site of the former basilica. The cathedral was conceived as a triple-aisled nave church, in the French idiom. Charles obtained the services of the French architect, Matthias of Arras.

Following the latter's death in 1352, the masons' and sculptors' workshop of Peter Parler (1332–99) took over the building. Under his direction the famous triforium arcade was created, along with the choir, the South Tower, and particularly the vaulting, for which Parler was famous.

The Wenceslas Chapel and the Golden Door, both evidence of a new synthesis of architecture and sculpture, can be attributed wholly to Parler.

After finishing St Vitus' Cathedral, Parler completed the Týn church (begun in 1365). Also designed by Parler's workshop are the windows of the Martinic chapel, the Bridge Tower of the Old Town and the chapel of Charles Church, modelled on the chapel of Charlemagne in Aachen. In 1357, under Parler's direction, work began on the Charles Bridge. Peter Parler was one of the most notable architects of the late-Gothic period. His style greatly influenced subsequent architecture.

and in the Lazarus House in the Jewish Quarter. The move to the Carolinum, today one of the oldest university buildings in the world, did not take place until 1356. Charles, who was a writer himself and one of the few educated medieval rulers, was able to gather leading thinkers and scholars of his time around him. Without doubt, Prague in the 14th century was one of the most important cultural centres of Europe. Among the early Humanist circle around Charles were men such as Cola di Rienzi, Ernest of Pardubitz (later Archbishop of Prague) and Johann of Neumark. The latter was Charles' chancellor and had considerable

the Poříčí. This area incorporated small settlements and several monasteries, among them the convent of Our Lady of the Snows and the Emmaus Monastery, which were founded in 1347 and planned to fit in with the designs for the New Town. Also in 1347, the foundation stone of the Charles Church was laid.

Neither the plans nor the name of the architect have survived, but an analysis of the basic town plan, which remained almost unaltered until well into the 19th century, shows clear evidence of creative and far-sighted planning. The official founding charter was granted by Charles on 3 March 1348 – probably

influence on the spread of the New High German language. He was also well known as a fine translator of Latin prayers and Bible texts.

A masterpiece of civic planning

Charles made his most noticeable mark on the development of Prague, however, by founding the New Town (Nové Město) and thereby almost doubling the city's area. The New Town spread in a circle from the southeast of the Old Town to the river below the Vyšehrad and to

LEFT: Charles IV laying the groundstone for one of Prague's landmarks, Charles Bridge.
ABOVE: Charles IV with the imperial regalia.

the day on which the foundation stone for the city walls was laid. Settlers who wanted to live in the New Town were assigned plots of land and, in return for tax concessions, had to complete their houses within 18 months.

The New Town was designed to fall into four large sections: the central section is constructed around Wenceslas Square (the former horse market); the south is centred on Charles Square (formerly the cattle market); and the north is dominated by the former merchant street of Hybernská. The lower area, the former settlement of Slup, planted with orchards and vineyards, was hardly built up at all.

The scale of the plan is remarkable. Ječná

(Barley Street) is nearly 27 metres (89 ft) wide, and Charles Square, with a length of 520 metres (1,706 ft) and an area of 8 hectares (20 acres), is the largest square in Europe. Nor were Charles' building schemes confined to the castle and the New Town. On the left bank of the Vltava a new wall was built and the area of the Malá Strana increased considerably. At the same time, building began on Petřín Hill.

The Hradčany settlement was also fortified. Part of this fortification is known as the "Wall of Hunger" because Charles ordered its construction during a time of widespread poverty in order to provide employment. In the Old

pages 224–5) served as the currency for the entire region. In alliance with the kings, foreign merchants, notably Germans and Italians, became economically and politically powerful.

First signs of unrest

But social stability was undermined by the emergence of guilds of craftsmen which were often torn by internal conflicts. Poor inhabitants provided a further volatile element, as the taxes necessary to fund such development placed a disproportionate burden on the poor. The uneven social structure, both social and national, as well as between inhabitants of the

Town, too, the monastery and St James' Church were rebuilt, alterations made to the churches of St Aegidius, St Martin, St Castullus, St Gall and St Nicholas, and the church of the Holy Ghost was constructed.

After the boom time of Charles' rule, Prague, at the end of the 14th century, consisted of two castles and four towns with an area of 800 hectares (2,000 acres) and a population of over 50,000. Within the city area, there were around 100 monasteries, churches and chapels and several dozen markets. Prague had been promoted to an imperial residence, an archdiocese, the seat of a papal legate, and a university town. The Czech money minted at Kutná Hora (*see*

Old and New Towns, resulted in a break between the two in 1377.

When Charles IV died on 29 November 1378, he left Prague with a lot of building sites, and a lot of problems smouldering under the surface. Nevertheless, he was one of Europe's outstanding figures, and his country undoubtedly flourished during his reign.

Wenceslas IV

Charles' son, Wenceslas IV, succeeded his father's position, but he faced strong political opposition within the Empire and had to accept a considerable loss of authority. Hence, Prague decreased in importance. Building work slowed down, economic difficulties arose and led to a depression that brought social unrest. Dissatisfaction of large sections of the population, especially the poor Czech inhabitants of the New Town, was focused on the rich (mostly foreign) patrician families and on the clergy.

In 14th-century Europe, opposition to the luxurious and often immoral lifestyle of the monastic orders was growing. In Prague they had already come under critical fire during the reign of Charles IV. In the mid-14th century, Konrad Waldhauser (d. 1369) and Jan Milic Kromeriz (d. 1374) were prominent preachers who attacked monastic lifestyles.

In 1391, the Bethlehem Chapel was founded (*see page 174*). The simplicity of its exterior (the chapel was rebuilt exactly to original plans in 1950–53) marks it as a response to criticisms of decadence. In 1402, the religious reformer Jan Hus (1370–1415) began to preach here against the secularisation of the church.

The Hussite Wars

Hus's ideas for reform were very popular among Prague's citizens, and even with Wenceslas IV. The clergy, afraid of losing power, rejected him.

In 1398, Hus was appointed to the university as professor of philosophy. Here he continued to expound his ideas, but he was defeated in a vote by the "nations" – most academics condemned his thinking. In 1409, the dispute reached a crisis: it was no longer purely a theological quarrel, but had nationalist overtones. Hus managed to obtain the Decree of Kuttenberg (Kutná Hora) from his patron, Wenceslas IV. This granted the Bohemian "nation" in the university a majority of votes.

After strong protests, German academics moved out of Prague en masse and began an empire-wide campaign against the university. Prague's clergy reacted with a series of arrests and repressive measures. They were backed by the nobility, disturbed by the social and political applications of Hus's ideas as proposed by the radical preacher Jan Želivský.

Escalation of the conflict came on 30 July 1419, when an angry mob led by Želivský marched to the Town Hall in the New Town and demanded the release of a group of Hussite prisoners. The councillors refused, and the enraged citizens stormed the building and staged the first defenestration, hurling the councillors and seven other citizens from the window. Unrest spread rapidly. Soon the Hussites occupied the Town Hall and elected their own councillors. Wenceslas made no effort to suppress them and, in August, approved the new appointments. Perhaps he hoped to calm the conflict, but the signal came too late. Wenceslas IV died on 16 August 1419. The next day, the Hussites stormed the Carthusian monastery in Ujezd and continued the revolution. ❏

PREACHER OF THE PEOPLE

Jan Hus was born around 1372 in Husinec, Bohemia. He became a priest in 1400 and was influenced by English theologian John Wyclif (1328–84). Like Wyclif, Hus urged a return to the Bible and a lesser gap between clergy and laity. He made fiery speeches against the worldliness of the Catholic church and the immorality of clerics. He was forbidden to preach by the archbishop of Prague, but when he refused to obey he was charged with heresy and viciously burned at the stake in 1415. One of the most charismatic figures in Czech history, a statue of him dominates the Old Town Square and the anniversary of his death is a national holiday.

LEFT: Jan Hus being led to the stake in Constance.
RIGHT: in the shadow of his father Charles; Wenceslas IV faced strong opposition within the Empire.

THE URGE TO DEFENESTRATE

*As a punishment, it was crude but effective. Three major events in Prague's
history involved hurling someone out of a convenient window*

For centuries, defenestration – throwing people out of windows – has been a peculiar practice in Prague. Here are some of the more dramatic examples, and the events which prompted them.

The first two defenestrations

On 30 July 1419, a stone was thrown from the window of the New Town Hall at a procession of armed Hussites. The long-smouldering conflict finally erupted. The Hussites stormed the Town Hall and threw three consuls and seven citizens out of the windows. The Hussite Wars, named after their inspiration, Jan Hus (*see page 29*), had begun.

Then again, on 23 May 1618, enraged Protestant citizens of Prague threw three Catholic councillors out of the window of Hradčany castle into the moat. This confrontation between Catholics and Protestants led to the Thirty Years' War.

In order to consolidate his power in Bohemia, Ferdinand II had agreed to the terms of Rudolf II's "Letter of Majesty," which guaranteed religious freedom and the unrestricted building of churches. But the Catholic Ferdinand soon showed himself to be a staunch supporter of the Counter-Reformation. His harsh and merciless actions led to open revolt. Protestant churches in Bohemia were closed, and some were even torn down.

The Defenestration by the enraged Estates of Prague had far-reaching consequences. The monks of the Strahov Monastery and the archbishop were exiled and in 1619 Ferdinand II was deposed by the Bohemian Estates. A year later the army of the Estates, dependent on foreign help and led by Frederick V of the Palatinate, was defeated by the imperial army in the Battle of White Mountain, near Prague. The power of the Habsburgs was re-established. In the subsequent "Bloody Trial" in Prague, 22

Czech and five German noblemen were tortured and executed in the Old Town Square.

Defenestration or suicide?

Early morning on 10 March 1948, the caretaker in charge of heating the Černín Palace, Karel Maxbauer, found his employer, the foreign

minister of the Czech republic, Jan Masaryk (*see page 47*), dead in the courtyard.

Masaryk, son of Tomáš Masaryk, the founder of the Czechoslovak Republic, was the only non-Communist cabinet member left after the "bloodless" coup in February 1948. One month before, 12 non-Communist ministers had resigned from Klement Gottwald's coalition cabinet. Under pressure from the Communist militia and the threat that Soviet troops might invade, President Edvard Beneš appointed a Communist cabinet. The sole exception was Jan Masaryk. But full details of his mysterious death, and whether he jumped or was pushed, have never been uncovered. ❑

LEFT: portrayal of the Defenestration of Prague, on 23 May 1618, at Hradčany castle.
RIGHT: Jan Masaryk is dead.

RUDOLF II AND THE HABSBURGS

The reign of Rudolf was a relatively benign period in the city's history.
Then came the Thirty Years' War

The winners in the Hussite revolution were, for the most part, the Czech nobility. During the decade 1430–40 the Catholic city governors were driven out, church property was confiscated and Prague's independence was legally confirmed – triumphs for the Bohemian Estates. Only Czechs of Hussite persuasion were allowed to vote on the Prague city council. Rome agreed to religious freedom with the *Four Articles of Prague*. However, the Catholic church was merely biding its time.

Catholics and Utraquists

But for now the people of Prague acclaimed their first Hussite king. In 1458, George of Poděbrady was crowned. A Czech and an Utraquist (the more moderate Hussites), he was King of Bohemia for 13 years, and Prague, laid waste by the revolution, blossomed once more. George had the towers of the Týn church and the Bridge Tower in the Malá Strana built. But he had little more to do before Rome incited the people against the "heretic king".

During the rule of George's successor, Prince Vladislav II of the Polish Jagiellon dynasty (1471–1516), another defenestration occurred. Vladislav had let the Catholics back in. They occupied the Old Town Hall, arming themselves against the Utraquists. But their dark plots were made public, and on 26 September 1483 an angry group of people stormed the Town Hall and threw the spokesman and the mayor of the Old Town out of the window.

In 1484, Catholics and Utraquists made peace once more, with the Treaty of Kuttenberg (Kutná Hora). The unrest had badly affected King Vladislav, whose residence was in the royal palace in the Old Town. He decided to move to the castle, and have it renovated. The masterpiece of the renovation is the late-Gothic Vladislav Hall which was designed by Benedikt Rieth (1454–1534).

LEFT: Van Dyck's portrait of General Wallenstein, commander-in-chief of the imperial forces.
RIGHT: Prague flourished under the rule of Rudolf II.

It was the teaching of Martin Luther that split the Utraquists into two in the early 16th century. The Old Utraquists were against the German Reformation; the New Utraquists supported it. Catholicism also found support in the reign of Vladislav's son Ludwig (1516–26). Following Ludwig's death while fighting the Turks

in Hungary, the Estates chose another king. They made a fatal choice: the Austrian Archduke Ferdinand I of Habsburg (1526–64).

The Habsburg rule

During Ferdinand's reign Prague became the most important prop of Viennese rule, and Rome found more support for its fight against the Utraquists. The Hussite era was facing its final defeat. Ferdinand soon quarrelled with representatives of the Bohemian Estates and relieved them of political power.

Ferdinand's great achievement was the construction of the Summer Palace, which finally helped the Renaissance to establish itself in

Prague. The Belvedere, on a hill opposite the Hradčany, became the model for the palaces of the nobility. John of Lobkovic had his palace built in the latest Italian style. In the early 18th century it belonged to the Schwarzenberg family; it still bears their name, and is now the Museum of Military History (*see page 123*). Ferdinand was also responsible for constructing of the Star Hunting Lodge at White Mountain just outside the city. Before this, however, there was more fighting to be done.

In 1546 open conflict broke out once more. Ferdinand went to war against the Protestant German princes, although the Estates in

A cultural rebirth

However, Prague acquired new fame in 1583, although it was no longer politically independent, as the residence of Rudolf II of Habsburg. Many historians compare the Rudolfine era with the glorious reign of Charles IV. Life came back to the city: diplomats, political observers, adventurers, traders from all over the world, craftsmen, professional soldiers, musicians and many artists followed the ruler.

While Rudolf indulged his passion for collecting works of art, political and religious conflicts continued to seethe, hardly noticed by those in the castle. Meanwhile, Rudolf acquired

Prague refused to support him in a war against their religious brethren. However, the king returned victorious, with one thought clearly in mind: revenge. On 1 July 1547, Archduke Ferdinand's mercenaries swooped down on Prague. Never again would the city dare deny him either obedience or support.

Ferdinand took away all the privileges won by the glorious Hussite revolution. The city became a vassal of the Habsburgs – all public property had to be surrendered, and the way was open for the return to power of the Catholic church. In 1561, Ferdinand appointed a new Bishop of Prague – a post which had not been filled since the Hussite revolution.

A CURIOUS COLLECTOR

As well as art, Rudolf was also interested in all kinds of curiosities and rare objects. An inventory records: "In the two upper compartments all kinds of strange sea fish, underneath them a bat, a box of four thunder stones (meteorites), two boxes of lodestones, and two iron nails, said to come from Noah's Ark, a stone that grows which was a gift from Herr von Rosenberg, two bullets taken from a Transylvanian mare, a box of mandrake roots, a crocodile in a bag, a monster with two heads…" Despite his indiscriminate passion for collecting, Rudolf II undoubtedly made Prague into the "artistic treasure house of Europe". Sadly, much was later lost during the Thirty Years' War.

and hoarded artistic treasures – paintings and drawings were his particular passion. His favourite painters were Dürer and Pieter Brueghel the Elder. If he couldn't get hold of the original, he had it copied by Jan Brueghel or Pieter the Younger. Rudolf also amassed paintings by other leading artists of the Renaissance: Titian, Leonardo, Michelangelo, Raphael, Bosch and Corregio.

In 1578 Jesuits began work on St Saviour's Church. The basic construction still adheres to the old Gothic pattern, but windows and sills, reliefs and vaulting are built in a more modern style. The great church of the Jesuits was the

In 1611, after a failed attack on Prague, Rudolf had to surrender the crown to his brother. He died barely a year later defeated and, some say, mentally deranged.

The Thirty Years' War

In all ages there have been places in the world where political observers can feel the pulse of the times beating, places where a *zeitgeist* is created. Prague in the early 17th century must have been such a place. The gulf between the House of Habsburg and the Bohemian nobility, between Catholic and Protestant, was a reflection of the political situation throughout

symbol of growing Catholic strength in Prague.

But conflict was growing between Rudolf II and his ambitious brother, Archduke Matthias, who took control of the army during a war with the Turks between 1593 and 1609. This family quarrel was a long-awaited trump card for the Protestants. Rudolf, under pressure from Matthias, had to make concessions. In 1609, the Estates forced the king to issue the *Majestát* (Letter of Majesty) guaranteeing religious freedom throughout Bohemia.

LEFT: Prague's forces fight against the Swedes on the Charles Bridge (1648).
ABOVE: the murder of Wallenstein in Cheb (1634).

Europe. The conflict here had a long tradition unparalleled anywhere else. It was no surprise, then, that Prague was the place over which the storm clouds of war, which had been hovering threateningly all over Europe, broke first.

In 1617, the oppressor of the Protestants, Archduke Ferdinand of Styria, was crowned King of Bohemia. Soon, Protestant churches were burning in the surrounding countryside. Representatives of the Bohemian Estates were enraged and stormed the Court Chancellery in the castle on 23 May 1618, led by Count Thurn. "Follow the old Czech custom – throw them out of the window!" a voice from the crowd is said to have shouted. The Protestant nobles needed little encouragement: Count Martinic, Governor Slavata and their secretary Philipp Fabricius were thrown 16.5 metres (55 ft) to the ground, landing in a dung heap, which saved their lives. Prague was in uproar. The Thirty Years' War began, and the city became the centre of the revolt.

A year after the Defenestration, the Bohemian Estates got rid of Ferdinand II and made Frederick V, Elector of the Palatinate, King of Bohemia. From his base in Vienna, Ferdinand resolved to pay them back. On 8 November 1620, the combined armies of the Emperor and the Catholic League were drawn up on White Mountain outside Prague, facing the Bohemian

Estates army. The outcome of the battle was decided within hours. The Protestant army fled back behind the city walls, and Frederick retreated to the Netherlands. Prague was defeated. Enemy troops plundered the city, the damage running to millions of gilders.

A dreadful revenge indeed. The leaders of the revolt were arrested. On 21 June, 15 citizens of Prague, 10 members of the nobility and two citizens of other estates were executed in the Old Town Square. The heads of the 12 leaders were impaled on the Bridge Tower in the Old Town as a permanent warning. Even before the executions were carried out the emperor had reinstated the Catholic clergy. In the same year all non-Catholic clergy, including the eminent philosopher and teacher Jan Amos Comenius, were forced to leave Prague. The emperor had torn up Rudolf's Letter of Majesty with his own hands. In the years that followed, Protestant families emigrated, and the Catholic Church attained heights of power unknown since before the Hussite Revolution.

Wallenstein's Palace

During the 30 war-torn years only a few new buildings were constructed in Prague. One of them was the palace of Albrecht von Wallenstein (or Waldstein) in the Malá Strana. Wallenstein had helped crush the Bohemian revolt and been appointed commander-in-chief of imperial forces. He built his residence between 1624–30 on a site that had formerly contained 23 houses, a brickworks and three gardens. The palace still stands (*see page 141–2*), but Wallenstein's ambition of becoming the supreme authority in a united Germany was never realised: he was murdered in Cheb in 1634. A year later the Treaty of Westphalia ended the war and left the Habsburgs in control, to the detriment of the economy and culture. German became the dominant language, and remained so until the late 19th century.

Under the rule of Maria Theresa (1740–80) and Joseph II (1780–90) religious freedom returned to Prague. Joseph II proclaimed the *Edict of Tolerance* in 1781, the same year that serfdom was abolished. The age of religious wars was at an end, but freedom of religion was not the only aim of the Bohemian Estates. ❑

Left: Joseph II, the son of the "mother of the nation", Maria Theresa, Empress of Austria and Queen of Bohemia (**right**).

THE ROUTE TO THE REPUBLIC

*By the 19th century, the Czech people were tired of battles and strife and began
to campaign for independence from their increasingly troubled rulers*

After the Thirty Years' War, any last glimmer of post-Hussite Czech national consciousness was extinguished at the Battle of White Mountain in 1620. Twelve heads hung on the Bridge Tower, gruesome symbols of the destruction of Czech culture.

In the following centuries, the Czech language disappeared from the Estates, and the Czechs became a people of peasants, small-time craftsmen and servants. In the 18th century, the upper classes and nobility were German. Language differences often made communication between people and administrators impossible. Empress Maria Theresa commanded that all justices and civil servants should know the "vulgar tongue", and teachers began to teach Czech once again.

Return of the Czech language

The late 18th century was a great period for theatre in Prague. In 1781, the Nostitz Theatre (today the Estates Theatre) was built by Count Anton Nostitz-Rieneck. When it opened, the German upper classes flocked to see Lessing's *Emilia Galotti* and, in 1787, Mozart's *Don Giovanni*. Czechs struggled to stage performances in their own language. In 1785 they gained permission to do so, but only for a time.

Czech players moved to the Bouda (shack), a little wooden theatre in the Horse Market (now Wenceslas Square). The Czech language could no longer be suppressed. Czech books and newspapers returned, and the language was again taught at the university.

In 1833, the Englishman Edward Thomas began the production of steam engines in Karlín. The rapid economic development of the industrial revolution created a proletariat in and around Prague, and the native Czech population rose. Tension increased between Germans and Czechs, although at first they both had a common enemy: the all-powerful

---

LEFT: Jewish synagogue and town hall in the late 19th century.
RIGHT: the former Nostitz (now the Estates) Theatre.

Viennese State Chancellor Metternich. The 1848 revolution was the last time that Germans and Czechs together manned the barricades for a common cause.

The goals were not common to both parties: the Czechs were no longer interested in Bohemian, but in Czech freedom; German

Nationalists wanted a united Germany. In February 1848 there was a revolution in Paris, and Metternich resigned on 13 March. There was rejoicing in Prague, but opinion was divided – the Germans wanted to attend the Frankfurt Parliament; the Czechs wanted their own state as part of a federal Austrian Empire.

Violence at the Slavic Congress

The First Slavic Congress met on 2 June 1848 in the museum building of Prague. One of its main demands was for equal rights for all nationalities. The leader of the movement was the Czech František Palacký: "Either we achieve a situation where we can say with pride: 'I am a Slav', or we shall stop being Slavs," he pronounced. The congress came to a violent end. After a Slavonic mass, the Prague militia fired into the crowd, and the nationalist movement was crushed in bloody fighting.

Following the revolutions of 1848, all the nations of the Austrian Empire came under the rod of Absolutism; the Czech language was even forced out of civil service departments. But after the Austrians were driven out of northern Italy in 1859, their power weakened. On 5 March 1860 an "extended imperial council" was called. Representatives from different lands sat with councillors appointed by the emperor. In 1861, a Czech could become mayor of Prague, but nationally the emperor favoured German-speaking Bohemians. The Czechs remained loyal to the emperor in the struggle with Prussia in 1866, but were not rewarded with equality or autonomy.

The Czechs could win only minor battles. Their long-awaited national theatre finally opened on 15 June 1881 with a performance of Smetana's *Libuše*. The theatre burned down two months later, but was quickly rebuilt and remains a symbol of Czech national sentiment today. Work began on the Rudolfinum in 1876, and in 1893 the National Museum was built. The university was split in 1882 into separate Czech and German universities.

World War I and independence

By the start of World War I, Czechs were still fighting the Germans for equal rights. The war increased the estrangement: Germans fully supported the war effort of the Central Powers; Czechs opposed it.

Tomáš Garrigue Masaryk, who represented Czech causes in Vienna, where he led the People's Party in the Imperial parliament, led the campaign for independence. Together with his former student Edvard Beneš and Slovak astronomer Milan Štefánik, he devised a union between Czechs and Slovaks. He contacted his exiles in Allied nations and organised them into the Czech League, to fight on the side of the Allies. He convinced Allied leaders including US President Woodrow Wilson of the importance of "autonomous development" for Austrian-Hungarians. A declaration favouring a union of the Czechs and Slovaks was issued in Pittsburgh on 31 May 1918.

After the recognition of the Czechoslovak National Council by France, other Allies followed suit, and on 18 October simultaneous declarations of independence were issued by Masaryk and Beneš in Washington and Paris. The Habsburg monarchy, on the point of collapse, had to accept the terms. The Czechoslovak Republic was proclaimed by the Prague National Committee on 28 October 1918, a move that was repeated by the Slovak National Council two days later. ❑

TOMAS GARRIGUE MASARYK

The first President of the democratic Republic of Czechoslovakia was a philosophy professor. Born in Moravia, Masaryk (1850–1937) planned to be a blacksmith. But armed with intelligence he eventually received a doctorate in philosophy from the University of Vienna. During World War I, Masaryk went into exile, gaining foreign support for a state of Czechoslovakia, and in 1918, Masaryk became president. During office Czechoslovakia flourished as a centre of culture, industry andl freedom. He did not live to see his country crushed by Nazis, but his legacy lives on in the ideals of an ethnically diverse society based on democracy.

LEFT: World War I caricature of Austria-Hungarian emperor, Franz Josef, who ruled from 1848-1916.
RIGHT: Tomáš Masaryk, a leading Slavic nationalist.

TWENTIETH CENTURY

Hitler and Stalin inflicted immeasurable suffering on the country.
The 21st century, the Czechs hope, can only be better

On 28 October 1918, the Czechoslovak Republic was declared in Prague. But the borders were still not confirmed: the Sudeten Germans wanted to join with German-speaking Austria, the inclusion of Slovakia in the Czech Republic had not yet been decided, and Poland was claiming the coal mines in the former duchy of Teschen.

Sudeten Germany

On 14 November, Tomáš Masaryk was elected president of the republic and was welcomed back by the enthusiastic people of Prague after four years of exile. Foreign Minister Edvard Beneš – who would be Masaryk's successor in presidential office – made skillful use of the last weeks of the war and the time after Germany's surrender. The uneasy powers of the Entente had no clear idea of how Europe should look once peace was declared. Beneš had managed to obtain the incorporation of Slovakia into the Czech state, against Hungarian opposition and the opposition of the Slovak populace, who also wanted autonomy. Continual internal unrest was guaranteed by demands for "national autonomy for Slovakia".

The incorporation of the Sudetenland had even worse consequences. Some two decades later, it would give Adolf Hitler a welcome excuse to liquidate Czechoslovakia. Following the formula of the US President Woodrow Wilson, representatives of the Sudeten Germans had declared an "autonomous province of the state of German Austria", to which Czech troops retaliated by occupying German-settled areas. The Peace Conference decided in favour of Czechoslovakia. Without a plebiscite being held, the German areas went to Czechoslovakia. Those parts of Teschen which were incorporated were not all in favour, either. After the Treaty of Versailles (1918), opposition flared up all over the country.

PRECEDING PAGES: Wenceslas Square, before 1900.
LEFT: the anniversary of the Communist regime, 1949.
RIGHT: Hitler crossing the border to the Sudetenland.

An "oppressed" minority

The Sudeten Germans saw themselves as an oppressed minority, disadvantaged by language rulings, land reform, and the unfavourable position of the German education system and industry. The economic effects of "Black Friday", on 4 October 1929, strengthened opinion.

Around two-thirds of the 920,000 unemployed in the winter of 1932–33 were Germans. In 1933, Konrad Henlein, a gymnastics teacher, founded the *Sudetendeutsche Heimatfront* (SHF), the Sudeten German Home Front. In 1935 the party, now known as the *Sudetendeutsche Partei* (SdP) – the Sudeten German Party – took part in elections. They won 68 per cent of German votes, making them the strongest group in parliament, and they began to demand autonomy for German areas.

It did not take long for Henlein to make contact with Hitler, and soon he and his party became puppets of their mighty patron. The SdP's demands became more and more radical over the years, and their goals shifted from equal rights to inclusion in the German Reich. In 1937, Henlein drew the conclusion that "today even the broad mass of Sudeten Germans no longer believe in equal rights with the Czech people in a Czech state".

Nazi occupation

Afraid of war, France and Britain finally gave in to pressure from Hitler. On 30 September 1938, Chamberlain, Daladier, Mussolini and Hitler signed the Munich Agreement. The Sudeten lands now belonged to Germany. On 22 October, Beneš went into exile in England, and on

14 and 15 March 1939, Hitler declared a "sovereign" Slovak vassal state and established the Protectorate of Bohemia and Moravia. German troops marched into Prague on 15 March. A puppet government and head of state dealt with domestic affairs, and the Czechs were defined as second-class persons under Article 2 of the Treaty of the Protectorate.

The chief of the *Sicherheitsdienst* (security forces), Reinhard Heydrich, known as "the hangman", attacked the Czech intelligentsia. Czech universities were closed. Academics were not allowed to work in their professions. Some newspapers were banned, and the famous Barrandov Studios outside Prague were

forced to make propaganda films. Thousands of people were imprisoned in the concentration camps of Dachau and Oranienburg. (*For the treatment of Prague's Jews, see page 48.*)

Heydrich was assassinated in May 1942 by members of the Czech resistance (*see pages 193–4*), but his work was continued by General Kurt Daluege. A terrible reprisal was exacted for Heydrich's death: all the inhabitants of the mining village of Lidice were shot or incarcerated in concentration camps and the village was wiped off the map.

Apart from such atrocities, the number of victims the Czechs mourned in 1945 was small compared with those from Poland, Russia or the Ukraine. Except for two exiled groups, one in England and another in Russia, Czechs did not fight against Nazi Germany during World War II. However, no other country had lost such a high percentage of their intellectuals and artists under Nazi rule. In the years 1939–45, the Nazis in the Protectorate of Bohemia and Moravia systematically exterminated the academic and creative élite of the nation.

On 5 May 1945, three days before the war ended, the people of Prague rose up against the Germans. When the Russian Red Army marched into the city they were greeted as liberators, as well as brother Slavs.

The rise of Communism

In postwar Czechoslovakia the path to socialism had been smoothed as in no other country. Before World War II, the country was one of Europe's highly developed nations, with modern light and heavy industries, and efficient agriculture. Above all, it had a confident, highly qualified proletariat and a class of educated intellectuals and artists, who were, if not actually members of the Communist Party, nonetheless mainly left or liberal-left in their views. The relationship

> **SET IN STONE**
>
> In 1952 the largest statue of Josef Stalin in the world was erected in Prague's Letná Park to honour the Communist leader. It was demolished ten years later.

later, Foreign Minister Jan Masaryk, the only non-Communist still in government, was found dead in the courtyard below his office (*see page 31*). The Communists could still count on the support of the majority of Czechoslovaks, but disillusionment was just around the corner.

The Stalin years

The name of this disillusionment was Josef Stalin, who mercilessly forced the Czechoslovaks to accept his version of Communism. From 1948 onwards, the Czechoslovak

of the Czechs to the Soviet Union and socialism was positive. Following the rebirth of nationalism in the early 19th century, the Czechs viewed Russia as a Slavic older brother.

In the last free elections for more than 50 years, the Communists won 38 per cent of the votes, and Klement Gottwald became leader of a coalition government. However, this was not enough for the Soviet Union, and in February 1948, the Communists gained control of Czechoslovakia in a bloodless coup. A month

FAR LEFT: a Czech stamp with Hitler surveying Prague.
LEFT: Communist propaganda poster.
ABOVE: Stalin monument (1955), demolished in 1962.

Communist Party, by now Stalinist in orientation, succeeded in destroying any idea of a specifically Czechoslovak road to socialism. In 1960, the country's official title of "people's republic" was changed to "socialist republic".

The rule of the Stalinists, first under Gottwald and then under Antonín Novotný, had dire consequences for Czechs and Slovaks. In the late 1950s and early 1960s scepticism and cynicism spread throughout Czechoslovakia. Hardly anyone still believed in Marxism or Leninism, or even in the idea of just and fair socialism. What is more, the Czech economy, subject to a series of Five-Year Plans, was at rock bottom by 1963. The events, five years

The Holocaust

The Prague ghetto is one of the oldest in Europe, dating back to at least the 11th century. It was established over several centuries when laws segregating Jews kept the community within a designated part of the city. By the 17th century, despite periods of oppression, it was a flourishing community and a focal point for Jewish culture in Central Europe.

The Jewish community in the city was allowed to develop freely after 1848, when the laws segregating the Jews were finally repealed.

Although the ghetto was largely demolished for health reasons in the 1890s (one sign of the prejudice inflicted on the Jews was that the area had never been given sufficient sanitation), the community remained active until the Nazi occupation of the country in 1939. Today there are some 3,000 members of the Jewish community (this number also includes foreigners who practice their faith here), and about 1,500 people of Jewish descent living in Prague.

The Nazis systematically planned and carried out their Final Solution to the "Jewish problem" here as elsewhere in Europe. The Jews were first of all forced to register, then excluded from economic activity, then physically separated from the rest of the population. They were marked, insulted, sentenced to perpetual poverty, and evicted from their homes. They were deported to concentration camps, starved and tortured. For those who could no longer work, the death sentence was inescapable.

In the so-called Protectorate of Bohemia and Moravia the Jews suffered the same fate as those in Germany and elsewhere in occupied Europe. Immediately after the occupation of Bohemia and Moravia by Hitler's army, the Nuremberg Laws, passed in 1935 "to protect the German race", were enforced retrospectively. These laws had deprived German Jews of their citizenship and turned them into "subjects of the state". The same now happened to Czechoslovak Jews. One persecution rapidly followed another – culminating in the mass deportations of 1941.

The first five transports, each with 1,000 people mainly from the Jewish intelligentsia – doctors, artists, lawyers – were deported to the so-called Litzmannstadt Ghetto in Lódź, which the Nazis themselves designated a starvation camp. A month later the old fortress of Terezín (Theresienstadt) in Bohemia was declared a Jewish ghetto, and received deportees from all over occupied Europe (*see page 215*). Terezín was not itself an extermination camp, but from here the Jews were sent on for so-called selection and thence to the gas chambers of Auschwitz.

However, even in times of the greatest debasement of humanity there remained artists in Prague who had enough courage to lessen the impact of the humiliations they suffered. Authors wrote under false names; cultural afternoons to discuss contemporary poetry were held in private apartments. An amateur drama group, led by the famous Shakespearian translator Erik Saudek, performed plays. Poet Norbert Frýd's verses, called *A Horse Decorated with Flowers*, an introduction to the alphabet, were set to music by Karel Reiner and performed for the children in the community orphanage. These few rays of hope helped keep spirits up during the darkest days Prague's Jewish community had ever known.

Memorials to those who did not survive the Nazi holocaust are to be found in the Josefov district, most notably at the Pinkas Synagogue, where the names of all victims are painstakingly painted on the synagogue's walls (*see page 177*). ❏

LEFT: a Prague public library, where Jews were not allowed to borrow books.

later, which came to be called the Prague Spring, had already begun, with the failure of the latest plan and the near collapse of the whole economy of the country.

Literature and politics

In the years before the Prague Spring of 1968, a literature independent of the previous party censorship machine developed in Czechoslovakia. Since the rebirth of Czech national consciousness in the early 19th century, writers have played a vital role in both shaping and responding to nationalist aspirations.

When the crisis of Czechoslovak society and socialist beliefs eventually came, in the early 1960s, it was authors such as the future Nobel Prize-winner for Literature, Jaroslav Seifert, the lyric poets Vladimír Holan, František Halas and others, who replaced the functionaries at party headquarters as political and moral institutions. By 1965, at the latest, the Czechs and Slovaks had realised that this form of socialism could not continue, and, searching for something to cling to, they rediscovered their poets, authors and filmmakers. The term "Socialism with a human face" is usually associated with Alexander Dubček, who became an internationally known figure in 1968. It was, indeed, an ideal which Dubček wished to realise, but its programme was developed not by the Communist Party and not by the exhausted and insecure ideologists, but by the writers and artists of the Prague Spring.

End of a dream

"Socialism with a human face" was not Utopia but, had it been realised, it would have been a great step forward, laying the foundations for a more equitable society. The Action Programme embodied a number of reform ideas which included federal autonomy for the Slovaks, long overdue industrial and agricultural reforms, a revised constitution that would guarantee civil rights and liberties and democratisation of the country and the party. Behind these proposals lay a bitter admission and an undertone of despair: up until the spring of 1968 the face of socialism in Czechoslovakia had obviously not looked very human at all.

The dream of an efficient, just and happy socialist society came to a final end with the collapse of the Prague Spring, when the Soviet Union marched in with soldiers from five socialist countries on 21 August 1968 and destroyed the Czechoslovak hope of national independence. They left behind them the power structure of a totalitarian, Stalinist state, which, although it called itself socialist, had very little to do with the ideals of true socialism, which Prague reformers under Dubček had believed they could achieve.

Under the regime of Dubček's successor, the hard-liner Gustav Husák, many writers, composers, journalists and historians, as well as

PROTESTORS FOR PEACE

On 16 January 1969 a philosophy student named Jan Palach hit the headlines across the world, by setting himself on fire in Wenceslas Square, as a shocking protest against Communist rule and Soviet oppression. The protest would turn out to be suicide, when Palach died three days after the event, and he became hailed as a national hero, who died for his people. The act inspired the others, and about a month later, on 25 February, Jan Zajíc set himself alight. Twenty years later, Václav Havel was imprisoned yet again for attempting to lay flowers on the spot where they stood aflame. Today there is a small stone memorial to the two brave men.

RIGHT: citizens wave Czechoslovak flags during the Soviet invasion of August 1968.

scientists, found themselves unemployed and forced to accept menial jobs to earn a living. Some left the country, and those who stayed and tried to continue the struggle were silenced. But despite the indifference of the mass of the population, discontent continued to simmer.

It erupted again in January 1977, when a group of intellectuals signed a petition, known as Charter 77, in which they aired their grievances against the Husák regime. The spokesman of the group, Václav Havel, had already written, in an open letter to President Husák two years before: "You have chosen the

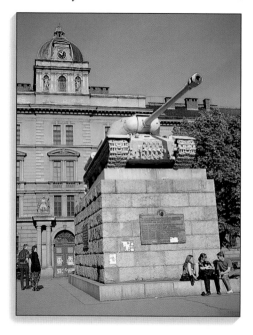

path that is the most convenient for you and the most dangerous for the country: the path of maintaining external appearances at the cost of internal collapse... the path of merely defending your power, at the cost of deepening the spiritual and moral crisis of this society and the systematic erosion of human values".

A political earthquake

After the massive changes in other Eastern Bloc countries in the late 1980s, the power-hungry Czech government could not hope to save itself. The citizens of Prague demonstrated in Wenceslas Square in their thousands and, despite the obstinate stance of the authorities

and the contingents of police and security forces, their voices could no longer be silenced. Remarkable though it would have seemed just a few months before, one of the last Communist governments in the world was about to come toppling down. After the peaceful revolution in East Germany, a "Velvet Revolution" now took place in Prague in November 1989.

Václav Havel was a central figure in the protests. On 29 December 1989, he was elected president by the parliament in Prague. Dubček, veteran leader of the Prague Spring, was voted president of parliament.

In the summer of 1990, in the first free elections for two generations, the Civic Forum party received the endorsement of most of the electorate. But like most revolutions, even velvet ones, its leaders gradually drifted apart as the common enemy disappeared. The differences of opinion surfaced, for example, during debates on the "outing" of those who had held any high office in the Communist Party or who had had any connection with the secret police. Known as *lustrace*, the controversial process was meant to be a spiritual cleansing, an atonement by a handful for the rest of society, and a practical measure to bar tainted officials from public office for the next five years.

Going separate ways

A key question for Czechoslovakia was how to achieve the economic reforms that would lead to a free market. When the economy began its shift away from socialist planning after the revolution, the Slovaks were on the receiving end, suffering disproportionately from the effects of transition to a market economy. Economically irrational but emotionally understandable, Slovak separatism was a symptom of uncertainty, a force liberated by changed circumstances at a time when the state's institutions were not strong enough to contain it. Havel tried to prevent a divorce, but the official split of Czechoslovakia took place on 31 December 1992, and two new countries emerged 1 January 1993: the Czech Republic and Slovakia.

An "economic miracle"?

In the new Czech Republic, market reforms in the early- to mid-1990s soon reached breakneck speed under the abrasive but dynamic new prime minister, Václav Klaus (with Havel as president). A highly ambitious privatisation programme – including a coupon scheme which gave every adult the chance to buy shares in the state firms being privatised – was accompanied by an apparently successful balancing of the budget, with an increase in exports, reduced inflation, low unemployment and impressive growth rates. Such a consistently upbeat picture could hardly fail to attract foreign investment and commentators began talking openly about an "economic miracle" emerging in the Czech Republic.

The high point was reached in 1995, when the Czech Republic became the first post-Communist state to join the Organisation for Economic Cooperation and Development (OECD), an important step on the road to the country's long-term goal of full membership in the European Union. (The country, along with Hungary and Poland, joined NATO in March 1999, and the Czech Republic is now aiming, rather optimistically, for full membership in the European Union on 1 January 2003.)

The consumer boom created a huge demand for western goods and services at the expense of domestic suppliers, leading to a ballooning trade deficit. But by the late 1990s, as inflation rose and then rose again, and the coupon-privatisation scheme floundered, ordinary Czech savers were hit by a spectacular wave of banking collapses, amid worrying allegations of fraud and corruption.

Into the millennium

Today, the country is ruled by a minority government of the left-of-centre Czech Social Democratic Party (ČSSD), with Miloš Zeman as prime minister, on the basis of an agreement with the opposition right-wing Civic Democratic Party (ODS), headed by former prime minister Václav Klaus. Havel remains president.

However, it is all a surprisingly stable political arrangement for the Czech Republic. The government also has the occasional support of the Communist Party; but because of its pact with the main opposition party, the ODS, its room to manoeuvre is limited, and it must rely on the support of the centrist Christian Democrats. So far, Zeman has been very skillful in keeping his government afloat and

in being able to pursue at least some of his proposed programme, which includes a minimum wage, increased pension payments, more social welfare and in general a stronger social network. He has also made an attempt to rectify the corruption of the Czech Republic's difficult privatisation programme.

The road ahead will not be an easy one. There are still many problems to solve and there are bound to be even more shocks and setbacks, but politicians and the Czech people alike are facing them with a guarded determination. They know now that there is no turning back. The Czechs are firmly on their way back to Europe. ❑

VACLAV HAVEL

Havel, a playwright and poet, had been a prominent participant in the Prague Spring of 1968. Following the Soviet clampdown, his works were banned and his passport confiscated. During the 1970s and '80s he was repeatedly arrested and served four years in prison for his human-rights activities. In between imprisonment, he was obliged, like many other intellectuals, to earn his living doing manual work. Havel remains president, but his health is uncertain. His new, second wife, a former actress with a talent for tactless remarks, has also lost him some popularity. But he will always be associated with "saving" the country from Communism.

LEFT: Square of the Soviet tankmen, painted pink after the revolution.
RIGHT: President Havel and Queen Elizabeth II.

PRAGUE TODAY

In today's Prague, it can often seem as though nothing is permitted but everything is possible

Prague, to all appearances, is a fairy-tale city: it has not one but two castles, its tiny romantic streets in Staré Město (Old Town) and Malá Strana are lined with ornate houses and buildings sporting whimsical façades in pastel colours. Horse-drawn carriages cut a swathe through the Old Town Square. And for visitors from the west, Prague has an additional appeal: it can be very, very cheap.

Some aspects of Czech society will be readily apparent to casual or even first-time visitors. They will hear the word *"prosím"* (please) exchanged constantly; in Czech it has the same sense of the German *bitte,* and means both "please" and "you're welcome" as well as "here". They may take notice that, for a city of over 1.5 million, Prague in many ways exhibits the warm familiarity of a village, where Praguers will often chance upon an acquaintance or old school friend in a shop or on the street, or even while hiking in the woods elsewhere in the Czech Republic.

Visitors will also notice, for example, how young people practically leap to their feet to offer a seat to an elderly or infirm person on a tram or city bus. Such civility and consideration on public transport is one of the nice and unusual things about living in Prague, and can be refreshing for visitors accustomed to the every-man-for-himself hard-scrabble attitude on city transport in the west.

Behind the *politesse*

Czechs, though, even so many years after the revolution, must often grapple in daily life with a frustrating inflexibility and incomprehensibility in what would seem to be basic transactions for goods and services. There remains a sense, probably a holdover from communism, that people in "authority" positions – from sales clerks to doctors to officials – need to be and expect to be buttered up, in order to be persuaded to per-

form their function. Every conversation with a stranger from whom one might require a service thus begins *"Prosím Vás"* (an extra-polite "please") or a humble *"Nezlobte se, ale..."* ("Don't get annoyed, but ..."). The *politesse* and personal touch that is so special about friendly Prague encounters are also still virtual require-

ments for what would be, in other societies, normal, emotion-free professional relationships.

Medical patients still expect to offer a gift to their doctor and/or his or her nurses in order to receive more than cursory care, and patients can be afraid to ruffle their "good relationship" with their doctor by seeking a second opinion or even by asking questions or broaching concerns about treatment. (And with reason: the national health insurance is so strapped for cash that harmonious relationships with doctors and especially their staff are absolutely necessary in order to receive the slightest extra attention.) Sales clerks are frequently grumpy and often apparently reluctant to make a sale,

PRECEDING PAGES: guards changing at Prague Castle.
LEFT: a city gent is a face in the crowd.
RIGHT: demonstration for a better environment.

entertain questions from a potential customer or emerge from behind the counter to assist a client: their attitude gives the impression that they can't wait for the customer to leave the shop so they can return to chatting with their co-workers. Waiters in restaurants may disappear from view and take a long while to return. (The flip side, of course, is that it makes for a very leisurely meal, and no one is hurrying you along.)

Trying to arrange what would seem to be a normal business transaction, for example, such as requesting a transfer of funds at a major bank, may quickly degenerate into a byzantine

tation of the west. Daily life in Prague requires a talent for improvisation, and personal connections are still necessary, if not vital. In addition to "*prosím*" you will frequently hear "*To není možné*" ("that's impossible"). But as everyone here knows, everything is possible, with politeness, persistence and that important personal touch.

Family life and strife

Under communism, Czechs generally retreated into family life as a refuge from the restrictions and frustrations of society. The family is still the centre of society for most Praguers,

and troublesome complication, as if such a seemingly simple procedure is extremely unusual and has never been attempted or even conceived of by the staff before.

Many vestiges of the communist period, and perhaps also of the Austro-Hungarian period as well – such as the feeling of powerlessness on the part of many citizens, a general suspicion of strangers, and for some a need to retaliate in petty ways – have carried over in modern life. Since the revolution people have been free in many aspects of their lives, yet they still feel tethered within their particular economic and social confines, especially since the gap between rich and poor grows ever wider, in imi-

although its hold may be weakening, due to time-consuming jobs and other pressures.

Several generations may live together in the same flat or house, adult children (single or with their spouse) live with their parents or in-laws long after such arrangements would dissolve naturally in the west. Grandmothers still play a very important role in raising children, since most mothers work outside the home. Women still do most of the housework in addition to holding down jobs; men while away their free time in the local pub. It remains to be seen whether this division of sex roles can continue, given the current economic pressures.

An added problem for families – and

certainly for young couples who'd like to venture out from the family fold – is the persistent shortage of affordable housing in Prague. There always was a housing shortage in Prague, even under Communism, but the problem has grown worse since the revolution, due to the influx of foreigners who can afford high rents and the rising class of *nouveaux riches* for whom money is no object. There simply aren't apartments that a young couple (or middle-income individuals) can hope to afford – unless they

RETURNING HOME

After the 1989 revolution, much of the property that had been taken over by the state was returned to its pre-1948 owners, but generally in very poor condition.

daughter who is not married by the age of 30 is quite unusual. In spite of the overall conservatism, however, homosexuality is, surprisingly, accepted. The Czech legal system is considering a very liberal law which would give same-sex couples the same rights as married couples.

It is also an assured fact in Prague and elsewhere in the Czech Republic that the elderly still play a role in society: they are the ones selling tickets at the cinema, for example, or working the box office at castles and museums, or

have extraordinary luck or personal connections. Persistence won't help in this situation.

It used to be that most young people were married and already having children by the age of 23 or 24; since the revolution, however, and with all the changes that it has brought in work opportunities, pressures and increased responsibilities, this age seems to be edging upwards as more people in their twenties pursue careers, higher education or other interests. Still, Czech society remains conservative, and a son or

FAR LEFT: Czech couples are getting married later.
LEFT: young Czechs have more time for socialising.
ABOVE: Prague is overrun by tourists.

working as guards at the *vrátnice* (reception) in an office building, deciding who may and who may not enter. They generally brook no nonsense. They will decide whether you can or cannot enter a gallery wearing your coat or toting your bag, or whether these items must be checked at the *šatna* (cloakroom), which charges a fee.

Crime afoot

Uppermost in many people's minds is the city's steadily increasing crime rate, both in violent crime and in economic, white-collar crime. Both are generally expected to go unpunished, because the justice system is still finding its bearings and corruption is common. (Race-motivated crimes against Romanies – gypsies – are generally acknowledged to receive shoddy investigations and the culprits are accorded light sentences at best.) The government is seen to lack the political will to truly grapple with economic crime, since many officials, who also go unpunished, are considered to be on the take. The Mafia from the former Soviet Union and former Yugoslavia is understood to have a strong presence in Prague. no. 22, which both ply the main tourist routes.

In all this, both police and judges, for their part, assert that they are poorly paid and under-staffed, and therefore don't have the adequate resources to do their jobs.

TAXI TACTICS

Taxi ranks are often illegally controlled. To avoid being overcharged hail a cab in the street, ensure the meter is running and ask for a receipt.

Something in the air

It was not until after 1989 that the people of the then Czecho-slovakia were confronted with black-and-white evidence of what many of them had suspected for a long time: that they were living in what was, ecologically speaking,

People have little faith in the police; in justice, as in life, one can only hope for the best.

Violent crime is still less prevalent than in the west, but it is increasing; car thefts and auto break-ins are common. The city's taxi problem, with drivers regularly overcharging tourists, has earned Prague a distinct notoriety in the western press, but the problem is seemingly no closer to being solved. Pickpocketing, the crime that visitors to the city are most likely to encounter, (unless they have the misfortune to be drivben by a shady taxi driver), has also given Prague a bad reputation in recent years, and it is practically institutionalised on two of the city's major tram lines, the no. 9 and the

one of the most threatened countries to be found anywhere in Europe.

Air pollution is still a serious problem in Prague, because the city lies in the middle of a geographic "bowl" surrounded by hills and, at the outer edge of the country, mountains. Visit Prague or nearby villages between October and March and you won't be able to avoid the acrid smell of burning coal. The main cause of air pollution lies in heat and power generation, which are heavily dependent on fossil fuels and the release of sulphur, carbon and nitrogen oxides. The worst threatened area is northwest Bohemia, where pollution exceeds all safety levels. On four or five days in winter pollution is so bad in the city that cars are banned from the centre and children and the elderly are advised to stay indoors.

A people apart

The situation of the Czech Romanies (gypsies) has caught the world's attention and has posed several human-rights questions for the nation.

After the creation of the First Republic, President Masaryk encouraged many Romanies to move from Eastern Slovakia and settle in the industrial centres that were emerging at that time. Following the expulsion of the Sudeten Germans in 1945, a similar migration of Romanies occurred into that area, where labour was in great demand. Large communities of Romanies still live there today, as well as in Prague. Life is hard; many have no work or only manual labour and live in basic conditions. Children are condemned to the "slow" programmes at schools if, as is often the case, they don't speak Czech very well, only Romany.

While under communism racism was kept tamped down, violent acts of racism, as well as casual, run-of-the-mill, "acceptable" racism – remarks expressed by everyone from lorry drivers to college professors – has now flourished in Prague and elsewhere in the country.

Since 1989, life has become less tolerable for Romanies living within the Czech Republic. In their settlement areas in Ostrava in Moravia, the northern Bohemian towns of Teplice and Most, and in the Prague neighbourhood of Žižkov, the *Cikáni*, as they are derogatorily referred to, are forced to confront hatred on a daily basis.

But quieter, more insidious forms of racism are also commonplace, and people of colours other than white are accorded a derision mixed with an almost admiring yet condescending wonderment at their "otherness". A visiting American jazz musician to the city, for example, may be referred to in the Czech press as "a black American jazz musician" or someone is described as "a black writer" or "a black singer". Jokes about Romanies and blacks are not unusual fare for television comedy and for tasteless magazine cartoons.

Tourists, tourists everywhere

It is a curious paradox that Prague can often appear to be both supported by and destroyed by tourism. Czechs are proud of their history

LEFT: grafitti can be found all over the city.
ABOVE: former lead singer with The Doors, Jim Morrison, has left a worldwide legacy.

and also proud that their capital city is one of the most beautiful and best preserved in the world. They also readily acknowledge that tourism is a huge source of income for the city and for the many individuals who work in the tourist sector. But there is a significant price to pay in the crowds they generate.

Almost every day of the year, tourists in packs of 30 or more, following a guide holding aloft a coloured umbrella or stick, clog the lanes and streets of the Old Town, Hradčany and Malá Strana.

Often tourist groups can virtually take over a city tram, bus, or underground car, and their loud revelries – they are on holiday, after all – disturb the Czech sense of propriety, of *"slušný"* (decent) behaviour, especially for the older generation. Not many would care to return to the days of the past, but it can be frustrating to fail to find a fellow Czech-speaker in the centre of Prague from whom to ask the time of day.

Mixed feelings about foreigners

Aside from pleasure in all the freedoms that the revolution has brought, and of course the huge influx of money to the city, Czech people who work with foreigners often feel patronised and

LANGUAGE BARRIERS
Although the Czech and Slovak languages are different, even with basic nouns, Czech and Slovak are mostly mutually comprehensible.

exploited – and they are, since they are usually paid much less than they would be for an identical service in the west.

While Czech managers at the highest levels in international companies with branches in Prague can expect to earn the same or almost as much as their counterparts in the west, this is not the case for most other Czech employees. A recent university graduate from a business programme is lucky to earn about 20,000 Kč a month (about £400/US$650 a month) in Prague, while in a Western European country a similarly qualified person would earn £1,500/US$2,400 a month.

Praguers also have cause to worry about unemployment. It is lower in Prague (about 1.5 per cent) than elsewhere in the country, but the rate is growing steadily.

Cottage culture

A major part of Prague social life doesn't take place in Prague at all. It takes place at the weekend cottages *(chaty)* that so many Praguers maintain outside the city limits or deep in the countryside. There seems to be a mass exodus from the city on weekends almost year-round, but particularly in summer, when it would seem as though no Czechs at all have remained except for the obligatory tour guides, waiting staff and sales clerks.

For many Praguers, their weekend *chata* forms the real centre of family life. Over the years many families have transformed what was once their simple cottage into quite a comfortable dwelling which truly expresses their personality. One of the good things (or perhaps the only good thing) about the communist regime was that it was generous in doling out land and building credits to provide this small pleasure for people who didn't have the right to travel abroad. The *chata,* besides giving a modicum of personal freedom, usually gives city-dwellers the opportunity to maintain a vegetable and flower garden, and offers a welcome respite of fresh air. Today, many Czechs consider their *chata* to be a valuable birthright. And, for Praguers of course, it is by far the best way to get away from all those tourists. ❏

LEFT: Prague is seen by artists as an ideal city to paint, especially when it is covered in snow.

Czechs and Slovaks

The state of Czechoslovakia officially came to an end on 31 December 1992. It did not have a long history as a united country. Indeed, neither Czechs nor Slovaks had considered living together in one state until the end of World War I. The Czechoslovak National Council was formed in 1916 by Czech and Slovak exiles in the US, but not until the Habsburg monarchy was unquestionably collapsing did the Slovaks accept the ideas of the leader of the Czechs in exile, Professor Tomáš Garrigue Masaryk, and sign the Pittsburg Convention on 31 May 1918. In the future Republic of Czechoslovakia (of which Masaryk became the first president), both Czechs and Slovaks were to have equal individual rights.

Up until 1918 both Czechs and Slovaks lived under the Habsburg monarchy, though Slovakia was counted as a part of Hungary. However, the "Hungarianisation" of Slovakia was carried out with such thoroughness and brutality that by the beginning of the 18th century the Slovak language had almost entirely ceased to exist.

Influenced by the rebirth of Czech nationalism the Slovaks rediscovered their own lost language, which is very similar to Czech, and began to develop it further. After 1918, the Prague government tried to reinforce the Slovak education system and encouraged the Slovaks to develop their own intelligentsia. But Czechs taught in Slovak schools and colleges, and worked in administrative positions, in the judicial system and in other departments, so Czech became the dominant language in the republic.

Of course, this led to misunderstandings – the Slovaks felt first patronised then oppressed by the Czechs. The Pittsburg Convention of 1918 had stated that the Slovak people were equal partners in the new republic, but this was soon forgotten in Prague, and many Czechs looked on Slovakia as their "colony".

Discontent in Slovakia found its expression in the programme of the separatists, the Slovak Populist Party. In October 1938, just after the Munich Agreement had been signed, the separatists felt that their moment in history had come. Under the Catholic priest, Monsignor Jozef Tiso,

they proclaimed Slovakia an independent unit within the Czechoslovak state. In March 1939 they went one step further and declared the state of Slovakia fully independent of the republic. Needless to say Hitler quickly stamped on this idea, and soon forced them to accept the "protection" of the German Reich, with all its attendant humiliations.

By the end of August 1944, the Soviet Red Army had reached the northern borders of the Slovak state. Slovak patriots, together with the Communists, organised a popular revolution, which was crushed by the Germans but was of historic importance to the Slovaks. The Czechs and Moravians

did not rebel against the Nazis until Germany was already on the point of surrender.

Over the next 45 years the two national groups, united once more, obviously had their differences, but the Soviet-backed government kept political dissent to a minimum, and was itself the chief object of dissatisfaction. It was only when the Communist system collapsed that stronger nationalist tendencies and seemingly irreconcilable differences came to the fore.

Since 1 January 1993 Czechs and Slovaks have constituted two separate republics: the Czech Republic and Slovakia. In these two new nations, they are now learning to live amicably as neighbours, but not compatriots. ❑

RIGHT: Czech and Slovak national pride is most notably expressed in national dress.

PRAGUE'S STREET PERFORMERS

Prague's long reputation as a city of music and theatre is not confined to stark auditoriums; local performers love to bring art onto the city's streets

In the heady days following the 1989 Velvet Revolution, it was almost impossible not to encounter some guitar-strumming musician on the Charles Bridge playing Beatles melodies with a large circle of locals and young backpackers gathered around singing along. Those carefree days, however, are now mostly gone. The city administrators cracked down on unlicensed street performers several years ago, and the open-air jamming sessions that take place today are, it is true, perhaps more polished, but a certain sense of spontaneity is lost. But it is hard to keep Prague's entertainers down.

DANCING IN THE STREETS

While buskers may not be as common a sight on the Charles Bridge today as they once were, they have found plenty of other venues and still draw enthusiastic crowds – until the authorities tell them to move along. Music is not the only artform filling Prague's romantic squares, bridges and lanes. Puppeteers, mime artists, sword- and fire-eaters all appear on the city streets when the weather turns warm.

The best place to get a feel for the wide variety of street performances is still on or around the Charles Bridge, but also at the base of Wenceslas Square and along Karlova and the other narrow streets radiating from Old Town Square, especially Celetná and Melantrichova. Among the licensed performers visitors might see on the Charles Bridge are a Dixieland-style jazz band that draws regular appreciative crowds or a musician playing classical favourites on a set of crystal goblets filled with different levels of water to produce all the tones of the scale. In high summer, other outdoor entertainment is also on offer, including an open-air Shakespeare festival and classical music concerts in some of the city's most beautiful parks and gardens.

△ **MINSTREL PLAYERS**
It is almost a tradition for visiting ensembles, like this French troupe, to give the city an impromptu performance on Old Town Square.

◁ **MUM'S THE WORD**
Mumming has a long tradition in Bohemia, and an open-air mime performance is a real treat.

◁ **KNEE PLAYS**
The Charles Bridge is the venue for all types of entertainment, from the sublime to the silly. These knee puppets put a new twist on tradition.

△ **ROCK ME AMADEUS**
Prague sometimes seems plagued by Mozart clones pushing leaflets at you, all trying to lure you to one of the evening's many classical concerts.

PULLING THE RIGHT STRINGS

As the many marionette shops in the city attest, Prague and puppetry are closely linked. The art form goes back centuries, and Prague is even home to a "puppet college", where students from all over the world come to learn puppet-making and marionette theatre from acknowledged masters of the craft.

The Charles Bridge makes a fine outdoor stage for a puppet performance, or you can happen upon a puppetry demonstration (which is in fact a well planned sales pitch) in the doorways of the marionette shops around Charles Bridge and along the Royal Way. In October, there is an annual festival of puppet theatre. In the summer, there are performances by the National Marionette Theatre (Národní divadlo marionet) of *Don Giovanni*. The Black Theatre (Cerné divadlo) blends live performers, puppets and projection in an innovative way.

△ **TAKING A BOW**
A romantic stroll across the Charles Bridge at sunset can be lifted to more magical heights with the accompaniment of a violin serenade.

▷ **MAIN SQUEEZE**
The accordion plays an important part in Czech folk songs (*lidovky*). Its melancholic strains can often be heard on Prague's narrow lanes.

PUBS AND BARS

The social life of Prague has centred around beer halls for centuries, and it's worth seeking out authentic pubs that still offer fine beer and atmosphere

There is perhaps no better introduction to Czech beer culture than to spend an evening in one – or several – of the city's classic beer halls (*pivnici*). This time-honoured institution, with its long wooden tables and its atmosphere heavy with cigarette smoke and spirited debate, is sadly becoming harder to find in the central districts of Prague.

The recent past has seen the closure of a number of Prague's storied old beer halls. For those in search of an authentic pub experience, it is no longer sufficient to just wander aimlessly through Prague's ancient winding streets and happen by chance into such a place. But although they may be fewer in number, some of these old-time haunts have steadfastly hung on, although more of an effort must be made now to seek them out.

Historic beer halls

Some still-thriving places have been serving beer continuously for centuries, while other long-established pubs are lacking the authentic ambiance that their long tradition would confer because they now cater heavily to the tourist trade. U Fleků in the New Town, a 14th-century pub featured prominently in every Prague travel guide and usually packed to the rafters with jolly tourists, and U svatého Tomáše (St Thomas') in Malá Strana, on the site of an former monastery brewery, are two examples. U Kalicha in the New Town, made famous by Jaroslav Hašek as the rendezvous destination of the Good Soldier Švejk (*see page 91–92*) and his comrade at "six o'clock in the evening after the war", sadly now has the feel of a theme bar, with an on-site souvenir shop, inflated prices and often with rows of tour buses parked outside.

While visiting what is arguably the beer-drinking capital of the world, it is a worthy venture to seek out not only those pubs that

have real character, but even more important, that are known to pour an exquisite draft. For a proper mug of beer, not only must the beer be cellared at the proper temperature and be poured through regularly cleaned taps, but it must be pulled by a master of the trade – which is truly an art form.

An old-style pub in the Old Town that has tenaciously held on to its character, despite its discovery by hordes of tourists, is U zlatého tygra (The Golden Tiger), the former haunt of the beloved Czech writer and pub denizen extraordinaire Bohumil Hrabal, who died in 1997. This is the place – assuming you can find a free seat – to sample an expertly poured Plzeňský Prazdroj (better know by its German name Pilsner Urquell). While the Tiger is equally popular with tourists as the above-mentioned pubs, you will hear far more Czech spoken here than at the other three, which the locals mostly avoid. When President Clinton visited Prague, Václav Havel brought him here.

PRECEDING PAGES: Café Nouveau in Municipal House.
LEFT: a member of the enduring café society.
RIGHT: café life in Prague.

Pilsner Lager

Few Czech products are as famous as Czech beer. The brewing tradition in Bohemia extends over many centuries – in Prague, the oldest written record of the brewer's art is found in a document dated 1082. And yet the capital does not produce the country's best beer; that honour is uncontestably held by Plzeň (Pilsen).

Although the Prazdroj Brewery was founded as recently as 1842, Plzeň's brewing tradition stretches back much further. When the town of Plzeň was founded in 1290 it was granted the right

to brew its own beer. Numerous exhibits in the Museum of Beer Brewing, which has been established in a late-Gothic malthouse at Veleslavinova ul. six (*see page 231*), testify to a thriving brewing industry here in the Middle Ages.

Before the new Prazdroj Brewery opened, beer was produced in various private houses scattered through the town.

Like every other beer, Pilsner is produced by heating ground malt with water and hops before allowing the liquor to ferment at low temperature by the addition of a special yeast, the *saccharomyces carlsbergensis*. Despite all this, the flavour of Pilsner lager remains unique, and many attempts have been made to discover the secret. The water used in the brewing process clearly plays an important role in the determination of quality and taste; the local water is very soft and has an exceptionally low level of salinity. The secret of the beer's success lies in the preparation of the malt; only barley with a low protein content is used. But the characteristic taste and headiness of the beer is also achieved by the addition of first-class, oast-dried hops from the nearby town of Žatec. All these basic ingredients have been employed and tested in numerous foreign breweries, but to date, not a single one has succeeded in producing an authentic-tasting Pilsner Urquell.

Another secret must lie in the cellars in which the beer ferments and matures. They were driven deep into the sandstone cliffs and extend over a distance of 9 km (5 miles). Throughout the year, they are maintained at a constant temperature of 1–2°C (33–35°F). The walls of the cellars in which the beer is kept for two to three months are coated with a fungus similar to penicillin. Many "spies" have tried to kidnap the fungus from these cellars to establish it on the cellar walls of their own breweries. So far, nobody has been able to find a suitable habitat; sooner or later it always died.

Fourteen years after the brewery was set up, its lager was sold for the first time outside the country. The citizens of Vienna were the first to try Pilsner Urquell; by 1865, three-quarters of the brewery's total production was destined for export. From 1 October 1900, a "beer train" left Plzeň daily for Vienna. Somewhat later, a similar train travelled regularly to Bremen; there the lager was loaded onto ships for transportation to the United States.

Today the Prazdroj Brewery alone produces 1.3 million hectolitres (28.6 million gallons) of beer each year. In 1999, Prazdroj merged with the country's second-largest brewery, Radegast, and together the two are expected to command at least 45 percent of the domestic beer market; smaller breweries are feeling the pinch. If you visit the brewery at ul Prazdroje, which lies to the east of the inner city, you can study brewing techniques at your leisure (ul Prazdroje 7, tel: 019/706 1111; tours in English and German daily at 12.30pm). Having done so, you should treat yourself to a glass of the delicious brew in the adjoining pub. Be very careful, though – the alcohol content of Pilsner lager is unusually high, and many visitors overestimate their capacity. ❑

LEFT: an early advertisement for the famous Czech beer, brewed outside Prague in Plzeň.

While visiting the Hradčany area, don't miss the chance to have a draught at U černého vola (Black Bull), straight up the hill from Prague Castle and near the Loreta. It is reputed to serve the most expertly poured Kozel ("Goat") beer from Velké Popovice, which is among the best Czech beers. You can even feel virtuous about drinking here, as the pub is said to donate its profits to the school for blind children next door.

Czech beers on offer

Beer in Czech is called *pivo*. For a stronger beer, ask for *dvanáctku* (12-degree), or if you want something a little lighter ask for *desítku* (10-degree). Usually a pub will serve both lager (*světlé*) and sweetish dark (*černé*) beer from the same brewery. It is also possible to ask for *řezané*, or cut, beer, similar to a Black and Tan.

Pivnice Radegast, a Gothic beer hall just off Celetná, is a boisterous pub serving its namesake Radegast beer and good pub food. For a finely poured half-litre of Budějovický Budvar, the original Budweiser, stop in at U Medvídků (At the Bears), where you can also order up a plate of filling and fairly reasonably priced Czech fare such as goulash and dumplings (*see page 75*). Not far away from The Bears is U Dvou Koček (The Two Cats), where you can order a decent mug of Pilsner Urquell. While in the New Town, another good option is the Novoměstské Pivovar (New Town Brewery), a maze of vaulted rooms which tend to become very crowded. This relative newcomer to the area brews its own light and dark beer and serves tasty pub food.

Back across the river in Malá Strana, U Glaubiců opened in the early decades of the 16th century and has recently re-opened after being shut for years. Now restored to its 17th-century appearance, it serves reasonably priced light and dark beer specially brewed for it by the Velkopopovický brewery. Other places in Malá Strana meriting a visit are U Hrochu (The Hippopotamus), which though relatively new has acquired an impressive air of authenticity, and U Kocoura (The Cat), another place with a reputation for expertly cellaring and pouring its beer. Or perhaps you will choose to try the Malostranská hospoda on Karmelitská street for a foamy glass of refreshment.

RIGHT: sign outside a celebrated bar.

The new contenders

Though the historic districts have lost many of their classic pubs, what has come in to take their place is a new breed of establishments catering to the young and hip, with their laid-back ambiance and comfortable, deliberately mismatched furniture.

Still another type of watering hole new on the scene is the cocktail bar, where you can find a large array of Czech liquors and pricier imports mixed with flair. And paradoxically, some of the beer halls that are attracting in-the-know Praguers, such U Rudolfina in the Old Town, are actually of a newer vintage,

WINE BARS

Wine bars (*vinárny*) in Prague range from humble one-room bars to restaurants. One of the best *vinárny* is Blatnice, tucked away on Michalská in the Old Town. Šenk Vrbovec on Wenceslas Square or Michalská vinárna on the street of that name are also good bets. Here, the wine, from Moravia or Bohemia, is inexpensive and poured from barrels. More elegant *vinárny* serve vintage wines, such as V Zátiší on Liliová in the Old Town. Czechs prefer wine semi-sweet (*polosuché*), though a couple of grapes yield a dry (*suché*) wine. If you visit in autumn take advantage of the *burčák*. It is a sweet, young wine served in bars and by vendors at market stalls.

though they have quickly managed to acquire an air of having been there for centuries.

Theme pubs, such as Irish, English or American bars are also cropping up and are popular with young Praguers. Irish Guinness and screenings of soccer matches are commonplace.

A Prague pub crawl

Where is the best area to go in search of the true Czech pub experience, in a place not overrun with other tourists? The answer may well be Žižkov, a sub-

urb in Prague's third district. This former working-class neighbourhood, still a little unpolished in places, proudly claims the largest number of pubs per capita in all of Prague. Mixed in with plenty of authentic smoky pubs peopled by old-timers playing card games are a newer crop of equally smoky pubs but with a younger, trendier crowd.

If the idea of a Žižkov pub crawl appeals to you, one could take the Metro to the station Jiřího z Poděbrad on line A, three stops from Můstek, and start at U Sadu on Škroupovo náměstí, situated practically under the district's dominant landmark, the soaring television transmission tower. Then make your way over

---

A DRINKING FOG

The anti-smoking brigade that has captured most of the western world has not appeared to have reached Prague yet. Be warned: the city's pubs are thick with cigarette and cigar smoke.

---

to Akropolis on Kubelíkova, on down to Nad Viktorkou, with a stop at the Žižkovská hospoda on Koněvova and U vystřeleného oka (At the Shot-Out Eye), an artsy pub tucked away on a cul-de-sac off Husitská. The pub is named in honour of the one-eyed Hussite general Jan Žižka, whose enormous equestrian statue high on Vítkov Hill is this district's other dominant landmark. Don't despair if you wander off track; there is sure to be another agreeable pub just footsteps away.

Pub etiquette

When going into any of Prague's crowded pubs, if there is not a free table in sight, just find one with enough free space at it and ask if it is unoccupied by saying, "*Je tu volno?*" Once seated, put a coaster in front of you to indicate that you'd like to have a beer, and when the server comes around place your order for *pivo*.

In most pubs, when you order the first round the waiter will start a tab on a slip of paper left on the table, and keep making ticks for each subsequent round until you ask to pay (simply say "*zaplatit*", which means I would like to pay). Then it is often another member of staff who will come around and tally up the scratches on the piece of paper and announce an amount. In some pubs, it is assumed that your plan is to continue drinking one beer after another until the place closes. If an unbidden beer appears at your table after you've decided you'd like to leave, and you really don't have the time or inclination for just one more, firmly but politely indicate that you don't want it, and ask to pay up.

Whether a pub calls itself a *pivnice*, *hospoda* or *hostinec,* the important thing to all of them is that they take seriously their primary tasks: to serve up an expertly poured mug of beer and to foster a welcoming and convivial atmosphere. And remember: before you bring that frothy, thirst-quenching mug to your lips, don't forget to toast your table companions with "*Na zdraví!*" (To your health!). ❑

● *For further details on these pubs, please see the Travel Tips listing on page 257.*

LEFT: pulling a pint at the Corsair Bar.
RIGHT: the best pubs are in working-class areas.

FOOD

*Traditional Czech cuisine is simple, rustic and hearty, but international influences
are making their presence felt on Prague's restaurant scene*

Prague may still have a way to go before it rivals Paris or New York as a centre of gastronomy, but few other cities could claim to have come so far so fast. Prague's dining has acquired a more international flair in recent years, and a number of top-quality restaurants have sprung up to meet the demand of increasingly sophisticated gourmands, tourists and the city's foreign residents.

The availability of international food has risen sharply not only in quantity and variety, but also in quality. A few years ago it used to be that the non-Czech fare to be found was merely approximations of ethnic dishes. But now it is possible to dine on excellent French, Chinese, Indian, Japanese, Italian and even Lebanese food, as one would expect in other major cities.

Czech specialities

But great ethnic food can be found elsewhere. While in Prague, take the opportunity to sample the homey Czech specialities – especially if you don't mind dieting after your holiday. Classic Bohemian fare is most often a combination of meat and starch, usually in the form of dumplings or potatoes. The dumplings may be made either from bread (*houskové knedlíky*) or potato (*bramborové knedlíky*), and are ideal for mopping up the sauces served over the meat.

Most Czechs begin their meals with soup, and the choices range from simple meat broth with dumplings, to a thick potato cream soup or a bowl of tripe soup (reputed to be an excellent hangover cure). This might be followed with a main course of the speciality *svíčková na smetaně*, a cut of beef fillet in a slightly sweet cream sauce, garnished with cranberries, lemon and a dollop of whipped cream, and served with *houskové knedlíky*. Potato dumplings accompany smoked pork served with sweet red or white sauerkraut. These traditional dishes can be found in restaurants all over the city.

LEFT: Czech food stores dress up their window displays, particularly at Christmas time.
RIGHT: a waiter at Obecní dům.

For an introduction to Bohemian cooking in lively surroundings, head to one of the pubs that also offer a full menu. Try U Medvídků (At the Bears), or the Radegast *pivnice*, which serves up a first-rate *guláš* (goulash). The beer hall at Obecní dům also serves good Czech fare in a more serene environment.

The vegetarian problem

It is true that the classic Czech dishes and cuisine has very little to offer vegetarians. And just because a dish is meatless doesn't mean it's healthy. Aside from the ubiquitous *smážený sýr* (a thick slab of fried Edam cheese) served with chips and tartare sauce, other meatless options might be an omelette or deep-fried mushrooms. But be warned: if a dish is billed as *bez masa* (without meat), it doesn't mean a bit of bacon or splash of beef broth hasn't made its way into the meal.

Happily vegetarians can escape to any number of international restaurants serving pasta, pizza, salads, sandwiches or other meatless fare.

A haven for vegetarians is the U Govindy chain run by Hare Krishnas and serving fresh and tasty food for a nominal donation in two Prague locations. The branch near Náměstí Republiky also has a tearoom downstairs.

Czech desserts

When it comes to sweets Czech cuisine is not lacking, though this may not be apparent from the dessert offerings of the average restaurant. The most common offering is *palačinky,* warm, thin crêpes wrapped around ice cream, fruit,

chocolate or nuts. Ice cream sundaes or compotes of stewed fruit are also readily available. A relative rarity are delicious *ovocné knedlíky* (fruit dumplings). These dough balls, wrapped around plums, apricots or blueberries, drowned in butter, sprinkled with sugar, and usually topped with sweetened cheese, are filling enough to eat as a main course.

International restaurants offer a wider range of puddings, and it is difficult to go far without encountering the perennially popular *tiramisu,* with varying degrees of authenticity.

But for an even better glimpse at the Czech love of sweets, pop into a *cukrárna* (sweet shop) and choose from a tempting array of

cakes and pastries, which owe much to the Viennese tradition. A *cukrárna* is also the place to try locally made *zmrzlina* (ice cream).

> **FRUIT AND VEGETABLES**
>
> One of the best open markets for fresh fruit and vegetables is in Havelská, near Old Town Square. You can even wash off your wares in the fountain under the arcade.

Street food

If you are in a hurry, all up and down Wenceslas Square and in the Old Town Square, among other places, there are stalls that will sell you a *párek v rohlíku* (hot dog nestled into a warm roll) or a *klobasa* (a grilled sausage served with rye bread and mustard). A *langoš,* a garlic-slathered slab of deep-fried dough, might also hit the spot. In the colder months, many food stalls also sell warming cups of *svařené víno* (mulled wine) to wash down your food. A sweet street snack is an *oplatka,* a sugar-filled wafer put on a hot iron to caramelise the sugar.

Fine dining

For those looking for romantic dining, eschew the boisterous pubs for one of the city's excellent restaurants-with-a-view. Bellevue, as the name implies, offers stunning vistas of the river Vltava and Prague Castle. A couple of other good restaurants along the water are Ostroff on Střelecký Island and Kampa Park just off the Charles Bridge on Kampa Island.

A couple of Prague's best restaurants reside in equally stellar settings. The French restaurant La Perle de Prague, on the top floors of the "dancing building" (Tančící dům) built by Frank O Gehry and Vlado Milunić, heads this list. For fans of Art Nouveau, the restaurant Villa Voyta in the hotel of that name is worth the trip to Prague 4's Lhotka neighbourhood.

Restaurant listings

Prague dining is constantly in flux, and those who wish to dine well here should buy a copy of *Gurmán,* a restaurant guide that is updated twice yearly and is published in an English version. Or pick up the weekly English-language *Prague Post,* which offers restaurant reviews and lists a selection of restaurants.

In the high tourist seasons, it is advisable to call ahead for table reservations. For further details on the restaurants named above, see Travel Tips. ❑

LEFT: tucking into a real Czech meal – potato dumplings, duck and beer.

Coffee Houses

Praguers these days don't seem to have the time in their fast-moving lives to while away their days in the city's venerable cafés, that great institution of the interwar First Republic. At one time Prague café society was equal to that of Paris and Vienna. Many of the most storied cafés frequented by their forebears have faded into history – gone, for example, are the National and the Arco, the meeting place of the "Arconauts", who included Franz Kafka, Max Brod, Franz Werfel and others. But some of Prague's other illustrious cafés are still humming with a vibrant mix that includes students, entrepreneurs with their mobile phones, ladies of a certain age, and the inevitable tourists from all over the world.

Several of the city's time-honoured coffee houses (*kavárny*) have been given a facelift in recent years, and café society seems to be making a gradual comeback. The Malostranská kavárna underwent renovation in 1997, and the famed Café Slavia re-opened with much fanfare in November the same year. Once filled in its heyday with poets, painters and actors from the National Theatre across the street, the Slavia today still gets an occasional visit from one-time habitué and the current Czech president, Václav Havel.

Prague's coffee houses are excellent places for people-watching, and an afternoon can be pleasantly spent observing the comings and goings from a windowside table while sipping a cup of *espresso* or glass of herbaceous Becherovka, the national liqueur. Coffee is usually drunk black, although a Viennese variation, topped with whipped cream, is also popular and tourists have brought with them the *cappuccino*. In these cafés the staff won't mind if you spend half the afternoon nursing a single cup of coffee while you write in your journal or glance through the newspapers or magazines made available to customers. You can also nibble a pastry as an accompaniment or indulge in a light meal, or occasionally something more substantial, at most of these venues.

Most of the best cafés are ideally situated on lively pedestrian thoroughfares, and are a great place to escape from the bustle and just sit back and unwind. They often feature sumptuous interiors

RIGHT: the famous Obecní dum serves good Czech fare and great coffee.

that can quickly sweep you back to an earlier era when cafés were the nexus of Prague social life. A good place to start might be at the café in Obecní dům, whose Art Nouveau splendour was lovingly restored to great acclaim in the late 1990s. Or try the café in the Hotel Evropa on Wenceslas Square, with its still sumptuous, though slightly faded Art Nouveau interior.

In cafés such as the Slavia or the Café Louvre on Národní třída you are likely to find waiters and waitresses who take great pride in their profession, dressed smartly in bow-ties and crisp white aprons. Another good bet for its elegant setting is the Café Savoy, set back from Vitězná near the Legions'

Bridge, an airy and genteel space decorated with restored murals.

A few of Prague's cafés are attempting to resurrect the traditional connection between coffee houses and literature. The Literární kavárna G + G in the Vinohrady neighbourhood, which is connected with a publisher of the same name, hosts regular poetry readings in Czech and English for the clientele, as well as music recitals. And the expat-owned Globe Bookstore and Coffeehouse occasionally hosts readings by some of the big names among Czech and English-language writers passing through Prague. ❏

● *For further details on the coffee houses described above, see the Travel Tips listing on page 267.*

BOHEMIAN GLASS

One of the finest of the decorative arts to emerge out of Bohemia is its
unique decorated and cut glassware

Archaeological excavations have confirmed that glass has been used to make bead necklaces and bracelets in the area of the present-day Czech Republic for many hundreds of years. In the early Middle Ages the first blown glass was used to make drinking goblets, and at the same time windows, glass panes and

wall mosaics were being manufactured. During the reign of Emperor Charles IV, in 1370, the massive mosaic on the south portal of St Vitus' Cathedral was made, showing scenes from the Last Judgement. The splendid windows of St Bartholomew's Church in Kolín also date from around 1380. Glass for everyday use was, as in other Central European countries, mostly employed in the form of bottles and phials, in standard shades of green or brown.

By the beginning of the 15th century there is evidence that there were eight glassworks in Bohemia, five in Moravia and another eight in Silesia, which at that time was part of the Bohemian kingdom. The glassworks in

Chřibská, which still exist today, were mentioned as early as 1427, and had considerable influence on the development of the Bohemian glass industry. By the 16th century, the rustic glass made in the forests no longer satisfied the refined tastes of the aristocracy who belonged to the court of the first Habsburg rulers. Following Venetian models, thin, refined glass was produced, in harmonious and elegant Renaissance styles.

Towards the end of the 16th century, and particularly after 1600, cylindrical tankards formed the ideal basis for what would become the famous Bohemian enamelled glass.

Gem-cutters' skills

From 1600 to 1610, at the Prague court of Rudolf II, the jeweller Caspar Lehmann (1563–1622) of Uelzen had experimented with the engraving of glass. As gem-cutter to Rudolf II, he adapted these techniques, using bronze and copper wheels for working on glass. This was a new skill, and when it was perfected, engraved glass was highly prized.

In Bohemia the production of engraved glass did not begin until around 1680. From then on, glass was exported in great quantities to all parts of Europe. The names of aristocratic families such as Kinský and Harrach can be found among the production managers of glassworks in north and northeast Bohemia and in the Bohemian forest (Šumava).

The 18th and 19th centuries

After 1720, the variety of products was enriched by the addition of gilded glass and black painted decoration in the style of Ignaz Preissler (1676–1741). Engraved and cut glass from Bohemia was famous, as was the Bohemian chandelier with pendants of cut crystal glass. During the 18th century these chandeliers were being exported to the courts of France and Tzarist Russia.

After some stagnation towards the end of the 18th century, milky Bohemian glass with painted, colourful enamel decoration now became tremendously popular. Contrasting trends that developed around 1800 provided the market with plain, finely cut and engraved Empire- and Biedermeier-style glasses.

Yet a further success for the glassware industry came from 1820 onwards with the thick, coloured glass discovered by Friedrich Egerman: black hyalith (often used with gold Chinoiserie decoration), agate glass, lithyalin (which resembled semi-precious stones) and new uses for ruby glass and opaque white overlay glass, both carved and enamelled, were taken into production.

THE BOHEMIAN GOBLET

The classic shape of the Bohemian Baroque goblet, with its polished balustered foot and the many-sided beaker of fine, thin glass, was intricately engraved with ornaments featuring flowers, garlands or grotesques.

glass window in St Vitus' Cathedral. Other artists such as Loetz, Lobmayer and Jeykal used imaginative Art Nouveau shapes and utilised surprising colours and metallic effects. The Arts and Crafts School in Prague produced a particularly excellent generation of artists just after World War II, and they were successful in a number of important exhibitions during the 1950s and 1960s.

Apart from its usual domestic and technical functions, modern glass has become an art

The fame of Bohemian glass was increased in the 19th century by mirror and plate glass and by glass coral. The latter is still produced in Jablonec nad Nisou, under the name Jablonex.

Mucha's Art Nouveau

Bohemian glass entered the 20th century with artists such as Alfons Mucha, who used the medium to great effect, notably in his stained-

form. Bohemian glass is widely available in shops and galleries throughout the city in a range of designs, from huge chandeliers to simple vases, although its increasing popularity is raising the prices. A particularly good place to go for bargains is Karlovy Vary, where the Moser factory is based (*see page 237*). The factory shop offers glassware for sale considerably cheaper than in the tourist-orientated shops of the capital.

For those interested in learning more about the history of the Bohemian glassware industry and seeing some fine antique examples, pay a visit to the Museum of Decorative Arts, which can be found in the Jewish Quarter. ❏

PRECEDING PAGES: old spa glasses from Karlovy Vary.
LEFT: an Alfons Mucha stained-glass window.
RIGHT: a selection of Bohemian glass on sale.

PRAGUE'S WINTER BALL SEASON

Young and old, Praguers love to dance. Just as winter settles in, the ball season arrives to bring the city a flash of gaiety amid the snows

As the days grow short and the sky dons its pall of grey for the winter, the ball season gets into swing. On any given weekend night in winter, venues all over town are filled with the sounds of waltzes, foxtrots and polkas, as Czechs of all ages step out in their finery for a night of ballroom dancing. Most young people attend dancing lessons from an early age, and the graduation ball (*maturitní ples*) is a rite of passage for all Czech school-leavers.

TAKE YOUR PARTNER

Unlike in other cities, Prague's balls are truly for everyone, not just the social élite. Every aspiring Fred and Ginger should be able to find a ball that will suit his or her taste. Among the many choices for splashing out is the Moravian Ball, where attendees dress in traditional Moravian folk costume and dance to melodies from this ancient region. Or, for a slightly offbeat evening, check out the Hunters' Ball, where prizes of dead game are raffled off at midnight, and weary revellers may be seen trudging home at the end of the ball with a half-frozen pheasant in tow on one of the city's night trams. For lovers of the local brew, there is also a Beer Ball, where *pivo* and dancing are the focal points. Almost every profession, from doctors to journalists, has its own winter ball.

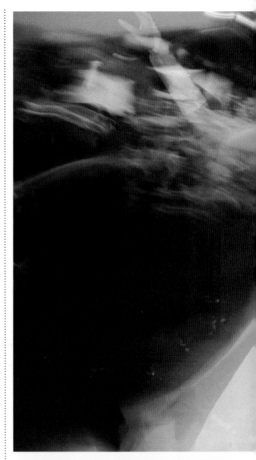

△ **SUITED SUITORS**
Anxious young men at the start of the dance relax once the music begins.

▷ **SHALL WE DANCE?**
Ballroom dance is a serious sport in Prague. Many young dancers move on to the world of competitive dancing.

▷ **TAKE FIVE**
Some ballgoers take a breather to watch from the balcony as others dance the night away.

GRADUATION COIN TOSSING

△ OLD TIES
Since the 1989 revolution, ties to that other dancing city, Vienna, have been re-established with an annual Prague-Vienna Ball.

◁ COSTUME BALL
At the Moravian Ball, people dress in traditional folk costume and dance to the region's lively songs.

A highlight for students graduating from their *gymnázium* (high school) is the *maturitní ples* (school-leaving ball). By the time this ball rolls around, they should be well prepared to demonstrate their ballroom dancing skills: most of the students will have spent months learning all the steps at dancing lessons.

At some point during the ball an ancient Prague ritual occurs, when parents and well-wishers shower the students with coins. The graduates run around, scooping up the crowns that have been rained upon them – the money collected is set aside for a later graduation party. It won't be their last chance to cash in on their school-leaving, however. In late spring, when exams are over, graduates can be seen in outlandish getups, hat in hand, requesting coins with cries of "*maturita*!" ("graduation!") from passersby, who cheerfully hand over their spare change to the colourful "beggars".

Mozart im Haufe Du...
Schek.

CITY OF MUSIC

Few other cities can claim such talent and determination of its musicians, from the early politically hindered composers to the modern-day jazz buskers

Paris may be the city of lovers and Milan the city of fashion, but Prague is without any doubt the city of music. David Oistrakh once described Prague as the "musical heart of Europe", and the city still beats as the centre of Bohemia's rich musical heritage, as it has done for centuries.

Bohemian musicians

The great flowering of Czech music, also known as "Bohemian classicism", took place in the 18th century. The popular saying "All Bohemians are musicians" dates from this time, and the fact that it seems to be true – or very nearly true – probably stems from Bohemia's traditional support for musical education. Documents dating from this time show that most cantors (school-teachers) had a musical education and saw to it that every pupil could play one or more instruments or, at the very least, they could sing.

Musical talent and education, in those early days, were an excellent means of obtaining material comforts and advantages. Peasants could be freed from serfdom and exempted from military service if their musical achievements came to the ears of their lords. And once a position as a servant was gained, those who went on to prove themselves as good musicians had the hope of rising to more elevated positions and perhaps even being released from service altogether.

When the English composer Charles Burnley visited Bohemia in 1772 he was so surprised by the level of musical skill in the country that he named it the "conservatory of Europe". The musical climate not only produced many folk musicians but also such a surplus of trained performers that they had difficulty in earning their living in their home country.

The unstable political situation of the 18th

century, together with religious persecution, forced many people to emigrate. Countless musicians were among them, and, thanks to their skills, easily found work all over Europe. Everywhere these emigrants went, they commanded respect, influenced the new instrumental style of classicism, and left definite

traces in the structure of its melodies. At the same time, Bohemian music became exposed to foreign influences, which it in turn incorporated successfully.

Mozart and Figaro

The visits of Wolfgang Amadeus Mozart (1756–91) should be seen in this international context. Mozart left his home town of Salzburg, Austria to build a career for himself in Vienna, but the Viennese public and the court did not always appreciate him. But Prague had gone wild about his opera *The Marriage of Figaro* when it was performed here. An invitation to visit the city followed, and he came in 1787.

LEFT: a portrait of Mozart, who captured the popular imagination of Prague with his *Marriage of Figaro*.
RIGHT: capturing the 18th-century musical spirit.

In Prague Mozart witnessed *Figaro*-fever, which had gripped the whole city and led to him receiving a commission for an opera from the impresario of what was then the Nostitz Theatre (now the Estates Theatre, *see page 174*). In contrast to other theatres in Central Europe, the Nostitz was not tied to a court, but was a relatively independent institution. The fact that in Prague opera had been available to the public for a long time explains the interest of the broad mass of people. The

MOZART MANIA

Men dressed in Mozart costumes are a regular sight all over the Old Town, but be aware that the concerts they advertise are often given over to tourism rather than musical quality!

middle classes claimed their share in the process of shaping cultural life. The centre of activity moved from aristocratic salons to public concert halls, and a new era dawned. It was shaped by two institutions which both left a definitive mark. One was the Society of Artists, founded in 1803 and modelled on its predecessor in Vienna; the other was the Prague Conservatory, which opened in 1811. This was the first in Central Europe and set the standards for the rest. The city of Prague, which

Prague premiere of *Don Giovanni* in the autumn of the same year, conducted by Mozart himself, was an unprecedented success.

Although Mozart spent quite little of his life in Prague, he has become a revered adopted son, as is evident from the Mozart industry in postcards and T-shirts and the interest shown in the Mozart museum, Bertramka, at Mozartova 169 in the district of Smíchov, which holds regular concerts.

The German influence

From the early 19th century on, the aristocracy of Prague gradually lost their position as the most important patrons of the arts. The rising

was still under the strong influence of the Mozart cult, was now being exposed to even more new influences.

Carl Maria von Weber, director of the Nostitz Theatre from 1813–16, acquainted Prague with Beethoven's *Fidelio* and the first Romantic operas. In the same theatre, Nicolo Paganini, the celebrated violinist and composer, enjoyed great successes. Beethoven concerts also took place in the Konvikt, a complex in Bartolomějská (now an art-house film club). Later in the 19th century, a concert hall on the Slavic Island (Slovanský ostrov), near the present-day National Theatre, became a venue for Berlioz, Wagner and Liszt. The scene was now defined by the flood of German music, and Czech music faded into the background.

Bedrich Smetana

The awakening of national consciousness during the troubled times of the early 19th century saw a generation of Czech artists faced with the task of creating their own culture. They were not alone in this: throughout Europe nationalists were rediscovering their pasts and forging links between political aspirations and musical and literary expression. In the Czech lands, this cultural resurgence did not take place until the second half of the century.

The name of Bedřich Smetana (1824–84) is inextricably tied with Prague, and in his work Czech music first reached its peak. Born in Litomyšl, Smetana came to the city to study music. He took part in the Czech nationalist revolution in 1848, and shared in the patriotic feelings which engendered it. His wish was to unite artistic expectations with the demands of an independent national culture. It was a long road, but his aim was eventually achieved with his operas. Apart from a five-year stay in Göteborg in Sweden, Smetana remained active in the musical life of Prague, while he tried, at first in vain, to establish himself as a conductor and composer. Not until the success of his opera *The Bartered Bride* (1866) did he achieve the position of conductor to the Czech Opera and widespread recognition.

After the loss of his hearing in 1874 Smetana gave up his career as a practising musician, but he continued to compose and created some notable works, including the symphonic poems *Má vlast (My Homeland)*, and the string quartet *Aus meinem Leben (From My Life)*. Smetana received the highest honour when his opera *Libuše* was performed at the official opening of the National Theatre, a ceremony that symbolised the peak of national aspirations.

Antonin Dvořák

While everyone in Prague was raving about Smetana, another Czech composer had already started to show his talent. Antonín Dvořák (1841–1904) was born near Prague and first attracted attention with his *Hymnus,* a

---

LEFT: a performance of Bedřich Smetana's *The Bartered Bride* at Prague's National Theatre.
RIGHT: bust of Antonín Dvořák.

nationalistic cantata based on Halek's poem *The Heroes of the White Mountain.* He attended the organ school in Prague, played in the National Theatre orchestra, and was organist at St Adalbert's from 1874 to 1877.

His talent was recognised by Brahms, who introduced his music to Vienna, sponsoring the publication of the *Klänge aus Mähren (Sounds from Moravia)*, which was followed by a commissioned work, *Slavonic Dances.* His *Stabat Mater*, performed in London in 1883, won him European acclaim. In 1892–5 he was director of the New York Conservatory. His ninth symphony *From the New World* had a distinct

Slavonic flavour. Returning to Prague in 1895, Dvořák remained true to the musical traditions of Bohemia and influenced musical life of the city. His home, Villa Amerika, is now open to the public (*see page 189*).

Modern music

The strong flow of national culture did not have a detrimental effect on Prague's open-minded attitude to modern European music. Gustav Mahler, in 1885 conductor of the New German Theatre's orchestra, had the first performance of his *Symphony No. 7* take place in Prague. The same orchestra was directed from 1911–27 by Alexander von Zemlinsky, who acted as a go-between with the great musical cities, Vienna and Berlin; Alban Berg (1885–1935) and Arnold Schönberg (1874–1951) both had the opportunity to get to know Prague. Schönberg's *Ewartung* (*Expectation*) was premiered here.

Contemporary Prague lives up to the musical aspirations of the past. The National Theatre, the State Opera, and the Estates Theatre have a feast of opera and ballet on offer. Smetana is particularly well represented. Visitors to Prague can admire a range of his romantic operas, from *Libuše*, to the world-famous folk opera *The Bartered Bride* (*Prodaná nevěsta*), and *The*

Brandenburgers in Bohemia (*Braniboři v Čechách*), which celebrated its first success in 1866 and has been in the repertoire ever since. Dvořák still has his opera *Rusalka* and several of his other works performed regularly.

Admirers of contemporary opera will mostly find their tastes represented by the works of Bohuslav Martinů (1890–1959) and Leos Janáček (1854–1928), whose first opera, *Jenůfa*, was performed in Prague in 1916. It still appears regularly in the National Theatre opera repertoire, as does his most famous operatic work, *The Cunning Little Vixen* (*Příhody lišky Bystroušky*).

All musical tastes

You don't have to enjoy opera to have your musical tastes catered for in Prague. A varied programme is assured by several symphony orchestras, chamber music ensembles, and soloists, together with visiting foreign musicians. The Czech Philharmonic has its home in the Dvořák Hall of the Rudolfinum. The Prague Symphony Orchestra is based in the Smetana Hall at the Obecní dům. The Czech National Symphony Orchestra also performs regularly.

Information about all performances is provided by the numerous ticket agencies, including the Prague Information Service (Old Town Hall, tel: 2448 2018), by leaflet distributors and by posters pasted up all over the city centre.

The traditional repertoire is dominant in the programmes of the concert halls, and Czech composers, both old and new, feature prominently. For those who like chamber music, various string quartets can be recommended, such as the Wihan Quartet, the Talich Quartet, and the Škampa Quartet. The Suk Chamber Orchestra, founded by violinist Josef Suk, a great-grandson of Dvořák, offers splendid renditions of music by Czech composers. Regular concerts also feature Prague ensembles which have received international recognition, such as the Prague Madrigalists, a vocal group, and soloists such as cellist Jiří Bárta.

Musical life of Prague culminates in the Spring International Music Festival, a tradition going back over 50 years and a fixed place in the international calendar (*see page 98*). ❏

UNUSUAL MUSIC VENUES

Many churches and palaces are venues for concerts that offer an opportunity to see places that are not otherwise open. The architecture of St Vitus' Cathedral is enhanced by the addition of an orchestra and choir, and medieval music breathes new life into St George's Basilica. The Bethlehem Chapel, St James' and St Nicholas' in Malá Strana also hold concerts. Historic rooms opened for musical events include the mirrored chapel of the Clementinum, the Martinů Hall in Lichtenstein Palace, the Spanish Hall in the castle and St Agnes' Convent. Open-air concerts take place in the gardens of Waldstein Palace and the Royal Gardens below the castle.

LEFT: the German composer Arnold Schönberg.
RIGHT: Czech composer Bedřich Smetana.

LITERATURE

From Kafka to Kundera, many Czech writers have won international
acclaim. And one – Václav Havel – even became president

During Franz Kafka's time, around the turn of the 20th century, Prague was a crossroads of Czech, German, Austrian and Jewish culture. Kafka himself was a microcosm of all these. As a German speaker among Czechs, he was in an élite minority; as a Jew among Germans, a smaller minority still. (Look up "Kafka" in several random encyclopedias and you'll find him labelled variously as an Austrian, Jewish, German or Czech writer.) Many believe that the sense of alienation that permeates Kafka's fiction springs from this confusion of identity.

The German influence

Kafka wrote in German, however, and thus belonged to the circle of German-speaking intellectuals, along with such literary contemporaries as Franz Werfel (1890–1945) and Egon Erwin Kisch (1885–1948). Werfel is best known for his book *Song of Bernadette*, but was regarded at that time primarily as a poet. Kisch was called "the Roving Reporter", a journalist whose scathing critiques of society often took him into the back-alley underworld of Prague, and whose personal exploits in getting a story were legendary. A plaque on the House of the Two Bears on Kožná commemorates the place of his birth.

But perhaps the most important person in this early 20th-century literary circle was Max Brod (1894–1968). Brod is not known today so much for his literary works, which are more or less forgotten, but for his tireless championing of other writers and artists, which made him a pivotal figure of the times.

If it weren't for Brod, Kafka would be known today only as an author of a few early published works. It was Brod, as Kafka's literary executor, who brought the writer's great novels to the public after his death. Although some – most recently and famously, the Czech émigré writer

Milan Kundera – charge that Brod's act was a blatant disregard of Kafka's wish that his unpublished manuscripts be burned, Brod claims that he told Kafka to his face that he would never carry out such a request. Tellingly, perhaps, the only memorial to Max Brod is a plaque in the New Jewish Cemetery, hung on a

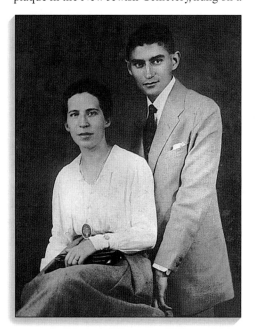

wall across from Kafka's grave. (Brod himself emigrated to Israel in 1939.)

But it was Brod's enthusiasm that managed to cross the Czech/German language and culture barrier. He was also a tireless promoter of the works of composer Leoš Janáček, and helped to promote the wider acclaim of the quintessential Czech novel, *The Good Soldier Švejk*, by Jaroslav Hašek (1883–1923).

The Good Soldier Svejk

Published in 1921, Hašek's story relates the serial misadventures of the hapless Josef Švejk, who frustrates the Austrian army's attempts to make a soldier out of him by his unique form of

---

PRECEDING PAGES: Theologians' Hall, Strahov Monastery. **LEFT:** Josef Lada's image of the Good Soldier Švejk. **RIGHT:** Franz Kafka with Felice Bauer.

smiling, servile sabotage. By appearing to follow all orders to the letter, Švejk makes a fruitful career of getting out of whatever work he is supposed to do, meanwhile getting into some very amusing scrapes along the way. It is a dark comic novel that offers very little in the way of optimism.

Because of its questionable hero, *The Good Soldier Švejk* (*Sweik* in German) has been criticised by some as being insulting and presenting a negative picture of the Czech national character. But don't tell that to the 23 Czech literary scholars, writers and historians who, in a 1998 survey published in *Týden*

magazine, voted *Švejk*, by a wide margin, the greatest Czech prose work of the 20th century.

The broad, beaming face of Švejk has been immortalised by the illustrations of the popular Czech artist Josef Lada that appeared in the first edition (and most editions since), and these images have become as much of a Prague icon as the brooding face of Kafka (although Švejk is much more likely to take the humourous form of a souvenir puppet). Strangely, much less is known of Švejk's creator, Jaroslav Hašek, who was as apparently as hard-living as Kafka was ascetic, and who died in 1923 at the premature age of 40.

DRINKING TO A LITERARY TRADITION

Fans of Czech literature can find many cafés and bars in the city which boasted writers among their clientele, aside from visiting the obligatory Kafka sites, and soak up the atmosphere that inspired these detailers of Prague life.

Both Hašek and his famous character, The Good Soldier Švejk, are today almost over-immortalised at the pub U Kalicha (The Chalice), where, in the novel, Švejk and a friend made a date to meet at "six in the evening after the war." The pub, which features a plethora of Švejk memorabilia on its walls, now caters mostly to the hordes of tourists wishing to drink in some of the spirit of the good soldier (*see page 69*).

Many people today still visit Bohumil Hrabal's favourite pub, U zlatého tygra (The Golden Tiger), where the well-known *bon viveur* was a regular fixture for many years.

The Café Slavia, which in turn was immortalised by the poet Jaroslav Seifert, was a second home for many prominent Czech artists around the turn of the 20th century. Later, during the Communist era, it was a hotbed for dissident writers whose works were banned by the government. After standing abandoned for many years, the Slavia was finally restored in the 1990s to the glory of its halcyon days, and today retains its unique air of *fin-de-siècle* sophistication.

Creating a national voice

Another early 20th-century Czech writer who made his mark was the prolific Karel Čapek. Although a radical journalist and author of numerous works of fiction, including *An Ordinary Life*, *Meteor* and *Stories From Two Pockets*, he was also a playwright who is perhaps best known for having coined the international word "robot" in his play *RUR*.

Gustav Meyrink's novel *The Golem* retold the legend of the real Rabbi Löw and the pretenatural creature he fashioned from the mud of the Vltava to defend the ghetto (*see page 179*). Alas, the Golem began to run amok

with other prominent Czech artists including Alfons Mucha, Bedřich Smetana, Antonín Dvořák, and Ema Destinnová, in the cemetery at Vyšehrad (*see page 200*).

Jan Neruda was another voice to mark the turn of the 20th century with his details of life in the Malá Strana. Neruda Alley (Nerudova) is named in commemoration of the writer.

Modern voices

Contemporary Czech literature lost perhaps its brightest light with the death of Bohumil Hrabal. The author of many works, including *I Served the King of England* and *Too Loud a*

and Löw was eventually compelled to destroy his creation and, rumour has it, lay it to rest in the attic of the Old-New Synagogue. Rabbi Löw's tombstone can be seen in the Old Jewish Cemetery, not far away.

Also influential in Kafka's time was Božena Němcová, whose lyrical work *Babička* (*Grandmother*), written in the 19th century, enjoyed a perennial popularity and was always high on Kafka's list of recommendations. Both Němcová and Karel Čapek are buried, along

Solitude, Hrabal is probably best known outside of his homeland as the author of *Closely Watched Trains*, set at the end of World War II, which was later made into an Oscar-winning film by Czech director Jiří Menzel in 1966. Hrabal fell to his death from a fifth-floor hospital window in 1997, an end eerily presaged in several of his later writings, particularly the disturbing collection of essays titled *Total Fears*.

Also prominent is the Czech writer Jaroslav Seifert (1901–86), the only Czech to date to win the Nobel Prize for Literature, in 1984. A pro-Communist who later turned his back on the movement, Seifert is best-known for his poetry, including an ode to the Café Slavia.

LEFT: admirers of Hašek's *The Good Soldier Švejk* tour Prague beer halls dressed in period costumes.
ABOVE: President Masaryk meeting Karel Čapek.

Notable among contemporary writers is Ivan Klíma (b. 1931), author of many works that focus on Prague, including *Spirit of Prague*, *My Merry Mornings*, and perhaps most notably, *Judge on Trial*, about a judge working within the Communist regime. But Klíma, although he lives in Prague and writes in Czech, is generally more popular abroad than he is in his homeland.

Writers in exile

Another Czech writer more popular in other countries is the expatriate author Milan Kundera (b. 1929), who may be, after Kafka and

Švejk, the name most associated with Czech literature for foreigners. His novels, such as *The Book of Laughter and Forgetting* and, most notably, *The Unbearable Lightness of Being*, were extremely well-received in the west. The latter was made into a popular film in 1987 starring Daniel Day-Lewis and Juliette Binoche, and provided many westerners with their first glimpse of what life was like in Czechoslovakia during the dark days of the Iron Curtain. Kundera left Czechoslovakia after the 1968 Warsaw Pact invasion, and chose to remain abroad after the revolution, taking French citizenship and writing his recent works in French. Many Czechs feel that his earlier

books, such as *The Joke*, about the Stalinist regime, are more important than those with which he gained an international reputation.

Czechs feel similar about another émigré, the humourous and disrespectful Josef Škvorecký, who is generally regarded in his homeland more for his 1950 novel *The Cowards* than subsequent works such as *The Engineer of Human Souls*, written in self-imposed exile in Canada.

The new wave

These more established authors are now beginning to have strong competition from a new wave of Czech contemporary writers who have found their voices in the post-Communist era. One of the most popular of these younger writers is Michael Vieweigh, whose novels *The Wonderful Years that Sucked* and *Bringing Up Girls in Bohemia* were not only best-selling books, but were made into extremely popular films as well.

And then there is Jáchym Topol – son of the playwright Josef (best known for his play *Nightingale for Dinner*) and brother of the firebrand underground rock musician and actor Filip – who has made an intense and disturbing impression on the Czech literary scene with his works, including the lacerating novel *Sister*.

The philosopher president

One of the distinctions of the Czech Republic is, of course, that its first president, Václav Havel was, before the revolution, a well-known playwright and political dissident. His works for the stage, such as *Private View*, *Garden Party* and *Largo Desolato*, functioned not only as drama but as allegorical tools of sabotage against the repression of the Communist regime. Havel also produced several books of thoughtful essays, philosophical reflections that draw on the experiences of his own life, among them *Letters to Olga*, a compilation of his letters from prison to his first wife.

Although Havel's main body of work was produced before his entry into political life, it is likely that the works of this "philosopher president," which spoke so eloquently to his times will maintain their place among the classic works of Czech literature. ❏

LEFT: paperback cover for Milan Kundera's most popular novel, *The Unbearable Lightness of Being*.

Franz Kafka's Prague

Few writers are as closely linked to their home towns as Franz Kafka (1883–1924) is to Prague. The author of some of the greatest works of 20th-century literature lived all but a few months of his life in the city, yet his relationship with Prague was ambiguous at best; he often expressed the wish to leave the town that he referred to as "the worst misfortune that had befallen" him and "a little mother with claws".

In a walk across Old Town Square, you can see the house where Kafka was born (U Radnice 5, now containing an exhibit dedicated to the writer); where he lived as a child (U Minuty House, Staroměstské náměstí 2); where he wrote most of *The Castle* (Oppelt House, Staroměstské náměstí 5); where he frequently attended a literary salon (House of the Unicorn, Staroměstské náměstí 18, which now bears a plaque to commemorate the luminaries who met there); and where he went to school (Staroměstské náměstí 12), the same building where his father had his haberdashery shop and which is now occupied by the Franz Kafka Bookstore. Kafka's university and several other family residences are only a stone's throw away from the square. It's no wonder that Kafka, looking out of his window down at the Old Town Square one day, drew several small rings with his finger and remarked to an acquaintance, "This little circle encompassed my entire life."

Apart from one early short work, however, *Description of a Struggle*, Kafka's stories were not set in Prague – or in any specific city. And yet, it's impossible not to see its influence in Kafka's fiction. "Kafka was Prague and Prague was Kafka," wrote one of his contemporaries, Johannes Urzidil. "Prague is contained … everywhere in his works."

Perhaps it would be more correct to say that it was Kafka's unique vision of Prague that was his real inspiration. Part of his perspective came from the fact that he lived almost his whole life with his parents and sisters (until the sisters married) in relatively small apartments, forcing him into an intimacy with his family that allowed for little privacy. One of his first published works was a short piece printed in a newspaper complaining

RIGHT: the house on Golden Lane where Kafka wrote *The Country Doctor* is now a Kafka museum.

about how noisy his family was. His strained relationship with his father, Herman, eventually produced *Letter to his Father*, in which Franz catalogues all his complaints. It was written as a letter that Kafka handed to his mother with the request that she deliver it to her husband. Wisely, she declined. Kafka's uneasy relationship with his family can also be seen as a major influence in his most famous story, *The Metamorphosis*.

Prague isn't mentioned in Kafka's two great novels, *The Trial* and *The Castle*, tortured tales of hapless people who struggle against a faceless, incomprehensible and malevolent bureaucracy. But there's no doubt that Kafka's job at the Worker's

Accident Insurance Company for the Kingdom of Bohemia in Prague, where attempting to negotiate the maze of Austro-Hungarian red tape was his daily routine, gave him food for thought.

Apart from the Old Town, Franz Kafka lived in two other Prague locations. The house on Golden Lane (Zlatá ulička 22) was rented by his sister Ottla as a place to meet her boyfriend. Kafka saw its potential as a quiet place to write, and spent his evenings there penning the stories later collected as *A Country Doctor*. One of the few apartments that he rented for himself was in the Schönborn Palace in Malá Strana. The author of *Amerika* could not know that the building at Tržiště 15 would one day house the American Embassy. ❑

THEATRE

The Czechs' love of theatre is still going strong despite financial difficulties, and a wide range of performances caters to all tastes

Theatre in Prague has a long and venerable tradition – as you would expect in the capital of a country which, in 1989, chose a playwright, Václav Havel, as its first post-Communist president.

Just over two hundred years earlier, in 1785, the people of Prague had lobbied their Austro-

Hungarian rulers for the right to put on plays in their own language in the newly-built Nostitz Theatre (today the Estates Theatre). And in 1881, when the brand new National Theatre burned down shortly after completion, sufficient public subscriptions were raised within a matter of weeks by the theatre-loving citizens to ensure that it was rebuilt again only two years later.

That same spirit is still very much alive today. Open any newspaper or listings magazine, read the posters plastered all over the city, and you will realise that the citizens of Prague think that theatre is still important. In an average week you might find productions of

Hamlet, Cabaret and *The Inspector General*, together with a wide selection of original Czech plays, a revival of *Fiddler on the Roof* and perhaps a quite unique performance of Mozart's *Don Giovanni*, set to recorded music in the original Italian and "performed" by elaborately costumed puppets.

And all that is without including the numerous fringe and alternative venues, or the two other theatrical forms for which Prague is perhaps best-known, in addition to puppetry: mime and a speciality, "Black Light".

Mime and Black Light theatre

Mime has a long and popular tradition in the Czech Republic and it can be seen at various theatres in the city. A new generation of mime artists operates from a little theatre in the middle of a courtyard surrounded by blocks of flats, called *Divadlo Mimů Alfred ve dvoře* (Alfred's Mime Theatre in the Courtyard). This unorthodox venue was founded by Ctibor Turba, a popular clown who teaches non-verbal theatre in Prague and France, and it offers both traditional and outlandish performances of mime and physical theatre.

Black Light is a postwar concept and was an idea first introduced in 1958 at the World Exhibition in Brussels. Since then it has gone from strength to strength in Prague. During the performances films and slides are projected on to multiple screens while actors, dressed completely in black to render them invisible, perform on stage, accompanied by a clever play of coloured lights.

A certain amount of acrobatic skill is also often required of the actors. Among the Black Light companies, *Laterna Magika* (Magic Lantern) is the most popular, and has made its home at the modern, gleaming glass Nová Scéna opposite the more traditional National Theatre in the New Town (*see pages 192–193*). Divadlo Image, the All Colours Theatre, and Černé divadlo Animato are three other venues in Prague where these popular and ingenious performances are staged throughout the year.

Puppet theatre

Puppet theatre in Prague is surprisingly popular with adults as well as children, and, like mime and Black Light shows, it often appeals to tourists, as language is not a problem. The most traditional shows, using the time-honoured characters of Josef Skupa can be seen at the Spejbl and Hurvínek Theatre, while the avant-garde all-purpose theatre Divadlo Archa frequently puts on innovative, original performances by theatre artist Petr Nikl.

THEATRE TICKETS

Theatre ticket prices have risen in recent years, but are still very cheap compared to in the West. Tickets are available from the venues or from ticket agencies.

intimate Divadlo v Řeznicke in the New Town is a favourite for both actors and audiences due to its unconventional approach.

Traditional theatre

If you like your theatre traditional, there is no shortage of venues. The most prestigious is the National. This splendid building with a rich history is the setting for top quality, classical theatrical works, and opera and ballet performances. The Estates (Nostitz) Theatre, a lovely Neo-Classical building in which the

world premiere of Mozart's *Don Giovanni* was held in 1787, is part of the National Theatre network (as is the nearby chamber theatre Divadlo Kolowrat) and presents National Theatre ensembles in classical theatre, opera and ballet performances.

The Praguers' love of puppets is also clearly evident by the many brightly coloured dolls available for sale throughout the city.

Fringe theatre

Among the fringe theatres dotted around Prague, the Divadlo na Zábradlí (where Václav Havel was based as a playwright) is particularly outstanding, as is the aforementioned Divadlo Archa. The music club Roxy regularly stages theatre performances by new dramatists. The

Theatre in Prague, as in many other cities in the world, is experiencing funding problems and, as in the west, the city's theatres must now scramble for private sponsorship. Still, it remains vibrant and exciting, with something to offer audiences of all kinds. ❏

● *Details of the theatres mentioned here, and a selection of other venues, are given in the Travel Tips section on pages 268–9.*

LEFT: a puppet performance on Charles Bridge.
ABOVE: the opulent interior of the National Theatre (Národní divadlo) in the New Town.

CULTURAL FESTIVALS

In spite of, or perhaps because of, the restrictions imposed by the Communist regime, Prague keenly celebrates its artistic heritage with annual festivals

Prague's main strength as a cultural capital lies in its reputation for presenting excellent concerts year-round, and there is always one music festival or another taking place in the city. Sometimes these "festivals" are simply programmes cobbled together featuring local ensembles and performers who

already perform regularly; but visitors should make special plans to come to Prague during the following world-class festivals.

Music festivals

The **Prague Spring International Music Festival** is the most famous and important of Prague's many music festivals, has gained world renown for the quality and variety of its programme. The festival has a tradition going back more than 50 years. It opens every year on 12 May, the anniversary of the death of Bedřich Smetana (*see page 85*), and ends on 3 June. Tickets sell out quickly, so contact the festival headquarters by the end of February for tickets

(Prague Spring, Hellichova 18, Prague 1; tel: 4202-530293; fax 4202-536040). Tickets are usually available through the city's main ticket agencies (*see page 268*).

A relatively recent arrival on the music calendar, **Prague Autumn** presents an appealing concert series by international ensembles and performers for two to three weeks during October and November.

Musica Iudaica is an annual festival, held for three weeks also during October and November, bringing international artists to Prague's concert halls for programmes of Jewish music. Synagogues, normally closed to concerts, open up at this time of year and provide beautiful venues in which to savour the music.

Two much anticipated annual festivals of popular music are the **E.T. Jam,** a three-day outdoor concert by top musicians and bands from the world of rock, pop, and dance music, held every June; and the **Respekt International Festival of Ethnic and World Music,** sponsored by the Czech alternative weekly newspaper *Respekt*, also held in June.

Prague film festivals

Prague offers a modest but enticing array of film festivals every year, and the audiences for these are continually growing as the festivals establish a firm place on the annual calendar.

In January, visitors can enjoy **FebioFest**, a week-long festival devoted to highlighting new Czech films and works for television. Of the approximately 200 films screened during the festival, though, the most consistently popular sections focus on the (unintentional) hilarity of stridently socialist films from the not-so-distant Czech past. FebioFest also presents previews of upcoming Hollywood films which will be presented in Czech cinemas in the coming year.

March brings the **Days of European Film**, a popular festival which offers the best in new European productions from each of the EU member states (as well as international co-productions), all in their original language. So far, this is the only festival of its kind in Europe.

In November, Prague's ambitious **Indies Film Festival** takes hold. The youngest festival in the city, Indies was inspired by the American festival Sundance, and presents daring independent productions mainly from Eastern and Central Europe. It usually includes a section of works by filmmakers from the former Yugoslavia, in co-operation with a similarly independent-minded festival in Sarajevo.

Karlovy Vary film festival

The most important Czech film festival, however, doesn't take place in Prague, but rather in the little West Bohemian spa town of Karlovy

in 1946, the first festival was held in Mariánské Lázně. In 1948 a jury began to judge the films that were shown. In 1950 the first international committee was formed and the festival became linked to an annual theme. From this point it was used as a tool in the Communist propaganda machine, and decisions about film selection and prizes were motivated less by artistic than by political considerations. It nonetheless succeeded in attracting filmmakers and enthusiasts from around the world. Among the prize-winning works of the festival have been *Diary of a Chambermaid* by Luis BuÉuel (1964) and Carlos Saura's bril-

Vary (*see pages 245–9*). For 10 days every July, the **Karlovy Vary International Film Festival** brings a cosmopolitan flair – and usually more than 400 films – to the town. It is the second-oldest festival of its kind in Europe – younger than Venice, but founded before those of Cannes, Locarno and Berlin.

Paradoxically, the origins of the Karlovy Vary Festival lie in neighbouring spa town of Mariánské Lázně (Marienbad). Immediately after the Czech film industry was nationalised

LEFT: Kyle Eastwood at the Prague Jazz Festival.
ABOVE: Hollywood actor Alan Alda arriving at the Karlovy Vary Film Festival in 1996.

liant film version of Lorca's *Blood Wedding* (1981). The Karlovy Vary film festival was the only one in the former Eastern bloc to achieve the highest international "A" rating, which it shares to this day with Cannes, Berlin and Venice. From 1950 until the 1989 Revolution the festival was held biannually: alternately in Karlovy Vary and in Moscow.

Since 1990, the festival has been independent and relies largely on private sponsorship, but it draws cinema-goers in droves. Celebrity guests also visit to introduce their projects to the Czech public, including such famous stars as Lauren Bacall, Gregory Peck, Warren Beatty and Leonardo DiCaprio. ❑

AVANT-GARDE ARCHITECTURE

Prague conjures up images of medieval buildings and alleys, but modern architects have not been shy at experimenting in this traditional city

Prague is essentially a Gothic city with a Baroque face. Nearly all of its numerous churches were either built or remodelled during the Baroque period, and many of the original Gothic houses were given a new Baroque façade in the frenetic period of building and reconstruction initiated by the Habsburgs in the 17th century. That said, Prague's historic centre is also remarkable for its harmonic blend of styles, from the Gothic to the avant garde. It is this lively interplay that gives the city its unique profile.

From Gothic to Classicism

Although most of Prague's original Gothic buildings may not be recognisable as such today, several fine examples of the style that flowered during the reign of Charles IV still stand in the heart of Prague. The best-known architectural legacy of the 14th-century ruler is the bridge named after him, Charles Bridge (Karlův most). Commissioned in the 1350s to replace the earlier Judith Bridge, it was built by Peter Parler, the architect of that other great Gothic landmark, St Vitus' Cathedral. Two other fine Gothic structures are on Old Town Square: the Church of Our Lady Before Týn (Kostel Panny Marie před Týnem), looking, when it's lit up at night, as if it's from Disneyland, and the Old Town Hall, with its clock tower and elaborately carved Gothic doorway.

While it's the city's more modern styles that make Prague truly distinctive, a few highlights of the Baroque period that dominates Prague's historic core should be mentioned. After the Thirty Years' War, the Habsburg rulers re-Catholicised Czech lands, in part by building grand Baroque churches that were meant to inspire awe – and obedience – among the masses. The best of these churches is, without doubt, St Nicholas' Church (Kostel svatého Mikuláše) on Malá Strana's Malostranské

náměstí, begun in the early 1700s by Christoph Dientzenhofer, continued by his son Kilián Ignaz, and finished by Kilián's son-in-law Anselmo Lurago. Kilián Dientzenhofer also built Prague's "other" St Nicholas Church, the much more modest church that anchors the northwest side of Old Town Square.

The Habsburgs dominated architectural style in Bohemia until Czechoslovakia's independence in 1918, but towards the end of the 19th century there were rumblings of national feeling appearing on the Prague cityscape. The three most notable examples of the National Revival style of the late 1800s, marked by its monumental Classicism, are the National Theatre (Národní divadlo), the Rudolfinum and the National Museum (Národní muzeum).

Prague's Art Nouveau

Along with Paris, Vienna and Berlin, Prague was one of the centres where the avant garde used revolutionary ideas to shape architectural

---

PRECEDING PAGES: house façades in Pařížská.
LEFT: the distinctive profile of Obecní dům.
RIGHT: Živnostenska Banka's Art Nouveau exterior.

styles in a way which would reflect their ideals and reject tradition. A progressive atmosphere was created by close cultural and economic ties between the cities. In this environment, architecture flourished, and Czech architecture soon won a place in European artistic journals. The various building styles that emerged in pre-World War II Prague were both internationally influenced and Bohemian-inspired.

The beginning of the modern period came with the advent of Art Nouveau (variously called Jugendstil and Sezessionist – *secese* in Czech), with its organic and flowing lines. One beautiful example is the Hotel Evropa on Wenceslas Square, designed by Alois Dryák and Bedřich Bendelmayer and built in 1903–4. But the greatest gem of Art Nouveau in Prague is Municipal House (Obecní dům) on Náměstí Republiky, by Antonín Balčánek and Osvald Polívka, completed in 1911, with salons decorated by Alfons Mucha and a huge mosaic, *Homage to Prague* by Karel Spillar. Wilsonova Station (Hlavní nádraží) designed by Josef Fanta and built between 1901–9, is another outstanding example of Art Nouveau architecture.

A student of the Viennese master Otto Wagner, Jan Kotěra was one of the first to introduce new trends to Prague. At first Kotěra was

STREET OF ALL STYLES

A stroll down Celetná, radiating from Old Town Square, is the starting point for a whirlwind tour of Prague's architectural history in a nutshell. Along this street it is possible to see a series of Gothic and Romanesque foundations (originally ground floors) lying below Baroque façades. The street also boasts a leading example of Cubism, in its House at the Black Madonna. Continue down Celetná to the Gothic-style Powder Tower and turn right onto Na Příkopě, then take in examples of other architectural styles, from the Art Nouveau Obecní dům, to the neo-Renaissance Živnostenska banka (Na príkopf 20), and the Modernist Palác Koruna.

strongly influenced by Vienna, as can be seen in his Peterka House at Wenceslas Square No. 12, built in 1900. With its slender windows and elegant ornamentation, it is considered one of the purest examples of Art Nouveau architecture in the city. Further development of Kotěra's ideas can be seen in the office block on Růžová and U půjčovny in New Town, dating from 1924, in which he incorporates Baroque forms.

The Štenc House at Salvátorská 8, near Old Town Square, is by Kotěra's pupil Otakar Novotný. Built for the photographer Jan Štenc in 1909–14, the house's striking appearance is due not to ornamentation but its play of proportions and light across its fine brick façade.

Another Otto Wagner pupil Bohumil Hübschmann marked the courageous transition to a starker architecture with his vertically articulated apartment house at Široká 5–7, built in 1910–11. Hübschmann also designed the covered entrance to the adjacent Jewish Cemetery.

Cubism

The second chapter of modern architecture in Prague was sparked by the exhibition of the first Cubist paintings by Picasso and Braque in Paris in 1909. The shock waves

---

ARCHITECTURAL LIGHT

An unusual example of Cubism is the street lamp with seat built in 1913–14 by Emil Králícek, in a quiet area of Jungmannovo Square, just off Wenceslas Square.

---

architecture flowered in Bohemia, the only place that the movement caught on.

In the heady atmosphere of the times, people saw Cubism, with its prism-like dissection and abstraction of surfaces, as a way projecting an image of the new age, and architects sought to translate the movement's formal qualities, such as fragmentation, spatial ambiguity and multiplicity, into habitable structures.

In addition to incorporating influences of the Parisian avant garde, Czech Cubist architecture

emanating from Paris soon reached Prague, and changed not only the development of painting, but also the style of buildings. By 1914, when the Mánes Society art gallery held an important Cubist exhibition, Prague had become the most fertile ground for Cubism outside Paris. It is perhaps not surprising that Cubism found ready adherents among Prague's painters and sculptors, but nowhere else in Europe did Cubism also spark such enthusiasm among architects. In a short but frenetic period, Cubist

---

LEFT: National Theatre mirrored in the glass of the Nová Scéna.
ABOVE: Nová Scéna's modern façade.

---

also had formal roots in the Art Nouveau style. Art Nouveau's later tendency toward a stronger geometric expression marked a transitional phase to the even starker geometry and dynamism of Cubism.

Perhaps Prague's best-known architectural work in the Cubist style – if for no other reason than its prominent location along the Royal Way – dates from 1912: the House of the Black Madonna (Dům u Černé matky Boží), by Josef Gočár, a pupil of Kotěra and one of the most important Czech architects of the 20th century. Located at Ovocný trh 19, the building was Prague's first Cubist building. It originally housed a department store and a café. Today it houses a branch of the Czech Museum of Fine Arts and features a permanent exhibition of Czech Cubist painting, sculpture and furniture. The house derives its name from the statue of the Madonna relocated from a former Baroque building at that site. This early Cubist work demonstrates that it was possible to build anew in the modern idiom without destroying the optical harmony of a historic district.

Emil Králíček was responsible for designing another striking Cubist structure, the Palác Dia-

> **TALKING SHOP**
>
> Urbánek house is also notable as the venue for a series of lectures entitled "New Architecture" in 1925, by such international masters Le Corbusier, Gropius, Adolf Loos and others.

Hill, all constructed in the heyday of Czech Cubism, rate as some of the primary examples of the style. Don't miss the Hodek Apartment House (1913–14) at Neklanova 30, with its bold Cubistic cornice.

A short walk away is another example of Chochol's work, the 1912–13 villa at Libušina 3, situated between two other noteworthy Cubist houses, one by Králíček to the south and one by Otakar Novotný to the north. The villa and its garden, originally landscaped in the Cubist manner, are surrounded by a gate

mant at Spálená 4 on the corner of Lazarská – a building whose ground floor now houses an automobile showroom. The Diamant building (1912) straddles the border between late Art Nouveau and Cubism. Notable is the Cubist frame around a Baroque statue adjoining the 18th-century Church of the Holy Trinity next door. Though controversial in its day, today we can see a sensitive solution to harmonise vastly different periods and styles.

One of the 20th century's most notable and radical architects among those working in the cubist style was Josef Chochol, who had trained for two years in the Vienna atelier of Otto Wagner. His buildings in the neighbourhood below Vyšehrad

that echoes the geometric planes of the house. Also worth a look is the architect's so-called Cubist Triple House (1913–14) – three connected private villas on Rašínovo nábřeží 6–10.

Rondocubism

The Cubist influence came at a time when the country was dissolving its centuries-old ties with the Habsburg monarchy and founding the Czechoslovak state. Against this political background, leading architects tried to create an independent national style, using Cubist methods combined with forms of vernacular architecture such as arches, cylinders and shapes in high relief. In their new designs, they were inspired by folk art: brightly painted Moravian portals, elaborately decorated cottages and the like. Roundness and colour were used as a counterpoint to sharp edges and greyness that to them symbolised the Germanic monarchy.

The style arising from this unlikely marriage of national feeling and radical modernity is known to art historians as Rondocubism – known locally as the National Style – and has had a strong influence on many buildings in Prague. A brief but fruitful period produced a number of notable houses, especially the colourful Adria Palace at Jungmannova 31 by Pavel Janák (1922–5), built for the Italian Riu-

CUBIST LIVING

Rondocubism was not confined to public buildings, however. There are many residential buildings which were worked on by noted architects. Novotný, for example, designed the façade for an apartment block on Kamenická No 35 in the residential Holešovice district in 1923–24. Gočár and Janák designed with František Zavadil a group of detached houses in the Strašnice district; Rudolf Hrabě used National Style forms and colours in the Prague Municipal Houses complex in the Holešovice district; and the style can also be admired here and there in the neighbourhoods of Dejvice, Žižkov, Bubeneč and Vinohrady.

nione Adriatica insurance company. Its neighbour at Jungmannova 29, built in 1923–6 by the same architect, features a similar, though more monumental, façade.

Both of these buildings are situated opposite the Urbánek House (also called the Mozarteum) by Kotěra. Built in 1912 as a house and concert hall for the music publisher Mojmír Urbánek, this building now contains a gallery exhibiting contemporary Czech and international art, and is well worth a visit to admire its interior.

LEFT: the Nová Scéna (Laterna Magika).
ABOVE: the striking new bank building above Budějovická metro station.

Otakar Novotný designed a number of buildings in the Rondocubist style, including three apartment houses of 1919–21 located at Elišky Krásnohorské 10–14 in the Old Town. Sometimes called simply the Cubist House, it has an effective colour scheme and geometric designs.

Gočár also produced one of Rondocubism's finest examples – the Czech Legion Bank on Na poříčí 24, built between 1921–3, with its dramatic red-and-white façade and semicircular window arches. Visitors can step inside to admire the bank hall, which combines lively elements of folk ornamentation with straightforward modernity and features a vaulted glass roof. The frieze, *Return of the Legionnaires*, is by Otto Gutfreund, arguably the greatest 20th-century Czech sculptor and one of the nation's pre-eminent Cubist artists.

Modernism and Functionalism

During the course of the 1920s the so-called National Style reached a blind alley, and architects sought to reconnect with European modernism. Alfred Loos, the Viennese architect active in Prague and an early opponent of Art Nouveau, believed that architecture devoid of ornament represented pure and lucid thought, going so far as to state that "ornament is a crime." The influence of Loos, as well as

tionalist style – typified by white façades, flat roofs, ribbon windows, elegant entry ways and attention to detail – are located in the city's outlying districts, but right off Wenceslas Square, tucked behind the church Our Lady of the Snows at Jungmannovo náměstí 17, is the small three-storey House of Musical Instruments built in 1938–9, with its lively interplay of vertical and horizontal planes.

Several other notable examples of Modernism's streamlined aesthetic can be seen on Wenceslas Square: the former Hotel Juliš by Janák dating from 1928–33 and the Lindt Department Store by Ludvík

Gropius and Le Corbusier, began to take hold.

Throughout the 1920–30s, these ideas found expression in the movement known as Functionalism, a doctrine stressing purpose, practicality and utility. One of Prague's most prominent examples of Functionalism is the Mánes Artists Association House built between 1927–30. Named in honour of Josef Mánes, the 19th-century artist and nationalist, this white, puristic building designed by Otakar Novotný protrudes into the Vltava River and forms a bridge between the embankment and Slovanský Island. It is still in use today as an art gallery, and a terraced restaurant.

Many of Prague's best examples of the Func-

Kysela from 1925–27. The glass façade of the Lindt house was restored in 1998. Another notable building by Kysela on Wenceslas Square is the Bat'a Department Store (1927–9), with a glass curtain wall over a reinforced concrete skeleton.

A remarkable building of a different style dating from this period is the Church of the Holy Heart of the Lord, designed between 1929–32 by Josip Plečnik, a Slovene architect who also initiated additions and adjustments to Prague Castle in his role as chief architect there. This bold creation is a major landmark in the area. Its lower two thirds are lined with vitrified bricks, while the top third continues the effect with a white-plastered band that features a rhythmical sequence of windows.

Postwar architecture

The architecture of the postwar years after the Communist takeover in 1948 yielded few buildings that are still admired today – and indeed many are considered downright hideous.

Mention should be made, though, of the design of the Prague Metro (underground) stations, completed in 1974. Although no rival to Moscow's system, several

is, perhaps surprisingly, the Tesco Department Store (Národní 26), designed in 1968 by the architects' collective Stavo-projekt Liberec. With its generous dimensions and its acknowledgment of modern construction materials, the building has won constant admiration and respect both at home and abroad.

One exciting and controversial addition to the Prague cityscape in recent years is the curvaceous Fred and Ginger building (in Czech, Tačící dům, or dancing building), co-designed by American

of the stations deserve mention. On line B (Yellow), for example, walls are covered with glazed ceramic tiles and decorated with mosaics: especially worth a look is the stop "Anděl" (formerly Moskevská, or Moscow) where the entrance hall was designed in co-operation with a Soviet architect. Coloured marble and bronze figure reliefs evoke Moscow scenes such as Red Square and the Kremlin.

One exception to the overwhelmingly depressing architecture of the postwar period

LEFT: a post-modern department store.
ABOVE: the bold Fred and Ginger Building makes its mark on Prague's modern cityscape.

architect Frank O. Gehry and his Zagreb-born colleague Vlado Milunić. Created to resemble the immortal Hollywood duo, the swooping glass-and-steel "Ginger" tower – a magnificent flight of fancy – plays off beautifully against the concrete tapering cylinder of the "Fred" tower. Even before it opened in 1996, the building attracted its share of critics, who charged that it clashes with the landscape and that it smacked of grandstanding.

Visitors can decide for themselves: the top floor contains one of the city's finest French restaurants, La Perle de Prague, and the view over the river, with its sweeping vista of the city's many architectural styles, is magnificent. ❏

PLACES

*A detailed guide to the entire city, with principal sites
clearly cross-referenced by number to the maps*

Prague used to be known as the "Five Towns", and although it
has now been divided into ten separate districts, most visitors
concentrate on the five historic towns: Hradčany; Staré Město
(Old Town); Malá Strana (Lesser Quarter); Nové Město (New
Town); and the former ghetto of the Jewish Quarter, or Josefov.

City administration was not unified until the rule of Emperor
Joseph II (1780–90), and the separate town halls are reminders of
previous autonomy. Gradually the city began to expand and by the
beginning of the 19th century, 80,000 people lived in the city. Gradually more districts were added to the original five towns, and the
population grew steadily. The incorporation of Vyšehrad, Holešovice
and Bubeneč brought the population to around 200,000 by 1900.
After World War I, the city's area tripled to a size of 550 sq. km (190
sq. miles). New suburbs such as Severní Město (North Town) with a
population of 80,000 and Jižní Město (South Town) with a population of 100,000 were built. The southwestern suburb of Jihozápadní
Město, intended for 130,000 inhabitants, is a site of ongoing expansion. Today, about 1½ million people live in Prague, and around 10
per cent of Czech industry is based within the city environs.

Each individual district of the city still has its own special appeal.
Hradčany Castle (commonly known as Prague Castle) and its surroundings, especially the Loreta Church and the Strahov Monastery,
have a distinct atmosphere. The Malá Strana and the island of Kampa,
with its ostentatious palaces built in the shadow of the rulers in
Hradčany Castle, is another, quite separate place, dotted with elegant
wine bars. The gardens of Petřín Hill, the view of the Vltava River and
the Charles Bridge by night all have a romantic fascination.

In earlier times, the inhabitants of the congested and dirty Old
Town and Jewish Quarter must have felt envious when they looked
across to the other bank of the Vltava. If you take a look from the
beautifully restored Old Town Square at the narrow alleys and courtyards surrounding it, you can easily imagine old Prague, the city of
Franz Kafka. Today the Pařížská is a splendid avenue in which companies such as Dior and Hermès have established themselves, and
luxury boutiques are sprinkled throughout Old Town's tiny lanes.

The far-sighted designs of Charles IV (1346–78) and his architects
which you see when you walk through the New Town are evidence
of planning well ahead of its time. The broad open spaces of Charles
Square and Wenceslas Square are products of a time when no one
dreamed of cars or trams, or the days when thousands of visitors
would come to admire the beauty of the Czech capital. ❏

PRECEDING PAGES: views of the Old Town across the Vltava; feeding the swans in
front of Charles Bridge; Jan Hus' monument in the Old Town Square.
LEFT: ascending the steep steps to Prague Castle.

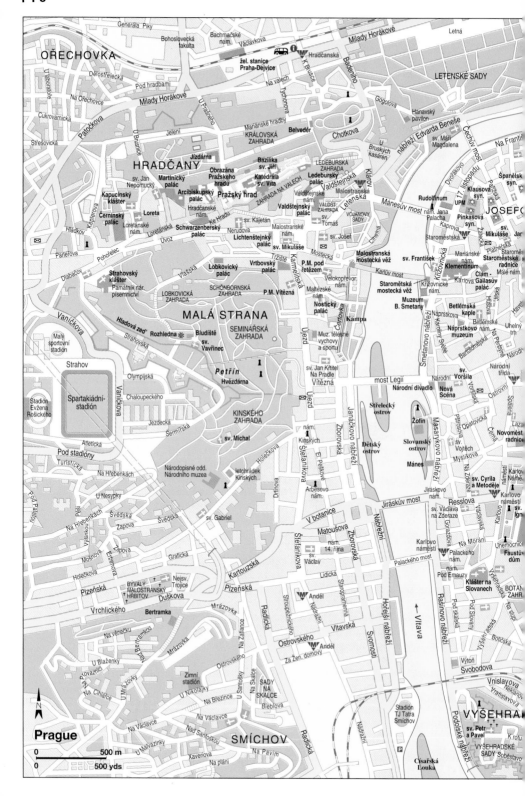

Prague

0 — 500 m
0 — 500 yds

HRADCANY AND PRAGUE CASTLE

The true history of Prague began with the construction of its castle in the 9th century, and even today the area is at the heart of Czech politics as the seat of the nation's president

Map on pages 124–5

The silhouette of Hradčany (Prague Castle) is perhaps the best-known view of the city. With the advantage of its exposed position, the castle dominates the skyline of the left bank of the Vltava. It is particularly impressive when floodlit at night, with the cathedral in the background.

The historical importance of this royal residence matches its imposing appearance. Its history is not only tied up with that of the city, but also with the history of the first independent Czech state and its destiny. A thousand years ago the fate of the country was decided here and, after several years of being ruled from Vienna, it has returned to its status as the ruling heart of the city. The castle is the seat of the president of the republic and still a centre of political power.

The building of the castle dates from the same period as the first historically documented prince of the Přemyslid dynasty, Prince Boleslav. He built what was at first a wooden fort on the site of a pagan place of worship. It then became the seat of the dynasty and secured the crossroads of important European trade routes which met at the ford of the Vltava. At the same time, Boleslav built the first church on the hill to replace the pre-Christian burial ground, as a sign of progressive Christianisation. In AD 973, when the bishopric of Prague was founded, the castle also became the bishop's seat.

After the turn of the millennium a Romanesque castle gradually evolved, with a princely (later royal) palace, a bishop's palace, several churches, two monasteries and fortifications. Every period has added its contribution to the development of the castle, but the castle as we see it today is mostly due to Empress Maria Theresa (*see page 126*).

PRECEDING PAGES: Prague *circa* 1860. **LEFT:** Hradčany, seen from the river. **BELOW:** detail above Matthias Gate.

Hradcany Square

Before you start your tour of the castle, look at the vast **Hradčanské náměstí (Hradčany Square) ❶**. A few interesting palaces have been built since the fire of 1541, which destroyed all of Hradčany and much of the Malá Strana lying below. Most notable for their façades are the **Arcibiskupský palác (Archbishop's Palace) ❷** next door to the castle, with rococo detailing, which is open to visitors once a year on Maundy Thursday (Thursday before Easter), and the Renaissance-style **Schwarzenberský palác (Schwarzenberg Palace) ❸**, on the opposite side of the square, has sgraffito decoration, in keeping with the Italian style. In here is the Vojenské historické muzeum (Museum of Military History) with its collection of European weapons, uniforms, medals and battle plans (open Apr–Nov: Tues–Sun; entrance fee).

The bold proportions of its façade draw attention to the early Baroque **Toskánský palác (Toscana Palace)** ❹, which ends the square to the west. Where Kanovnická joins the square you will see the Renaissance **Martinický palác (Martinic Palace)** ❺. When the building was restored, sgraffito decorations portraying Biblical and classical scenes were discovered.

To the left of the Archbishop's Palace as you face it a little alley leads off to the hidden **Sternberský palác (Sternberg Palace)** ❻, which maintains its Baroque splendour inside. This is the main building of the **Národní galerie (National Gallery)**, which houses a fine collection of European art, including Old Masters, from the 14th to the 18th centuries (open Tues–Sun; entrance fee).

On its south side, Hradčany Square opens up to the ramp leading up to the castle, from which you can get a superb view across the city. In the summer months you can get into the Castle Gardens (open Apr–Sept) through the entrance beside the New Castle Steps.

Entering the castle grounds

The main entrance to the castle is the **První nádvoří (First Courtyard)** ❼, which opens onto Hradčany Square. You enter this so-called Ceremonial Courtyard through a gate under a wrought-iron decoration. Two guards of honour are posted in front of statues, copies of the *Battling Titans* by Ignaz Platzer.

This is the most recent of the courtyards and was built on the site of the western castle moat during the alterations of Maria Theresa's reign (1740–80). The **Matyášova brána (Matthias Gate)** ❽ is considerably older; indeed, it is the oldest Baroque building in Hradčany Castle. It originally stood apart, like a triumphal arch, between the bridges that led over the moats. During the

BELOW: fanfare from the castle window.

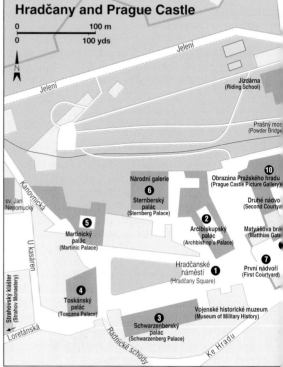

Hradčany and Prague Castle

rebuilding it was elegantly integrated into the new section as a relief. Since then, the Matthias Gate has been the entrance to the Second Courtyard. To the right of the gate a staircase leads to the reception rooms of the presidential apartments, which are closed to the public.

Map on pages 124–5

The **Druhé nádvoří (Second Courtyard)** ❾ has a somewhat plain appearance. Take a look first at the Kaple sv. Kříž (Chapel of the Holy Cross). The most valuable pieces of the cathedral treasure, including a collection of reliquaries, liturgical objects and interesting historical mementos, are kept in this former royal chapel with its magnificently decorated interior. This fascinating collection originated in the days of Prince Wenceslas, but most of it was acquired by Charles IV (1347–78). A great pragmatist in political matters, the emperor was at the same time an impassioned collector of holy relics.

The symmetrical, closed impression given by the Second Courtyard is thanks to Maria Theresa's innovations. Behind it, however, lies a conglomeration of buildings which has grown up gradually over the centuries. Each has its own complicated history. In the right-hand passage to the Third Courtyard you can see some remains of the Romanesque castle fortifications.

Czech national colours on the castle guards' uniforms.

The remains of an even older building, St Mary's Church, dating from the 9th century, were discovered in the **Obrazárna Pražského hradu (Prague Castle Picture Gallery)** ❿. Access to the gallery is from the passage in the north wing. Here you can see a collection largely put together by art-lover Emperor Rudolf II (1583–1611). This emperor has gone down in history as something of an eccentric because of his esoteric way of life (*see pages 34–35*), yet he was a great patron of the arts and sciences and collected a huge amount of art treasures, as well as countless curiosities. His collection was one of the most notable in

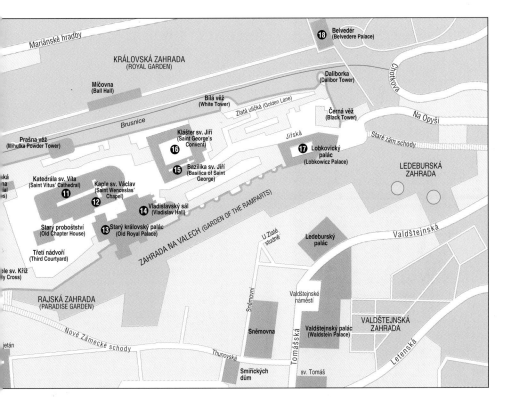

Europe in his day. When the imperial residence moved to Vienna, a great part of the collection went with it. Still more fell to the Swedes as loot during the Thirty Years' War. Yet another valuable collection was created, during the 16th century, from what remained, but much of it was taken to Vienna or sold to Dresden. What was left was auctioned off, and was thought to be totally lost.

Only in recent years were pictures discovered during rebuilding work. These were restored and then identified as paintings from the original collection. This small but valuable collection contains 70 paintings by, among others, Hans von Aachen, Titian, Tintoretto, Veronese, Rubens, Matthias Bernard Braun, Adriaen de Vries and the Bohemian Baroque artists Jan Kupecký and Petr Brandl.

Temporary art exhibitions are also housed in the next door Císařská konírna (Imperial Stables), decorated with Renaissance-style vaulting.

St Vitus' Cathedral

Once you have walked through the passage and into the Third Courtyard, you can hardly avoid stopping and letting your eyes follow the daring vertical lines of **Katedrála sv. Víta (St Vitus' Cathedral) ⓫**; the towering north portal is only a few steps away. The cathedral, the largest church in Prague, is the metropolitan church of the Archdiocese of Prague, the royal and imperial burial church and also the place where the royal regalia are proudly kept.

The 600-year history of the building of the cathedral began when the archbishopric was founded in 1344. Ambitious as ever, Charles IV used this opportunity to begin the construction of a cathedral which was intended to be among the most important works of the 14th-century Gothic style that was spreading from France. To this end, Charles employed the French architect Matthias of

BELOW: wrought ironwork on the cathedral façade.

ARCHITECTS OF THE CASTLE

The 14th-century architect Peter Parler was one of the most influential in creating the medieval image of Prague, much of which can still be seen today. As well as his founding work on St Vitus' Cathedral and the Royal Palace, Parler designed the original Charles Bridge, including the Gothic tower that still stands at the entrance to the Old Town. As well as work in the city, Parler completed the St Barbara's Church in Kutná Hora.

In the second half of the 18th century, Empress Maria Theresa commissioned the Viennese court architect Nicolo Pacassi to give the various buildings a unified, Neo-Classical façade and extensions. As a result, the original eclectic character of the castle has been transformed into something resembling a massive palace.

Then, in the 1920s, Josip Plečnik was appointed as chief architect of the castle, and he made various additions to the complex, including the granite obelisk in the Third Courtyard, as well as designing the presidential apartments. Although unpopular at the time, Plečnik is now hailed as a post-modernist genius. It is a credit to these three architects, and many others over the centuries, that the varying styles have blended harmoniously within the complex.

Arras, who had trained in the French Gothic school and was working in Avignon (at that time a papal city). Arras died after eight years and the work was taken over by Peter Parler, who influenced all later Gothic architecture in Prague.

After Parler's death, his sons continued the work, giving the building their own individual stamp, until construction was interrupted in the first half of the 15th century by the Hussite Wars. It was in this period that the choir, its chapels and part of the south tower were completed. Only a few alterations were made during the years that followed. For instance, the tower was given a Renaissance top some time after 1560. This was replaced by a Baroque roof 200 years later.

The task of completing the cathedral was not attempted until the 1860s, when a Czech patriotic association took it up. Following old plans and consulting Czech artists, they completed the building in 1929. The additions carried out across the centuries explain why the cathedral lacks a unity of style.

Before entering the cathedral through the western portal, take a look at its exterior, which dates from the last few years of the completion process. The **Rose Window**, more than 10 metres (30 ft) in diameter, portrays the creation of the world. On either side of the window are carved portraits of the cathedral architects. The towers are decorated with the statues of 14 saints. In the centre of the bronze gates the history of the building has been portrayed, and on the sides are images relating to the legends of St Adalbert and St Wenceslas.

Inside the cathedral

In the splendid interior of the cathedral the most notable features are the stained-glass windows and the triforium, a walkway above the pillars with a gallery of portrait busts. Leading Czech artists took part in creating the win-

Map on pages 124–5

A street musician in the castle grounds.

BELOW: St Vitus' Cathedral roof, once open to the public.

dows; among them Max Švabinský, who was responsible for the window in the first chapel on the right, the mosaic on the west wall and the great window above the south portal. The window in the third chapel on the left was designed by Alfons Mucha, who is perhaps best known outside the Czech Republic for his Art Nouveau posters featuring the actress Sarah Bernhardt (*see page 191*). However, all 21 of the chapels contain several notable works of art.

St Wenceslas' Chapel

TIP

Buy a ticket at the entrance to the cathedral or in the castle's ticket office in the third courtyard; tickets permit admission to the Royal Crypt, the Mihulka Tower, St George's Basilica and the Old Royal Palace, and are valid for three days.

The main attraction inside the cathedral and generally overcrowded is the **Kaple sv. Václava (St Wenceslas' Chapel) ⓬**, which protrudes into the south transept (Entry to the chapel is not possible; it must be viewed from its entryway). It was built by Peter Parler on the site of a 10th-century Romanesque rotunda, in which the national saint Wenceslas was interred. In keeping with the importance of the Wenceslas cult, the saint's sacred place is exceptionally splendid in its ornamentation. The frescoes on the walls, which are decorated with semi-precious stones and gold bezants, portray (in the upper half) Christ's passion and (in the lower) the story of St Wenceslas, prince of Bohemia. A little door leads to the Treasure Chamber directly above the chapel. Here the Bohemian royal regalia are kept, behind seven locks, the seven keys of which are held by seven separate institutions. The precious jewels are put on display only on special occasions.

The three central chapels of the choir, behind the main altar, contain the Gothic tombs of the princes and kings of the Přemyslid dynasty, and are the work of Peter Parler's masons. In the choir itself, on the left side, is a kneeling bronze statue of Cardinal von Schwarzenberg, by the Czech sculptor Josef Myslbek (1848–1922), who also created the Wenceslas Monument in Wenceslas Square (*see page 189*). On the right side is the overly ostentatious silver tomb of the 17th-century cleric St John Nepomuk, designed by the Baroque architect Johann Emanuel Fischer von Erlach. Also remarkable are the wooden reliefs in the choir, masterpieces of Baroque woodcarving.

Opposite the tomb of Count Schlick, designed by Matthias Bernard Braun, a staircase leads down to the Royal Crypt. Here are the remains of the walls of two Romanesque churches, as well as the sarcophagi of Charles IV, his children and his four wives, George of Poděbrady and other rulers. Emperor Rudolf II lies in a Renaissance pewter coffin. Above the Royal Crypt – just in front of the Neo-Gothic High Altar – is the impressive white marble imperial tomb of the Habsburgs, built for Ferdinand I, his wife Anna and their son Maximilian.

Don't forget to glance upwards to admire the lozenges adorning the roof of the choir. Peter Parler displayed a masterly ability to combine revolutionary technical solutions with elegant caprice. This is particularly evident on the south side of the choir, where the interplay of columns and struts and the remarkable complexity of the tracery are especially impressive. The organ loft originally marked the end of the choir on the west side. Once the Neo-Gothic part of the cathedral was completed, however, it was moved to its present position.

BELOW: St Wenceslas statue in St Vitus' Cathedral.

Third Courtyard

In order to see more sights, you have to walk around the former Old Chapter House which is pressed up against the side of the cathedral. Of special interest to art historians is the equestrian **statue of St George** which stands prominently in the courtyard. It is, however, a copy of the original Gothic sculpture, which is now in the St George Convent (*see page 132*) and is evidence of the highly developed art of 14th-century metal casting. The flat-roofed shelters next to the cathedral are to protect archaeological discoveries which have been made in the lower levels of the castle courtyard, visible through the grille.

From here you can get an impressive view of the complex system of buttresses and the south façade of the cathedral, which is dominated by the almost 100-metre (300-ft) tower. Its stylistically unusual top includes a gilded window grille, the letter "R" and the two clocks (the upper shows the hours, the lower the quarter hours) date from the time of Rudolf II. It is possible to climb the tower from April to September, but note that the stairs are steep, plentiful and often precariously crowded. The 360° views of the city, however, make the ascent more than worthwhile. The tower contains four Renaissance bells, among them Bohemia's largest, weighing 18 tons.

Unusual in both position and execution is the **Zlatá brána (Golden Gate)**, the distinctive portal that leads into the south transept. It is the ceremonial entrance to the cathedral, and it was through here that monarchs passed on their way to their coronation (*see pages 201–204*). Its remarkable triple-arched anteroom has an exterior mosaic, thoroughly cleaned in the early 1990s, depicting *The Last Judgement*. It was created by Italian artists around the year 1370. The anteroom itself is fitted with a grille depicting the individual months of the year.

Map on pages 124–5

Buttress detail on the cathedral's south façade.

BELOW: St George's statue on the fountain in the Second Courtyard.

The covered staircase in the left-hand corner leads to the Castle Gardens. These, in turn, lead to the **Starý královský palác (Old Royal Palace)** ⓭, which should not be missed.

A tour of the Old Royal Palace

In keeping with the rest of the castle complex, this was also built by many generations of rulers. New stories of the palace were layered one above the other on top of the original walls, which now lie deep under the level of the courtyard. A tour of the present building will enable you to gain deeper insights into the castle's past.

Go past the fountain decorated with an eagle, and from the courtyard you will be able to ascend the staircase leading to the anteroom. From here, you can start your tour of the palace, which until the 16th century was the residence of the Czech rulers. The first three rooms to the left of the entrance constitute the Green Chamber, a former law court and the audience hall, with a ceiling fresco, *The Judgement of Solomon*. Further along is the so-called Vladislav Bedchamber and the Land Records Depository. The Land Records were books in which not only the details of property ownership but also the decisions of the Bohemian Estates and the law courts were recorded.

Leave the anteroom and go on to the **Vladislavský sál (Vladislav Hall)** ⓮, named after King Vladislav II. This most imposing late-Gothic throne room was built by the architect Benedikt Rieth between 1493 and 1502. Numerous coronations and tournaments took place under the 13-metre (43-ft) high pillars. Immediately to the right of the entrance of this hall another wing of the building is joined. Continue on the same level and you come to the **Bohemian Chan-**

BELOW: the famous Defenestration Window in Prague Castle.

THE SECOND DEFENESTRATION

The Bohemian Chancellery in the Royal Palace became famous as the scene of the so-called Second Defenestration of Prague, which marked the beginning not only of the Bohemian rebellion but also of the Thirty Years' War. On 23 May 1618 more than 100 Protestant noblemen who marched on the palace in protest, and threw two Catholic governors, Jaroslav Martinic and Vilém Slavata, and their secretary Johannes Fabricius out of the eastern window. The governors were accused of breaking the terms of Rudolf II's *Majestát*, or "Letter of Majesty," by appointing the anti-Protestant Archduke Ferdinand to the throne. Rudolf's decree, which he had written a few years previously, had intended to guarantee the Bohemian nobility freedom of religion.

After a heated argument, the men were pushed out of the window and fell 15 metres (50 ft) – obelisks in the garden mark the spots where the two honourable gentlemen are supposed to have landed. No such honour was accorded to the secretary. All three survived the defenestration unscathed, if somewhat humiliated, for they fell directly into a dunghill in the castle moat. The Catholics of Bohemia explained their survival as an intervention of angels.

cellery. In the first room is a model which shows the appearance of the castle in the 18th century and compares it to the complex today. Go through a Renaissance portal and you enter the office of the former imperial governor.

Ascending a spiral staircase, you come to the **Imperial Court Chancellery**, which is situated above the Bohemian Chancellery. During Rudolf II's reign, the whole of the Holy Roman Empire was ruled from here.

Saints and fortifications

Under the three Renaissance windows on the narrow wall of the Vladislav Hall a staircase leads off to **All Saints Chapel**, which contains three remarkable works of art: the *Triptych of the Angels* by Hans von Aachen, the painting of *All Saints* on the high altar by Václav Vavřinec Reiner and, in the choir, a cycle of paintings by Dittmann. The latter portray 12 scenes from the life of St Procopius, who is buried in the chapel.

The next room leading off from the Vladislav Hall is the **Council Chamber**, in which the Bohemian Estates and the highest law court assembled. The royal throne and the furnishings date from the 19th century. To the left of the throne is the tribunal of the chief court recorder, built in the Renaissance style. The wall is decorated by the portraits of the Habsburg rulers.

The last room open to the public in this wing is the **New Land Records Office**, with the heraldic emblems of the Land Rolls officials decorating the ceiling and along the walls.

The **Riders' Staircase**, built to allow rulers and guests to enter and take part in the riotous festivities on horseback, such as jousting, leads out of the most recent part of the palace. The lower storeys are accessible and you can continue

Map on pages 124–5

BELOW: view of the courtyard from Prague Castle.

your tour to the left, going down into the early-Gothic levels of the palace. The lowest level is the Romanesque palace which contains the remains of fortifications dating from the end of the 9th century.

St George's Basilica

Romanesque art in St George's Basilica.

Leave the Royal Palace and go out into **Náměstí sv. Jiří (St George's Square)**. The red Baroque façade opposite the choir of St Vitus' Cathedral belongs to the **Bazilika sv. Jiří (St George's Basilica)** . This is the oldest church still extant on the site of the castle, and together with the adjoining monastery, it formed the hub of the complex in the early Middle Ages. It was founded in about AD 920 and rebuilt after a fire in the 12th century. Despite rebuilding programmes during the Renaissance and Baroque periods, the church has largely retained its Romanesque appearance and, following renovations at the beginning of the 20th century, it has been restored to its former glory.

The interior, in which concerts are held to take advantage of the excellent acoustics, is closed off by a raised choir. Remnants of the original Romanesque ceiling paintings can still be seen. To the right of the choir you can look through a grille into the Ludmilla Chapel, housing the tomb of the saint, the grandmother of Prince Wenceslas. The tombs of two Bohemian nobles are in front of the choir. The Baroque statue in front of the crypt – a corpse with snakes in its intestines – is an allegory of the transitory nature of life. The Baroque Chapel of St John Nepomuk is incorporated into the outer façade of the basilica. Its portal is decorated with a 17th-century statue of the saint by Ferdinand Brokof.

Adjoining the basilica on the left is the former Benedictine **Klášter sv. Jiří (St George's Convent)**. Founded in AD 973, but rebuilt several times, it today houses the Old Bohemian Art Collection, part of the National Gallery (open Tues–Sun; entrance fee). Among works from the 14th to the 18th centuries are paintings by artists who took part in the building of many of Prague's churches.

Along the north side of St Vitus' Cathedral runs Vikářská street which contains the **Prašná věž (Mihulka Powder Tower)**. In the late 15th century, while parts of the northern fortifications were being built, it served as a gunpowder workshop. Today it contains a small museum which records its earlier use as a metal-casting foundry and possibly an alchemist's laboratory. Individual storeys portray various aspects of crafts in the 16th and 17th centuries.

Golden Lane

Another part of the fortifications which can be seen behind St George's Convent, is the atmospheric **Zlatá ulička (Golden Lane)**, also known as Goldmakers' Alley. This is one of the most popular – and crowded! – attractions of the castle. In the part of the fortifications between the central Bilá věž (White Tower) and the outermost Daliborka (Dalibor) Tower, tiny houses crouch under the walkway on the castle wall, making a romantic backdrop. Legend has it that this is where the alchemists employed by Rudolf II tried to discover both the secret of eternal life and how to make gold. What is fact, however, is that Franz Kafka (*see*

BELOW: tourist groups being led through the castle grounds.

page 95) lived and worked for a while in No. 22, which now houses a tiny exhibition and Kafka-orientated bookshop.

The tour of the castle ends at the **Cerná věž (Black Tower)**, where Jiřská street reaches the eastern gate. Just before the gate, on the right-hand side, you come to the **Lobkovický palác (Lobkowicz Palace) ⑰**, which in recent years has been used for permanent as well as rotating exhibitions based on themes from the country's history (open Tues–Sun; entrance fee). On the other side of the eastern gate the Old Castle Steps and the street Na Opyši lead down to the Malá Strana (*see page 135*) and the Malostranská Metro station.

Belvedere Palace

The **Belvedér (Belvedere Palace) ⑱** lies outside the castle complex, but is worth a visit. Leave the Second Courtyard and go north, across the bridge (Prašný most), towards the former **Jízdárna (Riding School)**, nowadays an exhibition hall. From its terrace you can see an imposing view of St Vitus' Cathedral. Leaving the Riding School, follow Mariánské hradby (St Mary's Ramparts), which borders the Castle Gardens round to your right, to reach the splendid palace which art historians consider to be the only example of a purely Italian Renaissance building north of the Alps.

Emperor Ferdinand I built the palace in the mid-16th century for his wife Anna. The interior is unfortunately only open to the public during art exhibitions, which usually take place during summer months. Especially remarkable is the "singing" Renaissance fountain in the garden, which was cast with such skill that the falling water, striking the bronze basin decorated with hunting scenes, makes it ring. ❑

Map on pages 124–5

BELOW: beautiful 17th-century houses in Golden Lane.

MALA STRANA

*One of the best-preserved areas of Prague, the Malá Strana
abounds with ornate Baroque architecture and landscaped gardens,
as well as authentic beer halls and popular jazz clubs*

Map
on page
138

The Malá Strana (Lesser Quarter) lies at the foot of Prague Castle (*see page 124*). It is a totally individual quarter, almost like a picturesque island, separated from the rest of the city by broad parks and the wide, steady flow of the Vltava. Looking down from the hills, the impression gained is of a landslide of roofs which started to roll between the Hradčany and Petřín hills and came to a stop on the river bank.

In 1257, the Malá Strana was made a city, and is thus the second oldest of the five historic cities that make up Prague. The Malá Strana experienced its first boom during the rule of Charles IV. During this time it was extended considerably and received new fortifications. However, not until catastrophic damage was inflicted by the great fire of 1541 was there any sign of a major rebuilding programme. This rebuilding shaped the individual characteristics of the quarter which we can still see today.

The Malá Strana truly blossomed after the victory of the Catholic League over the Bohemians in the Battle of White Mountain in 1620, when many wealthy families loyal to the House of Habsburg settled here. True, most of the palaces were deserted once the political administration of Bohemia had moved to Vienna, but they have been spared major alteration to this day. Even the town houses, which often have much older foundations, have kept their mainly Baroque façades with their characteristic house signs. For this reason, the Malá Strana can be described as an architectural jewel, indeed as a complete work of art representing the Baroque style of Central Europe. The different creative styles of the town houses, the small, quiet squares, and the mansions with their attractive gardens designed to blend in with the slopes of the hill all came together harmoniously to form an original style – "Prague Baroque".

Of course, many things worth seeing remain hidden behind the façades. However, once off the main streets, you can enjoy the special atmosphere of the place. This is due not least to the fact that by no means everything revolves around the tourist, and the Malá Strana has its own everyday life to live.

PRECEDING PAGES:
strolling the streets
of Malá Strana.
LEFT: a tram along
narrow Letenská.
BELOW: pavement
café in Malá Strana.

St Nicholas' Church

The centre of the Malá Strana always was and still is the Malostranské náměstí, a square which is actually divided into two parts by the **Chrám sv. Mikuláše (St Nicholas' Church)** ❶ (open daily, Apr–Sept; Sat–Sun, Oct–Mar; entrance fee for evening concerts) and the neighbouring former Jesuit college.

The conspicuous dome of St Nicholas' Church and its slender tower can be seen from many different viewpoints in an ever-changing perspective. This unequal couple has become the symbol of the whole Malá Strana. The church itself is a masterpiece of Baroque architecture and one of the most beautiful examples of its kind. In the early 18th century the famous Bavarian architect Christoph Dientzenhofer built the nave and side chapels on the site of a Gothic church. The choir and the dome were added later by his son Kilián Ignaz. The building was completed in the mid-18th century by the addition of the tower, which was the work of Carlo Lurago.

Particularly outstanding among the special features of the interior is the monumental ceiling fresco by Johann Lukas Kracker in the nave. It is one of the largest in Europe and portrays scenes from the life of St Nicholas. Another valuable fresco, *Celebration of the Holy Trinity* by Franz Xaver Karl Palko, decorates the dome. The dome is 75 metres (247 ft) high – tall enough to accommodate the tower on Petřín Hill inside it (*see page 146*). The sculptures in the choir and the gilded statue of St Nicholas, patron saint of merchants, sailors and children, are the work of Ignaz Franz Platzer the Elder.

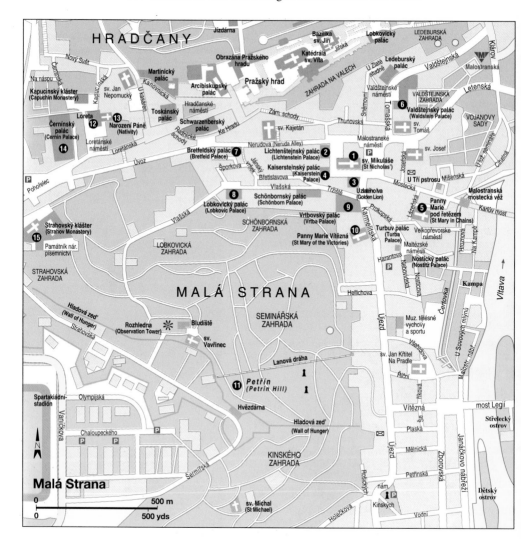

Around Malostranska namestí

Opposite St Nicholas' is the **Lichtenštejnský palác (Lichtenstein Palace) ❷** with its broad Neo-Classical façade. From 1620 to 1627 it belonged to Karl von Lichtenstein, the so-called "Bloody Governor" who was mainly responsible for the execution of the leaders of the 1618 rebellion (*see page 35*).

From St Nicholas' Church you will notice the **U zlatého lva (Golden Lion House) ❸** at No. 10. It is one of the few purely Renaissance houses in the Malá Strana and also contains the wine bar U Mecenáše (tel: 533881). These small wine bars, whose charm lies mainly in their ancient walls, are typical of the Malá Strana. Guests were served here as early as 1600. Nowadays, however, it's best to reserve a seat.

Cross Karmelitská and follow the arcaded passage, taking a peek at the court-yard on the right, which is still rich in atmosphere (despite a McDonald's, a cinema and an Irish bar). It lies almost hidden behind the arch of a gateway. All over the quarter, little surprises such as this await the observant visitor.

The lower side of this busy square is bordered on the right by the **Kaiserštejnský palác (Kaiserstein Palace) ❹**. A memorial plaque outside the house proclaims that the world-famous opera singer Ema Destinová once lived here. On the left side is the former town hall of the Malá Strana, now a jazz and rock club called the Malostranská beseda (tel: 539024). Another café, the **Malostranská kavárna** (tel: 533092) protrudes into the square and, in the summer months, provides a welcome opportunity for eating and drinking out of doors.

Leave the lively Mostecká street and on your right you will find that the streets have become quieter. Here you enter one of the quiet, dreamy corners of the Malá Strana. There is a passage next to the cinema 64 U Hradeb, or you

Map on page 138

Street artists are a regular sight in the Malá Strana.

BELOW: dome of St Nicholas' Church.

can turn off into Lázeňská street. House No. 6, **V láznich (The Spa)**, was a first-class hotel in the 19th century. Among the celebrities to have stayed here was Tsar Peter the Great. A memorial plaque proclaims that the French poet René Chateaubriand was also a guest. Another plaque, on the house called **U Zlatého jednorozce (The Golden Unicorn)**, marks the place where Ludwig van Beethoven stayed.

There is a beautiful Baroque interior in the **Kostel Panny Marie pod řetězem (Church of St Mary Beneath the Chain) ❺**, the oldest church in the Malá Strana. Remains of its 12th-century Romanesque predecessor can still be seen in the right-hand wall of the forecourt.

An excursion to your right will take you to the long sprawl of the **Maltézské náměstí (Maltese Square)**, with its sculpture representing St John the Baptist, the work of Ferdinand Maxmilian Brokof. Two palaces in this square are worth your attention: the **Turbovský palác (Turba Palace)**, now the Japanese Embassy, with its rococo façade, and the early Baroque Nostický palác (Nostitz Palace), now occupied by the Dutch Embassy, to the south. Adjacent to the church is another square, the Velkopřevorské náměstí. On one side is the **Buquoyský palác (Buquoy Palace)**, home of the French Embassy, and opposite is the former **Palace of the Grand Prior of the Knights of Malta**, one of the most beautiful in the area.

Kampa island

A little bridge connects the square with the island of **Kampa**. It is separated from the Malá Strana by a canal branching off the Vltava or Devil's Stream, the Čertovka. During the last decade of Communist rule, the island and the palace gardens became a favourite meeting place for the flower children of Prague.

They left behind lovingly executed murals, including one of John Lennon. This district of the city is known as Little Venice on account of its situation, water mills and gardens. The park has been formed by linking up the gardens of former palaces and offers a beautiful view of the Old Town. The small group of houses, lying directly by the water, between Charles Bridge and the mouth of the Certovka, are also known as the Venice of Prague, and are much sought after. Go up a double flight of steps and you will come onto **Karlův most (Charles Bridge)** described on page 159.

Map on page 138

Gardens and refreshments

Downstream from the Charles Bridge the palace gardens of the Malá Strana beckon. Some of them are open to the public between April and September.

Without leaving the bridge you can see **U Tří pštrosů (The Three Ostriches)**, with the remains of the sgraffito decoration which gives it its name. In the late 16th century the house belonged to a merchant who supplied feathers to the royal house. There was a coffee house established here in 1714 and it is now an elegant and expensive hotel and restaurant.

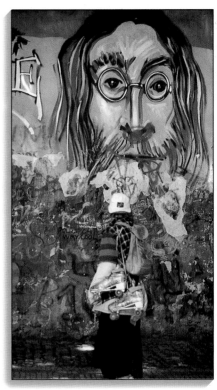

Mural from The Three Ostriches house, now a hotel.

This house points the way to U Lužického semináře, where **Vojanovy sady (Vojan Park)**, the former monastery garden, is situated. In this park, with its two Baroque chapels, modern sculptures are often exhibited.

If you not only know about Czech beer, but consider it to be an essential form of sustenance, you should visit the traditional inn **U sv. Tomáše (St Thomas')** in the same street, which specialises in dark beer, or *černé pivo*. The beer garden of this former monastic brewery (founded in 1358) is no longer in existence, and neither is the home brew, but Braník beer tastes just as good down in the cellar vaults.

BELOW: John Lennon mural.

A church is, of course, also part of this former Augustinian monastery, which was founded in the 13th century. Its present Baroque form is the work of Kilián Ignaz Dientzenhofer, and inside it is richly decorated with the works of Bohemian Baroque artists.

When making a tour of the Malá Strana gardens, you should also take a quick look at the **Metro station Malostranská**, which contains a copy of Matthias Bernard Braun's *Hope*. Some sculptures from his workshop can be seen in the courtyard garden. Your route now takes you on through Valdštejnská street, past palaces whose gardens lie on the slope beneath the castle, an ideal place for artists. Three of these terraced gardens, built for the nobility after Italian models, can be visited. The entrance is next to the Koloratský palác (Kolowrat Palace, No. 10).

Waldstein Palace and Gardens

Valdštejnská street, and Valdštejnské náměstí (Waldstein Square) into which it leads, border the complex of **Valdštejnský palác (Waldstein Palace)** ❻ (or Wallenstein, as it is also called) on two sides. This was the first Baroque palace in Prague built between 1624–30 for General Albrecht von Wallenstein.

The grandiose residence matches Wallenstein's political ambitions – it was intended to rival Prague Castle. He acquired the site for the building by buying up and dispossessing the inhabitants of more than 20 houses. Even the city gate had to go, in order to give the architects (all Italians) enough space to provide their patron with a palace featuring all possible luxuries available at the time. The palace today is used for state functions and is closed to the public.

However, the rather restrained outer façade facing the square does not give anywhere near the same impression as a visit to the **palace gardens** (open daily May–Sept). The greatest pride of the householder – apart from an artificial grotto, an aviary and a pond – was the triple arched loggia (*sala terrena*), richly decorated with frescoes. Today it serves as the podium for open-air concerts occasionally held here in the summer. The bronze statues of mythological gods and goddesses, scattered about the garden, are the work of Adriaen de Vries, court sculptor to Emperor Rudolf II. They are, however, copies – the originals were taken to Sweden as spoils of war in 1648 and are now located in the park of the Drottingholm palace near Stockholm.

Another work by this sculptor is the figure of Hercules fighting the dragon in the middle of the pond. The fountain with the sculpture of Venus and Cupid is also remarkable. Opposite the loggia is the former Riding School, where art exhibitions are held (open Tues–Sun).

Around Waldstein Square

BELOW: the Old Mill on Kampa Island.

Tomášská street leads from Waldstein Square back to Malostranská nam. Go past the house The Golden Pretzel (No. 12) and you will come to the Baroque house **The Golden Stag**, which bears one of the most beautiful and photographed house signs in Prague. The sculpture shows St Hubert with a stag, and is the work of Ferdinand Maxmilian Brokof.

Before house numbers were introduced, during the reign of Empress Maria Theresa in the 18th century, these house signs were used for identification. They were based on the profession or craft of the house owner, his status or the immediate environment of the house. Animal and other symbolic signs, both of a secular and a religious nature, were popular. If the house owner changed, the house retained its original sign. Sometimes the new owner even took over the name of the house.

Map on page 138

Go back to Waldstein Square and from there, make a short excursion into Sněmovní. This street and the adjoining cul-de-sac, U Zlaté studně (The Golden well) form a picturesque corner. Hidden away at the end of the little alley is a garden bar with the same name as the street. Also noteworthy is the Renaissance house The Golden Swan at No. 10, which hides a beautiful inner courtyard. Go back in the direction of Thunovská, which leads to the Zámecké schody (New Castle Steps). These so-called "new" steps are not to be confused with the Old, which lead to the other end of the castle. The New are actually much older than the Old – but that's just the way of things in Prague.

House signs marked the occupation of owners, such as this family of violin-makers at Nerudova No. 12.

Neruda Alley

Parallel to the Castle Steps lies **Nerudova (Neruda Alley)**, named after the famed Czech poet, author and journalist Jan Neruda (1834–91) who lived in the upper part of the street, in house No. 47, U dvou slunců (The Two Suns). His work was inspired by the everyday life of the Malá Strana. Incidentally, his name was adopted by Ricardo Eliecer Neftalí Reyes y Besoalto, now the Nobel Prize-winning poet Pablo Neruda.

Many of the middle-class houses in this street were originally built in a

ALBRECHT VON WALDSTEIN

General Albrecht von Waldstein (also known as Wallenstein, the eponymous hero of a play by the German playwright Schiller) was a man who made his way to the top by skillful strategy and leadership on the one hand and by intrigues and treachery on the other.

During the Thirty Years' War he enlisted under the Habsburg Ferdinand II. He won many important victories for Ferdinand and these brought him not only power and a ducal title, but also considerable wealth, which as a court favourite he was particularly well placed to increase. By 1625, he owned one quarter of all Bohemia. This process was helped not least by his participation in a grandiose coin swindle, so that in the end he was able to raise his own private army. Eventually, his services became so expensive that parts of the empire had to be mortgaged to afford him.

But Waldstein's rapid rise came to an equally rapid end when, in secret deals with the enemy, he initiated tactical manoeuvres which would have eventually led him to the Bohemian crown. However, Emperor Ferdinand saw through him and organised a group of mercenaries to get rid of him. They murdered him in his bed in the town of Cheb in 1634.

TIP

On Nerudova it's easy to pass by the unobtrusive tearoom U Zeleného čaje at No 19, but it's well worth a stop. Numerous kinds of teas from around the world are brewed in beautiful earthenware pots; the apple strudel is a welcome treat. Open daily from 11am–10pm.

Renaissance style and later given Baroque additions. They often bear house signs which don't match the names of the houses. For instance, house No. 6, The Red Eagle, has a sign showing two angels. In the case of house No. 12, The Three Violins, however, it is known that several generations of violin-makers lived here. More signs can be seen on The Golden Chalice (No. 16), St John Nepomuk (No. 18), and The Donkey and the Cradle (No. 25). A small pharmacological museum is housed in the former pharmacy, The Golden Lion at No. 32 (open Tues–Sun, entrance fee).

As is so often the case in Prague, two embassies have settled into the Baroque palaces in this street. On the left is the **Morzinský palác (Morzin Palace)**, the Romanian Embassy. Its unusual façade ornament – the heraldic Moors which support the balcony, the allegorical figures of Day and Night and the sculptures representing the four corners of the world – are the work of Ferdinand Maxmilian Brokof.

Somewhat higher up is the **Thun-Hohenštejnský palác (Thun-Hohenstein Palace)**, the Italian Embassy, which is decorated with two eagles with outspread wings, and is the work of Matthias Bernard Braun. The statues of Roman deities represent Jupiter and Juno. The palace is connected by two passages to the neighbouring church and monastery of St Cajetan, creating an architectural unity typical of the closing years of the 17th century.

From the end of Nerudova you can get a splendid view of the Schwarzenberg Palace (*see page 123*). The alley gives way to a romantic but steep stairway leading up to the castle; to the left, Loretánská street leads out of the Malá Strana in the direction of Strahov Monastery (*see pages 153–5*). This is also the way to reach the Loreta Shrine (*see pages 149–50*).

BELOW: painted house sign on Nerudova.

Map
on page
138

Neruda palaces

A maze of courtyards lies hidden at the back of the last houses of Nerudova. They fall in a series of terraces into the valley between the two hills. At the bottom are a few alleys that have almost a village character. If you go back a little, you will reach, at No. 33, the rococo **Bretfeldský palác (Bretfeld Palace) ❼**, with a relief of St Nicholas on the portal. In earlier years famous balls took place in this building, some of which both Mozart and Giacomo Casanova are said to have attended. The palace is not open to the public.

From here the steps Jánský vršek lead down and then turn right into Šporkova, which leads us along the slope mentioned above. It then curves and leads into Vlašská, directly opposite the **Lobkovický palác (Lobkovic Palace) ❽**. This magnificent Baroque palace now contains yet another embassy: this time representing Germany. The palace garden is partially open to the public and is worth visiting, if only because of the view.

If you want to visit the parks of Petřín Hill or the Strahov Monastery, you have to follow Vlašská to your right. However, you can also go on in the opposite direction and use the funicular railway, which runs between Újezd street and the peak of Petřín Hill.

On the way lies the **Schönbornský palác (Schönborn Palace)** in Tržiště, which now houses the US Embassy. Its splendid garden, which can be seen from the Castle Ramp, is not open to the public, but you can visit the particularly lovely Baroque terraced garden of the **Vrtbovský palác (Vrtba Palace) ❾** on Karmelitská. It is a small garden, but full of atmosphere, and has a *sala terrena* (pavilion) and sculptures by Matthias Bernard Braun. The views of the castle from the gardens are also magnificent.

BELOW: tourists pack Charles Bridge.

Map on page 138

TIP

The Petrín Funicular Railway stops en route at the restaurant Nebozízek (tel: 537905), which has a magnificent view over the city.

BELOW: a wooden carved door in Malá Strana. **RIGHT:** steep steps in Malá Strana.

Further along Karmelitská you come to the **Kostel Panny Marie Vítězná (Church of St Mary Victorious)** ❿, the first Baroque church to be built in Prague. It was built as a monument to the Counter-Reformation brought to Prague by the Habsburgs. The furnishings, which are all of a unified style, date from the 17th century; the saints' pictures by the altar are the work of Petr Brandl. It is in this church that the famous Infant Jesus of Prague is kept, a wax figure of Spanish origin, which is always clothed in one or another of its 72 costly robes. It is highly revered, and believed to work miracles.

Petrin Hill

Behind Nerudova is Prague's favourite park, Petrín Hill. It's not far from here to the **Petřín Funicular Railway** (*lanová dráha*), also known as a cable car, but the cars don't actually hang on cables, they run on rails. The fact that the contraption looks so curious is due to the original method of locomotion. The old cars had a water tank, which was always filled at the top and emptied at the bottom. In this way the cars going up were powered solely by the weight of the cars going down. The cable car was inaugurated in 1891. In the 1960s the water tanks were done away with, the hill slope repaired (it had partially collapsed) and re-opened in 1985, powered by more modern means.

The park on the **Petřín Hill** ⓫ was formed by linking up the gardens which had gradually replaced what had once been vineyards. On the level of the upper cable car station, a path offering a marvellous view of the castle and the Old Town below it leads all the way through the park to the Strahov Monastery. But apart from the delightful views of the city, the park also has many sights of its own which are worth taking the time to explore.

Starting in the most southerly corner, visit the Villa Kinský. On the way, in a northerly direction, lies a little wooden church, the Church of St Michael, a wonderful example of folk art of the 18th century. It comes from the Carpathian Ukraine and was rebuilt on this spot in 1929, a gift from the inhabitants of the small Ukrainian village of Mukacevo, which became part of Czechoslovakia after World War I and was annexed by the Soviet Union after World War II. A belfry from Wallachia stands next to the church.

The **Hladová zed' (Hunger Wall)**, which you will discover further on, leads down the slope and is part of the fortifications built by Charles IV. According to local lore, this project was undertaken to provide work for the starving and impoverished. Near the wall lies the People's Observatory, a popular meeting place of amateur astronomers from near and far.

On top of the hill is the **Rozhledna (Observation Tower)**, a scaled-down replica of Paris' Eiffel Tower, which is 60 metres (197 ft) high (open daily Apr–Sept; in winter during clear weather only; entrance fee). It was built for the Prague Jubilee Exhibition in 1891. Not far from the tower is Chrám sv Vavřinec (St Lawrence's Church) and the **Zrcadlová bludiste**, a labyrinth of mirrors inside a miniature castle (open daily; entrance fee). The latter, also built for the 1891 exhibition, brings the tour to a pleasant end, particularly for children. ❑

LORETA

Map on page 138

Prague's main centre of Christian pilgrimage is enclosed within a Baroque setting worthy of its religious importance. Nearby is the quaint 17th-century street Nový Svět

If you climb up from Hradčany Square towards the Strahov Monastery (*see page 153*), you can hear, every hour on the hour, a delicate tune played by bells as you walk between the palaces. Many years ago, during an outbreak of plague, there lived in Prague a mother and her children. One child after another fell sick, and with the last few coins that she had left she paid for the church bells to be rung whenever a child died. After they were all dead, she herself fell ill and died, but of course there was no one to have the bells rung for her. Then, all of a sudden, all the bells of Loreta rang out, playing the tune of a hymn to Mary. The same tune has been played up to the present day.

This little anecdote gives some indication of the importance that this shrine has for many people. It is not merely of historic and artistic importance, but is still considered to be a place of Christian pilgrimage.

The Santa Casa

In the mid-13th century the armies of Islam invaded and conquered the Holy Land. At that time two brothers were priors of the Franciscan monasteries in Haifa and Nazareth. When they fled, according to legend, they removed the Santa Casa (the Holy House) stone by stone, and rebuilt it near Renecati, now Loreta, in Italy. The house was visited by many pilgrims on their way to Rome, and was later decorated with rich marble reliefs, as the many copies show.

When the Catholic Habsburgs tried during the Counter-Reformation to convert their Hussite subjects back to the "true faith", they used the pious legend to serve their cause. They had replicas of the Santa Casa built throughout the land. The best-known and most attractive of these is Prague's **Loreta** ⑫. It stands on the Loretánske náměstí and was founded by Catherine of Lobkovic, who laid the foundation stone on 3 June 1626.

Unlike the simple original, the shrine became, across the centuries, an entire complex consisting of various buildings with several chapels, ornate cloisters and the Church of the Nativity. Dominating the group is the early Baroque tower, built in 1694, which has a carillon that rings out every hour.

Just as in Italy's Loreta, the shrine's outer walls are decorated with Renaissance reliefs. The interior also strictly follows the Italian model. As a result, you can see in the Prague Loreta a small, bare building which is probably the copy of a house in Palestine, and in which the **Loreta Madonna** is honoured. Dressed in a long cloak, she carries the infant Jesus in her arms.

The two-storey **cloisters** surrounding two courtyards were the work of the Bavarian Baroque architect Kilián Ignaz Dientzenhofer. Sadly, the

LEFT: the beautiful, ornate façade of the Loreta. **BELOW:** the "Golden Pear" tavern in Nový Svět.

Diamond monstrance in the Loreta's Treasure Chamber.

paintings in these cloisters have been over-restored and have lost their original beauty. However, the poetic images in the supplications to Mary are impressive: "Tower of David", "Gate of Heaven", and *"Oroduj za nas"* – pray for us.

Between the portal and the Santa Casa you can see the **Kostel Narození Páně (Church of the Nativity)** , with frescoes by Baroque artist Václav Vavřinec Reiner, and some macabre skeletons. The church was consecrated on 7 June 1737, exactly 111 years after the laying of the foundation stone.

Treasure Chamber

The Loreta's main attraction is the **Treasure Chamber**. As in other places of pilgrimage, pilgrims over the years have given votive gifts to the treasury as a sign of thanksgiving. The gifts of the Bohemian nobility were commissioned from notable goldsmiths of the time and include some of the most valuable works of liturgical art in Central Europe. The most remarkable is the **diamond monstrance**, which was a legacy of Ludmilla Eva Franziska of Kolowrat. The monstrance, made in 1699 by Baptist Kanischbauer and Matthias Stegner of Vienna, is studded with 6,222 diamonds and sends out its rays like the sun. It is almost 1 metre (3 ft) in height and weighs more than 12 kg (26 lbs).

Cernín Palace

BELOW: the Loreta is stunning in the snow.

If you leave the Loreta and walk right up to the square, you will be struck by the massive façade of the **Černínský palác (Černín Palace)** ⓮, an incredible counterweight to the light buildings surrounding the Santa Casa, which, seen from this point, almost seem to cower. Twenty-nine half-pillars run along the whole length of the palace façade, which is more than 150 metres (500 ft) long.

In 1666, Humprecht Johann, Count of Černín, bought the land, and work started on the palace, under the direction of Francesco Caratti. In 1673, Emperor Leopold I came to Prague to see the building about which there was so much talk in Vienna. It seemed as if the count, who had not received the imperial favour he expected, was building a palace out of pique. The emperor was displeased when the count claimed that it was nothing but a barn and he was going to replace the wooden doors with bronze ones. "For a barn, those wooden doors are quite good enough," the emperor retorted.

The Černín were an old Bohemian family and their members had excelled time after time in the service of the Bohemian crown. The house in Prague was to become a "Monumentum Cernín", and construction work continued for several generations until financial collapse put a stop to the project. During the Napoleonic Wars, it was used as a military hospital, and in 1851 the state bought parts of it and turned it into a barracks. In 1929, the authorities of the young Czechoslovak Republic had the palace renovated and made it the home of the Foreign Ministry it still is today. It was here that Jan Masaryk fell – or was pushed – to his death in 1948 (*see page 31*).

Novy Svet

Below the gardens of the palace runs an alley belonging to the old settlement in front of the castle. In the middle of this former poor quarter is **Nový Svĕt (New World)**, which draws many an artist and intellectual. Many of the houses have names displayed on house signs and often include the adjective "golden", a Prague tradition. You will see The Golden Leg, The Golden Star and The Golden Pear (U zlaté hrušky), which is now a romantic wine bar. ❑

Map
on page
138

TIP

Next door to the Prague Loreta is U Lorety, a pleasant example of a garden restaurant with views of the monastery.

BELOW: Nový Svĕt has a very peaceful atmosphere.

THE STRAHOV MONASTERY

The impressive grounds and church of Strahov Monastery have successfully survived numerous religious battles over the centuries, and now house an impressive library of Czech literature

Map on page 138

O utside the castle fortifications, away from the whole castle complex, on the age-old trade route from Nuremberg to Krakow, lies the **Strahovský klášter (Strahov Monastery) ⑮**. The oldest monastery in Bohemia, the complex sits on the slopes of Petřín Hill, the crown of the gently sloping valley, in a square now called Strahovské náměstí. The two towers of the Strahov, along with the green of the Petřín Hill and its miniature Eiffel tower replica, and the long line of the roof of the Černín Palace, together make up the distinctive skyline of the left bank of the River Vltava.

The first monastery of the district monks of the Premonstratensian order was founded in 1140 by King Vladislav II, but was completely destroyed by fire in 1258. The wars of the ensuing centuries also left their mark, with the result that very little remained of the original Romanesque building. Today, the monastery is predominantly Baroque in style, although it contains early Gothic and Renaissance elements. Only St Mary's Church, also known as the Church of Our Lady, retains visible traces of the Romanesque original.

The monastery continued to function until 1952. After the dissolution of all religious orders in Czechoslovakia under the Communist regime, it was declared a museum of literature and opened to the public on 8 May 1953.

LEFT: gleaming white Strahov Monastery.
BELOW: Strahov's Baroque interior.

Strahov library

The rapid transformation of the Strahov library into the **Museum of National Literature** (open Tues–Sun; entrance fee) was possible because of the vast resources of the monastery library, which had been slowly gathered over the centuries. Today, the monastery possesses not only the oldest and most extensive, but above all the most valuable library in the country. The collection was established at the time of the foundation over 800 years ago. Gradually added over the years were examples of almost the complete literature of western Christianity up to the end of the 18th century. Today, the emphasis is on national literature of the 19th and 20th centuries.

Entering the harmonious enclosure of the monastery, the first thing you will see is **chrám sv. Rocha (St Rochus' Church)**, built from 1603 to 1612 during the rule of Emperor Rudolf II, and nowadays used as a gallery. On the façade of the New Library (built from 1782 to 1784) is a medallion with the portrait of Emperor Joseph II, the ruler whose support of the Enlightenment led to the dissolution of the majority of monasteries in his domains (1783). Joseph's memory is honoured here because he allowed Strahov to escape the dissolution, and the monks of Strahov were permitted to buy the equipment for a new research library from another famous monastery in Moravia,

the Bruck monastery near Znojmo. These brown and gold gleaming shelves equipped the new hall, which was then designated the Philosophers' Hall, while the older hall was renamed the Theologians' Hall.

Theologians' and Philosophers' Halls

The **Teologický sál (Theologians' Hall)** was built by Giovanni Domenico Orsi in a rich Baroque style at a cost of 2,254 guilders. It was painted with splendid ceiling frescoes by Siardus Nosecký, a member of the order, between 1723 and 1727. The theme is true wisdom, rooted deeply in the knowledge of God. The brightly coloured scenes in their sturdy stucco frames radiate warmth and cheerfulness. In the middle of the room stand a number of valuable astronomical globes from the Netherlands, dating from the 17th century.

The ceiling fresco in the **Filozofický sál (Philosophers' Hall)** is beautiful but less easy to understand. The work of Anton Maulpertsch, it is in concept and technique a monumental finale to rococo ceiling painting in Europe. The fresco shows the development of humanity through wisdom – a theme that borders on the ideas of the Enlightenment. At the two narrow ends you can see Moses with the tablets of law and, opposite, St Paul preaching at the pagan altar. The lines of figures on the longer sides of the hall introduce great personalities of history who have made progress possible through their achievements.

The Strahov collection

BELOW:
Philosophical Hall in the Strahov library.

In 1950, the library contained 130,000 books. This number has now increased to around 900,000, as the Strahov has taken in the contents of a number of other monasterial libraries, particularly from central and northern Bohemia. One of

the most famous of all the manuscripts on display is the **Strahov Gospels**, the oldest manuscript in the library, dating from the 9th to 10th centuries, which was acquired during the reign of Charles IV.

Also among the most valuable treasures are rarities such as the New Testament, printed in Plzeň in 1476 and one of the first printed works in the Czech language. Another is the beautifully illustrated story of the journey of Frederick von Dohna to Rome, dating from the 17th century. A separate room is devoted to the great reformer Jan Hus (*see page 29*). The upper storey contains a vast number of documents relating to the writers who influenced the re-awakening of Czech national consciousness in the 19th century.

St Mary's Church and gardens

St Mary's Church, next door to the monastery, is usually closed to the public, although the interior can be seen through a grille. This Romanesque building was vastly altered and richly redecorated in the Baroque style during the 17th and 18th centuries. Much of the decorative work by Czech artist Jiří Neunhertz depicts scenes from the life of St Norbert, archbishop of Magdeburg and founder of the Premonstratensian order in northern France in 1120. It is believed that his remains were brought to this church during the 17th century. The organ, often heard emanating out across the monastery grounds, was once played by Mozart.

Also forming part of the monastery grounds are the large gardens, offering a wonderful vista of the city. These gardens fill the valley between Petřín Hill (once part of the monastery), and Castle Hill, right up to the edge of the Malá Strana. Once white-robed monks walked here; nowadays it is a favourite haunt of courting couples. ❏

Map on page 138

TIP

If you don't want to walk the steep hill back down to the Malá Strana, tram No. 22 travels from the Strahov Monastery to Malostranská Metro station, near Charles Bridge.

BELOW: Malá Strana seen from the monastery.

THE VLTAVA

Prague's river cuts through the city, dividing the 9th-century settlement from the medieval sites. Along the banks spectacular buildings and bridges indicate the river's importance to city life

Map on pages 118–119

The River Vltava (Moldau) is 435 km (270 miles) long and rises from two headstreams – the Teplá Vltava, rising on the mountain of Cerná hora, and the Studená Vltava. It flows first southeast, then north across Bohemia. Once a wild river whose floods threatened the city, the Vltava today flows peacefully and calmly. Dams – among them three large hydrodams with lakes that are also used for recreation – raise the water level and slow down the current. Up until the early 19th century, the river was prone to frequent flooding, necessitating raising of the embankments. When the river reaches the town of Mělník, it joins the Elbe (called Labe in Czech). The latter only becomes navigable from this point on, and by this route connects Prague with the German seaport of Hamburg. Thus, the Vltava forms an important link for river traffic between the Czech Republic and the North Sea. The Prague river harbour lies in the bend of the Vltava in the city district of Holešovice.

The Vltava has proved a vital source of power for the city, particularly since the industrial revolution. The hydroelectric plant on Štvanice Island, built in 1912, supplies electricity to the city, and various mills, weirs and waterwheels have assisted the city's businesses and supplied water to the citizens. Transportation of goods, too, has always been made easier along the route of Vltava, linking it to other towns and cities, rather than negotiating the ancient road systems.

LEFT: Prague's ancient bridges straddling the Vltava.
BELOW: catching some sun on a bridge wall.

Messing about on the river

Apart from freight and shipping, the river is also well used for recreation and enjoyment. Perhaps because their nation is land-locked, Czechs have always had a special fondness for water. Boats for river excursions leave from the Palacký Bridge. They travel daily, from April to September, in both directions, and are a wonderful way of seeing the city from a different perspective. Downstream you can sail to the small **Prague Zoo** (U trojského zámku 3; open daily; entrance fee) and the Prague suburb of Roztoky, and upstream to the artificial lake of Slapy. From here Prague's history is more immediately evident, from the ancient left bank still benefiting from undeveloped parkland, to the medieval right bank, the home of Prague's merchants since the 14th century.

Trips range from budget-style tourist services, to more expensive four-course river dining cruises, taking in the city by night. Tickets for either are available at the many river boarding points.

Rowing boats can also be hired cheaply from Slovanský Island (near the National Theatre, *see pages 192–3*) and are very popular – it is almost impossible to imagine the Vltava in summer without them. The unique winter fairs that once took place on the frozen

Map
on pages
118–119

A range of boats, from cruisers to pleasure craft such as this, journey up and down the Vltava every day.

BELOW: the Vltava seen on an icy winter night.

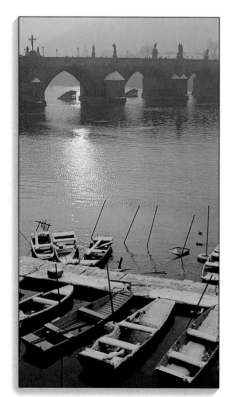

river are unfortunately a thing of the past, as the damming of the river has warmed the Vltava's waters and the river no longer freezes into sufficiently solid ground.

Bridges over the Vltava

From the hills of the left bank you can get a beautiful view of the layout of the bridges, which lie one behind the other. For 500 years the Charles Bridge was the only link between the two river banks. Not until the mid-19th-century industrial revolution were more bridges built. At about this time, too, a start was made on building the embankments. The Malá Strana bank in the vicinity of the Charles Bridge has remained largely unaltered in this way, though, and Kampa Island and the mouth of the Čertovka stream have remained in their original state (*see pages 140–1*).

The Vltava has been honoured in various different ways. A statue which is an allegorical representation of the river decorates a fountain on the exterior of the garden wall of the Clam-Gallas Palace, and commemorates all those who have drowned in these waters (*see page 173*). Its popular name is **Terézka**, and rumour has it that one wealthy citizen of Prague left his whole fortune to the statue. In the late 18th century, at the time of the birth of the Czech nationalist movement, the Vltava was a never-failing source of artistic inspiration. The Vyšehrad castle on its rock above the river (*see pages 207–9*) was famed in many legends, and during the Romantic period it fascinated many Czech artists who were beginning their search for a national identity.

Myths, legends and water spirits

The river and its myths found expression in countless songs, works of representational art and literature. Later, this tradition was continued by a whole generation of artists who took part in the construction of the National Theatre, the symbol of national rebirth. The building was, appropriately, sited on the bank of the Vltava, not far from the Vyšehrad rock, where it forms another dominant feature of the city skyline. The theatre was opened in 1881 with an appropriate performance of Smetana's *Libuše,* in which the prophesy of the mythological princess is heard.

According to another legend, which is generally omitted from the artistic versions, Princess Libuše, the Slavic ruler (*see page 21*), had a very prosaic relationship with the river. It is claimed that when she tired of her lovers she had them thrown from the Vyšehrad rock into the Vltava.

Smetana took up the Vyšehrad myth once again when he composed the symphonic poem *Má Vlast* (*My Homeland*). The second movement deals with the Vltava and is perhaps the river's most famous artistic representation.

Even today, the river influences people's imagination, though in a different way. Children in particular are familiar with the Vltava water spirits which appear in fairy tales: little men with green coats and pipes, who have lived in the water since time immemorial, and are always ready to offer help and advice. ❑

Charles Bridge

C harles Bridge (Karlův most), together with the silhouette of Prague Castle, has become the symbol of the city. A wooden bridge, linking the two banks of the Vltava at approximately this point, is mentioned as early as the 10th century. In 1165 it was probably replaced by the Judith Bridge, the second oldest stone bridge in Central Europe. After its destruction in a flood, Emperor Charles IV had a new one built by his cathedral architect Peter Parler. Named after the emperor, this bridge was also damaged by floodwater several times, but never collapsed. (According to legend, eggs were mixed with the mortar to give it durability.) It is no coincidence that the foundation stone was laid on 9 July, the day of Saturn's conjunction with the sun. The astrologers, who were often consulted when important decisions were to be made, considered it to be a most auspicious moment.

These and other theories have often been cited in an attempt to discover the secret of the bridge. Whatever the reason, this 600-year-old construction is worthy of admiration, especially as it even stood up to 20th-century traffic until it was declared a pedestrian precinct and given a well-earned rest.

The mainly Baroque statues (now partially replaced by copies) were created in the late 17th century, and modelled on the Ponte Sant'Angelo in Rome. In contrast to the Gothic architecture of the main structure, these give the bridge its characteristic appearance. The artist Johann Brokof, his sons Ferdinand Maxmilian and Michael Johann, and Matthias Bernard Braun were among the sculptors. The latter was responsible for what is artistically the most valuable sculpture: the group of St Luitgard (1710). It shows Christ appearing to the blind saint and allowing her to kiss his wounds.

The oldest statue on the bridge is that of St John Nepomuk (1683), designed by M. Rauchmuller and Johann Brokof. The reliefs around the base portray scenes from the life of the cleric, canonised in 1729. One relief is based on the legend of his death: the wife of Wenceslas IV had made her confession to Nepomuk, whereupon the king pressed him to disclose the details. Nepomuk refused to break the seal of the confessional, and in 1393 Wenceslas had him tortured then thrown from the bridge. His canonisation was probably an attempt to oust the memory of Jan Hus with the cult of a new saint. The statue of Bruncvík is on one of the bridge supports on the banks of Kampa Island. The sword of this legendary knight, associated with the Roland epic, is walled up, so it's said, in the bridge to be retrieved in the country's darkest hour.

At the end of the bridge are the Malá Strana Bridge Towers. The smaller tower is a remnant of the Judith Bridge, but its Renaissance gables and wall ornaments were added later. The higher tower complements the Old Town tower. The top is open to the public (Apr–Sept; entrance fee). Looking down towards the Old Town, you will see why Prague is known as the "city of a hundred spires". ❏

RIGHT: rubbing the statue of St John Nepomuk is thought to bring good luck.

STARE MESTO

Map on page 164

Prague's Old Town has always been the centre of activity in the city, as well as the site of many historic events. Today it is the tourist hub, where medieval buildings rub shoulders with souvenir shops

T he Old Town (Staré Město) of Prague is spread along the right bank of the Vltava and around the Old Town Square. The area's main streets – Národní třída, Na Příkopě and Revoluční – mostly follow the course of the city fortifications, which no longer exist. The name "Na Příkopě", which means "on the moat", indicates that it was built on the site of the moat which separated the Old Town from the New. Together, these two districts form the actual city centre of Prague.

The Old Town has kept its original character. The pattern of streets and squares has remained largely unaltered since the Middle Ages. Originally the Old Town lay some 2–3 metres (6–9 ft) below the modern street level. But the area was subject to repeated flooding, which is why the street level has been raised little by little since the late 13th century. Many houses have Romanesque rooms hidden in their basements.

The historic core of the Old Town is built on these foundations, and every age has left its signs for us to read. The overwhelming influence of the Baroque cannot be overlooked, but it only finds its expression in individual buildings and has not altered the basic structure of the district. The only large intrusion in the area is the massive building of the Jesuit College, the Clementinum. Here and there you can also see traces of the 19th and 20th centuries, for the development of the river bank gave the big city a chance to break in. However, apart from demolition of most of the Jewish Quarter at the end of 19th century, the entire district has hardly lost any of its charm.

The present-day appearance of the streets is marked by the succession of houses with a great variety of façades. This is a vibrant district with a well-balanced mixture of homes, offices, shops, small businesses, several schools and leisure facilities.

PRECEDING PAGES: Týn Church looming down over Old Town Square. **LEFT:** the House of the Stork on Old Town Square. **BELOW:** view from the Old Town Hall.

Prague's first settlement

The first settlements on the site of the Old Town for which there is any historical evidence date from the 10th century. They concentrated around the crossing of three important trade routes, which met at the ford across the Vltava, a little downstream from where the Charles Bridge stands today.

According to a contemporary report, a large market place with numerous stone houses covered the site of the present Old Town Square. As the years went by this market place grew, and was fortified with a city wall in the early 13th century. Around 1230, the settlement received its city charter. By this time it was possible to speak of a large town, in European terms. In 1338, John of Luxembourg granted the citizens of the Old Town the right to their own Town Hall, and in the years that followed, under Charles IV, the city experienced an immense economic and cultural boom.

The **Karolinum (Charles University)** ❶, the oldest university in Central Europe, was founded in 1348 (*see page 26*). Even if the importance of the imperial residence diminished later on, the Old Town kept its leading position in Prague. When the five independent towns became one unit in 1748, it was the Town Hall in the Old Town that became the seat of the administration.

Old Town Square

The busy streets near the border of the New Town lead to the **Staroměstské náměstí (Old Town Square)** ❷. They approach the square from all sides like the rays of the sun and make it a natural centre. The impressive memorial in the middle of the square honours the great reformer Jan Hus (*see page 29*) and was erected on the 500th anniversary of his death, 6 July 1915. The steps at its foot now form a central meeting and resting place for young backpackers.

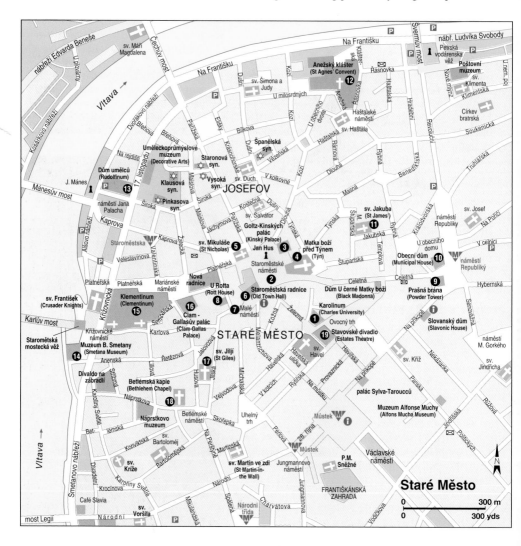

Map
on page
164

The houses on the east side of the square form a singular backdrop. This juxtaposition of varied building styles is typical of the Old Town and, together with the towers of the Týn Church, give the Old Town Square its special character. To the left you can see the **palác Goltz-Kinských (Kinský Palace)** ❸ with its late-Baroque façade, which incorporates some rococo elements. It was built by Anselmo Lurago, according to the plans of Kilián Ignaz Dientzenhofer. It was from here that Prime Minister Gottwald made his speech to the nation that brought in the Communist regime. The National Gallery's collection of prints and drawings is usually housed here, but it is currently undergoing reconstruction work and is closed to the public.

To the right of the palace, at No. 13, is the Gothic house **Dům U Kamenného zvonu (House at the Stone Bell)**, which has been restored and has had its original façade replaced. Various exhibitions and classical concerts are held in the interior, which is worth seeing (open Tues–Sun; entrance fee). The two neighbouring houses are connected by an arcaded passage with ribbed vaulting. To the left, the former Týn School, originally a Gothic building, was rebuilt in the style of a Venetian Renaissance. On the right is the early Neo-Classical house, U bílého jednorožce (The White Unicorn).

The Baroque façade of St Nicholas, over-looking Old Town Square, is one of the city's most beautiful.

Tyn and St Nicholas' churches

You can gain access to the **Chram Matky Boží před Týnem (Our Lady Before Týn Church)** ❹ through the Týn School passageway. (Hours to visit the interior can be erratic due to reconstruction, so it is best to try daily between noon and 2pm.) The church is a source of national pride to the Czechs, and the façade, particularly when floodlit at night, is the finest sight in the Old Town.

BELOW:
façades of the
Old Town Square.

A traditional pony and trap provides a relaxing means of touring the Old Town area.

BELOW: looking across Prague from the Old Town Hall.

Built in 1365, it was the third church to occupy this site, the successor to Romanesque and early-Gothic buildings. Up until 1621 this was the main church of the Hussites. The tall nave received Baroque vaulting after a fire. The paintings on the high altar and on the side altars are by Karel Škréta, the founder of Bohemian Baroque painting.

Other remarkable works of art are the Gothic Madonna (north aisle), the Gothic pulpit and the oldest remaining font in Prague (1414). To the right of the high altar is the tombstone of the famous Danish astronomer Tycho Brahe (1546–1601), who worked at the court of Rudolf II. The window immediately to the right of the south portal is a curiosity – through it you can see into the church from the neighbouring house. One resident who had this privilege was Franz Kafka, who lived in several different locations in the city (*see page 95*).

The beautiful, white Baroque **Kostel sv. Mikuláše (St Nicholas' Church) ❺**, on the other side of the square, is also the work of Kilián Ignaz Dientzenhofer, built between 1732 and 1735. The dark statues on the façade are by Anton Braun, a nephew of Matthias Bernard Braun. The unusual proportions of the church have come about because houses originally stood in front of the building, completely separating it from the square. It is interesting to see how the architect has succeeded in creating so perfect a building in such a relatively small space. However, the interior is somewhat disappointing in comparison, having suffered at the hands of Emperor Joseph II, who ordered the site to be used as a storage warehouse.

The house to the left of the church, which was on the spot of a childhood home of Franz Kafka (although only the portal survives), has been converted into a small but interesting Kafka exhibition (open Tues–Sun; entrance fee).

Old Town Hall

In times gone by, the area of the small park opposite the church was occupied by a Neo-Gothic wing of the **Old Town Hall (Staroměstská radnice) ❻**. It was destroyed by the Nazis in the last days of World War II. If you walk around the Town Hall Tower, which protrudes into the square, you have an unobstructed view of the historic part of the hall. Originally the house next to the tower on the left was purchased by citizens of the Old Town and declared a town hall. Later, three further houses were acquired.

The tower was built in 1364 and later had the oriel chapel added. But the most popular feature is the **astronomical clock**, which dates in its earliest form from 1410. It consists of three parts. In the middle is the actual clock, which also shows the movement of the sun and moon through the Zodiac, in accordance with the geocentric views of the time – essential to the Czech understanding of life in the 15th century. Underneath is the calendar, with signs of the Zodiac and scenes from country life, symbolising the 12 months of the year. The artistic work on the calendar is by the 19th-century Czech painter Josef Mánes.

The upper part of the clock is what draws the crowds. Every day on the hour the figures play the same scene: Death rings the death knell and turns an hour glass upside down. The 12 apostles proceed along the little windows which open before the chimes, and a cockerel flaps its wings and crows. The hour strikes. To the right of Death, a Turk wags his head. The two figures on the left are allegories of Greed and Vanity. Generally, a round of applause follows from hordes of delighted tourists.

There are frequent guided tours of the Town Hall (open Tues–Sun; entrance fee), which now contains some exhibition rooms.

BELOW: figure of Death on the astronomical clock on the Old Town Hall.

A CENTRE OF PRAGUE'S HISTORY

The Old Town Square has always been a central focus in Prague, and memorial tablets on the Town Hall Tower are reminders of the various important events that have taken place here over the centuries.

Following the Second Defenestration (*see page 31*) in 1618 and the defeat of the Czech Protestants in the Battle of White Mountain, "27 Bohemian gentlemen" were executed in the square on the orders of Emperor Ferdinand. Their heads were displayed on Charles Bridge, their punishment intended to serve as an example to others. The event led to the Counter-Reformation.

On 8 May 1945, the Nazis set fire to the Old Town Hall in a last-ditch attempt to hold the city. The following day, the Russian Red Army liberated Prague from German occupation by marching on the Old Town Square. The fire damage was repaired almost immediately. Three years later, Gottwald's speech from the Kinský Palace brought in the Communist government.

The Jan Hus monument in the centre of the square is in honour of the 15th-century religious reformer who stood up against the corrupt practices of the Catholic Church. Hussites and Protestants surround the figure of Hus, while a mother and child symbolise rebirth.

The Czechs' love of puppets can be seen in the many versions on sale in souvenir shops in the city.

BELOW: the Jan Hus monument is a popular meeting place.

Side streets

Malé náměstí (Little Square) ❼ is very evocative of medieval Prague. Surrounding the fountain, with its pretty Renaissance grille, are a number of fine houses, each with its own history.

In No. 11, a Signore Agostino of Florence established the first documented apothecary in the city (1353), and during the reign of Emperor Charles IV it became the home of a herbalist from Florence. Most spectacular is the multicoloured **U Rotta (Rott House) ❽** at No. 3, whose cellar was once the lower floor of a Romanesque town house. The first Czech Bible was printed here in 1488; at the turn of the 20th century an ironmonger had the building renovated, painting the façade with the original sign of three white roses and a selection of his wares inspired by the artist Mikuláš Aleš. The house now contains an excellent delicatessen.

In order to enjoy this change of atmosphere, you should make a short trip into the neighbouring side streets – busy Karlova, for instance, which bends to the left and is lined with souvenir shops, and then straight on into Jilská. Soon you will see on your left house No. 18, which in earlier years bore the name Two Stags with One Head. An unassuming arch (the so-called Iron Gate) is followed by a passage to Michalská. It links up with another passage through a palace courtyard with Renaissance arcades. However, there is another route on the left, which crosses the courtyard of a monastery containing St Michael's Church, in which Jan Hus preached. Both ways meet again in Melantrichova, just before Kožná leads into it. The first house on the left, The Two Golden Bears, is a beautiful example of Renaissance architecture. Kožná street leads you out of the labyrinth, back to the Old Town Square.

Map on page 164

Celetna

The street **Celetná** is named after the medieval bakers of small loaves (*calty*). It is one of the oldest streets in the whole of Prague, and its course follows the line of the old trade route to the east where it left the Old Town markets.

Following the large-scale restoration undertaken in recent years, most of the pastel Baroque façades in this model street shine in renovated glory. Of particular architectural interest is the late-Baroque **Hrzán Palace** (No. 12). Nearby is the wine bar U zlatého jelena (The Golden Stag), which is situated in what were originally the rooms of one of the oldest stone houses in Prague. An architectural rarity of quite a different order is the unique cubist house **Dům U černé Matky Boží (The Black Madonna)** at No. 34, designed by Joseph Gočár (1911–12), originally as a department store (*see page 105*). On the top floors it offers excellent rotating exhibitions and a permanent exhibition of Czech cubist art, including paintings and sculptures (open Tues–Sun; entrance fee).

At the end of Celetná is the late-Gothic **Prašná brána (Powder Tower) ❾**. It was built in the second half of the 15th century as an impressive city gate, replacing an older gate which had previously stood on this site. Its special status among the 13 gates of the Old Town fortifications came about because the Royal Court (no longer in existence), which acted as the royal residence in the 15th century, was right next door. It acquired its name when it was used as a gunpowder storehouse. The Neo-Gothic roof was added during rebuilding in the second half of the 19th century. The tower is open to the public daily from April to October and offers an interesting view.

The Municipal House

In the more modern **náměstí Republiky (Republic Square)**, which leads on to the New Town, on the site of the Royal Court, is the **Obecní dům (Municipal House) ❿**, built during the years 1906–11.

The splendid Art Nouveau building was created in response to the politically and economically strengthened national consciousness of the Czech bourgeoisie around the turn of the 20th century. A whole generation of artists worked on this building, including Alfons Mucha, who has left here some wonderful examples of his art. Every corner of the building, both inside and out, is elegantly decorated, and has been carefully retained over the years. It was also here that the independent Czechoslovak republic was declared in October 1918 (*see page 40*).

Today, the Municipal House is home to the Prague Symphony Orchestra, which plays in the Smetanova síň (Smetana Hall), including the opening of the Prague Spring Music Festival in May, performing *Má vlast* (*My Country*) by Czech composer Bedřich Smetana (*see page 98*). Some idea of the splendour of the Municipal House can be gained from its gorgeous café, where drinks, snacks and (very expensive) light meals can be enjoyed beneath ornate chandeliers. One-hour guided tours of the Municipal House are also available (entrance fee for one-hour guided tours in Czech; tours in other languages may be available upon request; tel: 2200 2129).

TIP

An excellent spot for a snack in the centre of the Old Town is the Dům Lahůdek in the Rott House, which has an extensive selection of gourmet salads, salamis, cheeses and Bohemian wines.

BELOW: the Old Town seen from Charles Bridge.

Another example of Prague late Art Nouveau (similar to the Viennese Secessionist style) can be seen at the **Hotel Paříž**, which is in Obecního domu, behind the Municipal House.

St James' Church and the Tyn

If you enter the little alleys at the back of these buildings, you soon come to the **Kostel sv. Jakuba (St James' Church)**  in Malá Stupartská. You can also get to it from Celetná, through one of two passages in houses No. 17 and No. 25. Like so many churches in Prague, St James', which was originally founded by the Minorites during the reign of Charles IV, was rebuilt several times until it attained its present Baroque form. Notable works of art are the reliefs on the main portal, the ceiling frescoes and the painting by Václav Vavřinec Reiner on the high altar. Particularly valuable from an artistic point of view is the tomb of Count Vratislav Mitrovic, the work of Johan Bernhard Fischer von Erlach and Ferdinand Brokof. A more gruesome feature is the 400-year-old decomposed arm hanging on the west wall, supposedly amputated from a thief who tried to steal the jewels from the altar, but who was stopped, legend has it, by the Madonna grabbing his offending arm. The almost theatrical quality of the interior provides a fine stage for the frequent organ concerts given on the ornamental and powerful instrument dating from 1705.

The cloisters of the former Minorite monastery adjoin the north side of the church. Musical instruments of all kinds can be heard in the former monks' cells in the upper storey, for the monastery is now a music school.

Between St James' and the Týn Church lies the Týn Court, also known simply as the **Týn**. It is a peaceful place, separated from the rest of the city, with plenty of atmosphere and elegant, up-market shops. Originally it offered protection to foreign merchants. The origins of the whole complex go back to the 11th century. You can use the street Týnská to get back to the Old Town Square. It leads around the Týn Court to the right to the north portal of the church. The covered end of the street, the Týn Court gateway and the church portal with the magnificent tympanum from Peter Parler's workshop, together make up one of the most picturesque corners of the Old Town.

St Agnes' Convent

The impressively proportioned Pařížská třída (Paris Street) leaves the Old Town Square by St Nicholas' Church and leads to the former Jewish Quarter (Josefov). You could combine a tour of this last district (*see page 181*) with a visit to the **Anežský klášter (St Agnes' Convent)** , which lies to the east of the area on Anežská street.

The convent is the first early-Gothic building in Prague (founded 1234). However, the whole complex, which included two convents and several churches, fell into decay over the years and parts of it were completely destroyed. After painstaking work lasting many years, restorers succeeded in bringing some rooms back to their original state. These were linked up to form the present-day historic complex by means of carefully reconstructed additions. The convent

BELOW: the Rudolfininum, a parliament building turned concert hall.

contains a permanent exhibition of 19th-century Czech painting and sculpture, including works by Mikuláš Aleš and the Mánes family, as well as excellent rotating exhibitions and frequent evening concerts of classical music (open Tues–Sun, entrance fee).

Returning to the centre of the Old Town via the street 17. listopadu, you reach the **Uměleckoprůmyslové muzeum (Museum of Decorative Arts)**, which has a very good collection of Czech and European crafts from the 16th through to the 19th centuries, in particular Bohemian glass, as well as rotating exhibitions and a small but unique gift shop (open Tues–Sun; entrance fee).

Rudolfinum

Located diagonally opposite the museum is the **Dům umělců (Rudolfinum)** , an impressive building in Neo-Renaissance style, which faces Náměstí Jana Palacha (Jan Palach Square). From 1918–38 it was the seat of the Czechoslovakian parliament, but today it has returned to its original use, as the seat of the Czech Philharmonic Orchestra. Its magnificent concert hall (the Dvořák Hall) is where many of the concerts in the Prague Spring Festival take place, and the Rudolfinum's gallery is an important venue for the work of well-known, often foreign, artists. (Box office for concerts: Alšovo nábřeží 12; open Mon–Fri; tel. 2489 3352. Art gallery: open Tues–Sun; entrance fee).

Across the Old Town Square there is a gorgeous view of the Charles Bridge, the Malá Strana and the castle from the banks of the Vltava. If you carry on upstream along the embankment and follow Křižovnická street you will pass the massive façade of the Clementinum and come to the Křižovnické náměstí (Crusader Knights' Square), with its monument to Charles IV.

Map on page 164

When the Nazis occupied Prague they wanted rid of the statue of the German Jewish composer Mendelsson from the Rudolfinum. Unfortunately they removed the statue of the revered German composer Richard Wagner by mistake.

BELOW: detail on St James' Church.

Crusader Knights' Square

Charles Bridge leads on to Crusader Knights' Square. On the first pillar of the bridge (*see page 159*) is the Old Town Bridge Tower, built, like the bridge itself, by Peter Parler. The remarkable statues which ornament the tower include figures of St Vitus, Charles IV, Václav IV, and the patron saints of Bohemia Sigismund and Aldabert and are also from the workshop of Peter Parler.

The **Kostel sv. Františka Serafinského (Church of the Crusader Knights)** on the riverbank side of the square is dedicated to St Franciscus Seraphicus. It once belonged to the monastery of the Order of Crusader Knights of the Red Star, the Bohemian knightly order at the time of the Crusades. The cupola of the church is decorated with the fresco *The Last Judgement* by Václav Reiner.

The buildings right on the waterfront were originally the municipal waterworks. The last one, which is decorated with sgraffiti, now contains the **Muzeum Bedřicha Smetany (Smetana Museum)** ❹ (open Wed–Mon; entrance fee), dedicated to the composer's life and work (*see page 85*). It is worth a visit for those interested in both music and architecture.

Opposite the Bridge Tower you can see the Baroque façade of Kostel sv. Salvátora (St Saviour's Church), which is part of the Jesuit college of the **Klementinum (Clementinum)** ❺. This broad complex was founded by the Jesuits, who were called to Prague in 1556 to help coax the country back into the Catholic fold. But not long after the building was completed, the Jesuits were exiled from the country, in 1773. Nowadays the National Library is based here, which is not open to the public, but classical concerts are often held in the spectacular Zrcadlová kaple (Mirrored Chapel) and the whole building is worth seeing at night, when its floodlights shimmer across the Vltava.

BELOW: sgraffito design on the façade of the Smetana Museum.

Charles Alley

The narrow and twisting Karlova (Charles Alley) has always been the link between the Charles Bridge and the Old Town Square. The astronomer Johannes Kepler lived at No. 4 for a while. A little further on, in **U zlatého hada (The Golden Serpent)**, the Armenian Gorgos Hatalah Damashki opened the first Prague café in 1714.

Map on page 164

Door knob in Staré Město.

Leave Karlova, following the outer wall of the Clementinum, and you have only a few steps to go to the **Clam-Gallasův palác (Clam-Gallas Palace)** ⑯, at the corner of Husova. It is a magnificent Baroque building, constructed by the Viennese court architect Johan Bernhard Fischer von Erlach from 1713 to 1730. The portal ornamentation of statues of Hercules is by Matthias Bernard Braun. Once containing a theatre, where Beethoven, among others, reputedly performed, the building now houses the city archives.

To the south of Karlova a network of tiny streets spreads out, inviting you to stroll along them. But follow Husova for now. On the right is a façade built in the Venetian Renaissance style. The house (No. 19) contains the Czech Museum of Fine Art, which holds exhibitions of contemporary Bohemian art (open Tues–Sun; entrance fee). A little further to the left is the **Kostel sv. Jiljí (St Giles' Church)** ⑰. By walking around it, you get the best impression of the clear, Gothic lines of the church exterior, which contrasts with the overloaded Baroque interior, decorated with paintings by Václav Vavřinec Reiner. The central courtyard of the monastery that adjoins the church to the left has an atmosphere of quiet solitude.

A road runs off at right angles to the right, and leads to Řetězová street. Further on in the same direction is the cosy little square Anenské náměstí.

BELOW: rococo staircase in Clam-Gallas Palace.

Map on page 164

Bethlehem Square

Betlémská kaple (Bethlehem Chapel) ⓲ (open daily; entrance fee), in the square of the same name (Betlémské náměstí) is an important Hussite memorial. Today's building is a faithful reconstruction of the original chapel founded in 1391, which became a centre of religious reform. It was here that mass was first said in Czech instead of Latin. The plain interior had the pulpit as its focal point and not the altar. It could hold up to 3,000 people. In the early 15th century, the reformer Jan Hus preached and worked here, and his ideas spread all over the country (*see page 29*). In 1521, the leader of the German peasants' revolt, Thomas Müntzer, also preached in this church.

A picturesque courtyard on the western side of the square contains the Náprstkovo muzeum (Ethnological Museum) with an exhibition of ancient artifacts from Asia, Africa and the Americas (open Tues–Sun; entrance fee).

Just a little out of the way, on the corner of Karoliny Světlé and Konviktská, lies the Holy Cross Rotunda (Rotunda sv. Kříže). This is a Romanesque round church dating from the beginning of the 12th century.

There is another curious church building in Martinská. Originally Romanesque, later rebuilt in Gothic style, the **sv Martin ve zdi (Church of St Martin-in-the-Wall)** was, as the name suggests, incorporated into the city walls. Here, in 1414, Holy Communion was first administered "in both forms" (i.e. both bread and wine given to the laity).

Back to Old Town Square

Our tour of the Old Town ends back in the neighbourhood of the Old Town Square. Martinská leads into the Uhelný trh (Coal Market) – now, unfortunately, home to the city's red-light district and not recommended at night – and some narrow old streets, such as the picturesque V kotcích, where time seems to have stood still.

Between Ovocný trh (Fruit Market) and Železná street lies the impressive Neo-Classical **Stavovské divadlo (Estates Theatre)** ⓳, which was opened in 1783 as the Nostitz Theatre. The oldest theatre building in Prague, it played a large part in the cultural life of the city; Mozart himself conducted the premiere of *Don Giovanni* here in 1787 – a fact Hollywood was keen to remember when it filmed the concert scenes of the film *Amadeus* here. It was also the site, in 1834, of the first performance of the Czech national anthem, *Kde domov můj?* (Where is My Home?), as part of a musical, *Fidlovačka*. (Box office open Mon–Fri, 10am–6pm; Sat–Sun, 10am–12.30pm, 3–6pm; tel: 2490 1448).

To the left of the theatre lies the **Karolinum**, the central part of the Charles University. The magnificent oriel window is the only true remnant of the original 14th-century Gothic building, although the courtyards were reconstructed to this style after World War II. The building is closed to the public.

Following Železná will bring you back to the Old Town Square. Alternatively, take Havířská and then Na Můstku to reach Wenceslas Square and the New Town (*see page 189*). ❏

BELOW: a Praguer dressed up as Mozart.
RIGHT: the popular astronomical clock of Old Town Hall.

ART NOUVEAU ARCHITECTURE

Art Nouveau swept through Prague around the turn of the 20th century, leaving a decorative and architectural legacy that still shines brightly

Known as Art Nouveau in Paris, Sezessionstil in Vienna and Jugendstil in Berlin, whatever name it goes by, the style Czechs called *secese* brought a definite aesthetic flourish to early 20th-century Prague. Dozens of buildings, especially in the city's New Town, bear the sinuous botanical lines, figures with trance-like expressions, mosaics and gilding that were the hallmarks of Art Nouveau style.

ALL THAT GLITTERS

Admirers of this flowery style only need to stroll around Wenceslas Square and Národní to sample some of the city's best *secese* architectural landmarks, including the Lucerna complex, built largely by Vácslav Havel, the president's grandfather. Not only buildings got the Art Nouveau treatment; decorative flourishes abound throughout the city and even some of Prague's most prominent sculptures were cast in the *secese* manner. One can't help but notice, for example, the statue of Czech religious reformer Jan Hus in Old Town Square, and the figure of nationalist historian Frantižek Palacký on the square named after him, both examples of Art Nouveau statuary.

If you still crave more decoration, there are two places to stop for refreshment: Obecní dům's café, which is Art Nouveau through and through, or the café of the Hotel Evropa, a gilded gem which retains most of its original features.

▷ **GLASS WITH CLASS**
The nation's leading artists of the day lent their talents to decorating every surface of Obecní dům, including the windows.

△ **NEW DEPARTURES**
Even if not traveling by train, don't miss Hlavní nádraží, the main station, for its *secese* decorations on the upper concourse and the façade.

▽ **ROOM WITH A VIEW**
Prague boasts several hotels built in Art Nouveau style, among the finest of which is the Paříž.

◁ **STANDING IN STYLE**
The monument of Jan Hus broods over Old Town Square. It was erected in 1915 to mark the 500th anniversary of Hus' martyrdom.

MONUMENTS TO CULTURE

After the reunification of Germany, the country found itself with one too many embassies. The Germans chose to keep the embassy in Lobkovický palác in Malá Strana, an area where many embassies are located. The former seat of East German diplomacy at Masarykovo nábřeží 32, facing the National Theatre, then became the Goethe Institute, the centre for German culture.

The Goethe Institute is in good *secese* company, as the Masaryk embankment is home to a number of Art Nouveau houses. An outstanding example is the Hlalol Choir Building at Masarykovo nábřeží 16. Built in 1905, the elaborate house is a monument to music, with its brightly coloured mosaic of a *musicale*. Above street level, spreading its wings above a door, is a multi-hued mosaic bird, dulled with age.

The ironwork balconies are decorated with aviary and floral motifs.

◁ **EYES RAISED**
While roaming Prague's streets, stop and glance upward so as not to miss splendid architectural details, such as this fine oreil on Vodičkova.

▽ **CROWNING GLORY**
Karel Spillar's mosaic *Homage to Prague* gracing the façade of Obecní dům is the *pièce de résistance* of Prague's Art Nouveau.

JOSEFOV

Map on page 182

The Jews of Prague suffered persecution by the Christians from the Middle Ages, but found some freedom in their own ghetto, now preserved as the Jewish Quarter and a memorial to their tenacity

The first Jewish community was founded in Prague in 1091. Throughout the centuries the Jews were alternately ostracised and accepted by the authorities and the Christian citizens. During the Age of Enlightenment in the late 18th century, the ghetto was renamed Josephstown (Josefov), in honour of the reforming Habsburg emperor, Joseph II. In the 1890s almost the entire area was demolished as the authorities deemed that its lack of sanitation made it a health hazard. Fortunately, the Jewish Town Hall, six synagogues and the old cemetery were spared, and are now administered by the Jewish Museum in Prague. With almost unbelievable cynicism, the Nazis intended to create a "museum of the extinct Jewish race" here, but after the liberation it became the home of the largest collection of sacred Jewish artifacts in Europe.

The easiest way to approach the Jewish Quarter is from Staroměstská Metro station, from which it is a short walk along Valentinská Street. The sites in the quarter are very close together and can be seen in any order, depending to some extent on opening times. (Tickets for the Jewish Quarter, with a sliding price scale depending on the number of sights you'd like to visit, are sold at the box offices at U starého hřbitova 3a and at Široká 3; most synagogues and sights open daily except Saturday and Jewish holidays; tel: 231 7191 for further information.)

PRECEDING PAGES: ancient gravestones in the Old Jewish Cemetery. **LEFT:** Thora Shrine in the High Synagogue. **BELOW:** High Synagogue façade.

Jewish Town Hall

The **Židovská radnice (Jewish Town Hall)** ❶ on Maiselova was designed in 1586 in Renaissance style by Pankratius Roder for the mayor Mordechai Maisel, although the newest, southern part dates only from the beginning of the 20th century. It is an attractive pink-and-white building with an unusual wooden clock tower and green steeple. In keeping with the Hebrew practice of reading from right to left, the clock hands move in an anti-clockwise direction. Today the Town Hall incorporates a kosher restaurant called Shalom, which is open for lunch only.

Old-New Synagogue

The **Staronová synagóga (Old-New Synagogue)** ❷ is the oldest surviving synagogue in Europe, built in the late 13th century. First called the New Synagogue, it gained its present name when another synagogue – now destroyed – was built close by.

The building is an unparalleled example of a medieval two-aisled synagogue. The building has a plain, rectangular shape, a high saddle roof and a late-Gothic brick gable. The consoles, the capitals of the pillars and the vaulting are all richly decorated with relief ornamentation and plant motifs.

In the main aisle, between the two pillars, is the

Almemor with its lectern for reading the Torah, separated from the rest of the interior by a decorated Gothic screen. In the middle of the east wall is the Torah shrine, called the Ark, formed of two Renaissance pillars on consoles, with a triangular tympanum. Next to the Ark is the Chief Rabbi's chair, decorated with a Star of David.

Men must cover their head when entering the synagogue (traditional Jewish skull caps, *kippahs*, are handed out when buying an entrance ticket). Services in Hebrew are held weekdays at 8am, Fridays at sundown and Saturdays at 9am. (Casual visits may not take place during the services.)

Josefov's other synagogues

The **Vysoká synagóga (High Synagogue) ❸** on Červená was originally part of the Jewish Town Hall but in 1883 was given a separate entrance. The central vaulting in the lower room with its rich stucco decoration, mirroring the profile effect of Gothic rib vaulting, shows how Renaissance forms adapted late-Gothic taste. Now, unfortunately, the synagogue is closed for viewing, but the ground floor contains a small, interesting gift shop of Judaica.

The **Maiselova synagóga (Maisel Synagogue) ❹** was founded in the 1590s, again by Mordecai Maisel, the wealthy leader of the community, as a place of worship for him and his family and was the most richly decorated synagogue in the district. It was destroyed by a great fire a century later and replaced by the present building, which was given a Neo-Gothic appearance, at the end of the 19th century. A permanent exhibition tracing the history of Jews in Bohemia and Moravia from the 10th to the 18th centuries is on view here, together with silver religious articles, textiles, manuscripts and prints.

BELOW: entrance to the Maisel Synagogue.

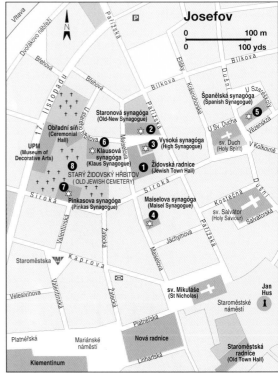

Map
on page
182

The newly-restored **Španělská synagóga (Spanish Synagogue)** ❺ was built in the 1860s on the site of an earlier place of worship. It has a square ground plan, and a huge dome covers the central hall. The Moorish-style stucco decoration of the interior, an imitation of the style widely used in parts of Spain, including the Alhambra, earned the synagogue its name. It holds a continuation of the exhibition in the Maisel Synagogue, looking at Jewish life in this region from the 19th century through to the present day.

The **Klausová synagóga (Klaus Synagogue)** ❻ at U starého hřbitova 3a is a Baroque building with a long hall and barrel vaulting. In 1694 it was built to replace the little "cells", three buildings which served as houses of prayer, classrooms and a ritual bath. The building has two rows of round arched windows in the south wall, facing the cemetery. The synagogue is now used to exhibit old Hebrew manuscripts, textiles, and silver religious articles, and a permanent exhibition entitled "Jewish Customs and Traditions", but religious services were held here until 1939.

Pinkas Synagogue

The **Pinkasova synagóga (Pinkas Synagogue)** ❼ is housed in a very beautiful Renaissance building. It came into being in 1535 in a specially adapted private house belonging to the prominent Horowitz family. It was rebuilt in the early 17th century and extended by the addition of a women's gallery, a vestibule and a meeting hall.

Since 1958 the synagogue has become one of the most important sights in the Jewish Quarter, as it serves as a memorial to the 77,297 Czech and Slovak Jewish victims of the Holocaust (*see page 48*). The inscriptions around the interior

Art of young Holocaust victims are a moving memorial in the Pinkas Synagogue.

BELOW LEFT: Jewish Town Hall detail.
BELOW RIGHT: Jewish musician in Prague.

Map
on page
182

The Hebrew name for the Old Jewish Cemetery – Bet Hayyim *("House of Life") – defies its purpose and pitiable circumstances.*

walls list the name, date of birth and date of deportation of each victim in horrifying succession. These names were obscured for some years, first because of damp and later through the reluctance of the Communist government to organise restoration, but between 1992–96 the names were carefully rewritten in their original style. A few remnants of the original wall can be seen.

The synagogue now also serves as a moving memorial to more than 7,500 children who died in Nazi concentration camps, and to the woman who encouraged them to paint while they were awaiting deportation from the holding camp at Terezín (*see page 222*), in the Elbe Valley, about 60 km (38 miles) north of Prague. The children's pictures, with their names and the dates of their death, line the walls of the first floor gallery.

Old Jewish Cemetery

The **Starý židovský hřbitov (Old Jewish Cemetery)** ❽, with entrances on Široká and U starého hřbitova, is both a moving and fascinating place. It came into being in the 15th century, when pieces of land on the northwest edge of the Jewish ghetto were bought up. Burials continued to take place here until 1787. The number of graves is much greater than the 12,000 gravestones would suggest – the true figure is probably closer to 100,000. Because this was the only place where Jews could be buried, graves are layered one above the other, giving the ground its uneven appearance. It is a tragic testimony to the prejudice and restrictions that beset the Jews of Prague, even in death.

The majority of the inscriptions on the stones consist of poetic texts expressing grief and mourning. The reliefs portray the family name or the profession of the deceased. Some families had their own symbol, which will be seen on a number of tombs, while tradesmen's memorial stones, such as scissors for a tailor, would depict the tools of the trade they followed.

The oldest monument in the cemetery is the tombstone of the poet Avigdor Kara, dating from 1439. Also buried here in 1601 was the leader of the Jewish community, Mordecai Maisel, and Rabbi David Oppenheim, Chief Rabbi of the city in the early 18th century. But the most famous tomb is that of Rabbi Löw (1520–1609), the scholar and supposed creator of the Golem. It is a Jewish custom to place small stones and written messages on the tombs of those they love or respect, and the graves of these eminent men are continually marked in this way.

The age and importance of the gravestones has meant that the cemetery is roped off to the public, but an organised path leads visitors past the most notable burial sites. The squawking crows overhead only add to the atmosphere.

The Neo-Romanesque **Obřadní šín (Ceremonial Hall)**, built in 1911, stands at the entrance to the cemetery on U starého hřbitova 3a. It was built for the Prague Burial Society, which performed charitable duties as well as burials. It continues the permanent exhibition relating to Jewish customs and traditions of the Klaus Synagogue, detailing medicine, illness and death within the Jewish ghetto in Prague and other areas of Bohemia and Moravia. ❏

BELOW: gravestone in the Jewish Cemetery.

The Golem

Every city with a long history has its stories, in which real events are either embellished or shrouded in shadow. Prague, too, has many such legends.

The legend of the Golem, the strangest tale of them all, was engendered by the mysterious epoch of Rudolf II (1576–1611). It was this eccentric Roman Catholic emperor, living in the midst of a country of Protestants, who created a fantasy image of Prague, as a city of alchemists and artists, of astrologers and scholars, who tried to lift the veil of divine secrets. It was a fitting world for the supposedly miracle-working Rabbi Löw and his monster.

They were strange times. The glory of the Renaissance was giving way to the twilight of the Baroque. The Renaissance had freed humanity from the superstition of medieval times, but the world was not yet convinced of the power of reason.

Here then is the legend of the Golem, the creature of mud and clay created by the cabalist, astronomer and magician Rabbi Löw. The *Sippurim,* a 19th-century collection of Jewish legends, relates that he breathed life into the Golem with a magic word, the "*Shem*", in order "to send it out to protect his community, to discover crimes and to prevent them". One evening, Rabbi Löw forgot to remove the sign of life from the mouth of the Golem, which began a rampage of destruction in Löw's house. The spark of life was removed and the creature turned back into mud and clay, to lie forever under the roof of the Old-New Synagogue.

The origins of the legend itself are based on the *cabala*, the mystical teachings and writings which are mentioned in the Talmud, but which say nothing about an artificially created human being. Not until the commentary of Eliezer of Worms, in the 13th century, does the word "Golem" in the sense of an artificial creation appear (along with exact instructions for making such a creature). In the medieval stories, the Golem is portrayed as a perfect servant, its only fault being that it interprets its master's instructions too literally. By the 16th century, it was seen as a figure that protected the Jews from persecution, but it had also acquired a sinister aspect.

Not until the middle of the 19th century do we find any connection in writing between these tales of the "creative" rabbi and the real-life figure of Rabbi Löw, alchemist, scholar and director of the Talmudic school. According to this version, Rabbi Löw, clothed in white, went one dark night to the banks of the Vltava and there, with the help of his son-in-law, he created the Golem from the four natural elements, earth, fire, air and water, while continually chanting spells.

This story forms the basis of the German novel *Der Golem* by Gustav Meyrink, in which the Golem rampages the streets of Prague once every 33 years. In the 1920s it was made into a film, which became a classic of German silent cinema. The Golem became the model for many other man-made monsters in literature and film, including the most famous one of all, Dr Frankenstein. ❑

RIGHT: Rabbi Löw's gravestone, littered with candles and prayers.

NOVE MESTO

Map on page 190

The name "New Town" is misleading – much of the area was actually built up in the 14th century. However, it is largely the New Town that has witnessed the political upheavals of the 20th century

N ové Město is the New Town district of Prague. Despite its name, much of it dates from the early 14th century, commissioned by Charles IV, with a lot of 19th-century redevelopment. It does not have quite as many interesting sights to offer as the other central districts, but you should not miss taking a stroll through the area, even if you do have to cover considerable distances on foot, if only because it is this area that will give you the best impression of everyday life in Prague.

Wenceslas Square

Nearly a kilometre (half a mile) long, **Václavské náměstí (Wenceslas Square)** is not really a square at all, but a wide boulevard, reminiscent of Paris' Champs Elysées. Nowadays, it is dominated by hotels, bars, restaurants, cafés, banks and department stores. It is a busy area, along which half the inhabitants of Prague seem to stroll in their leisure time, joined by masses of tourists. What you can't find here, it's said, won't be found anywhere in the Czech Republic.

The gently rising, gigantic former Horse Market is crowned by the martial-looking equestrian **Socha sv. Václava (Statue of St Wenceslas) ❶**, erected by Josef Myslbek in 1912 after taking 30 years to plan and design. The people of Prague always choose to congregate in the shadow of their patron saint in times of crisis. This is where proclamations have almost always been made and demonstrations have been started. Huge crowds assembled here in 1918 and again in 1939. In the television age, during the Prague Spring of 1968, and during the Velvet Revolution of 1989, pictures of Wenceslas Square were transmitted on news reports around the world.

Two of the more horrifying events to happen here were the deaths of student protesters Jan Palach and Jan Zajíc, who both set themselves alight to show their hatred of the Communist regime (*see page 49*). Today, a formalised memorial to these two men and the many other **Victims of Communism** (obětem komunismu) is regularly adorned with flowers in memory of those who gave their lives in the fight for political freedom.

The old two-storey Baroque houses that once lined the square have been replaced by six- and seven-storey buildings, of which only a few, such as the **Hotel Evropa (Europa) ❷**, still retain their Art Nouveau façades (*see pages 176–7*). The ground floor interior of the hotel has also been preserved, with large flamboyant mirrors and chandeliers.

Behind the statue of St Wenceslas, so redolent of history, the square is enclosed by the **Národní muzeum (National Museum) ❸** (open daily, except first Tues of

PRECEDING PAGES: shop front in Nové Město.
LEFT: Hotel Europa.
BELOW: Koruna Palace, Wenceslas Square.

each month; entrance fee). A close contemporary of the National Theatre in Národní třída, it was built in 1885–90 by the Prague architect Josef Schulz. Although he was assistant to Josef Zítek, the architect who designed the National Theatre, Schulz did not display the same flair. The building that was intended to become the spiritual and intellectual centre of the Czech nation now seems rather unfortunate and clumsy.

Next door, replacing the old Produce Exchange, is a conspicuous glass building, the New Parliament Building. Almost in its shadow, at Wilsonova 4, lies the **Státní opera (State Opera House)** ❹ (box office open daily; tel: 2422 7693). It was built in 1888 as a successor to the wooden New Town Theatre which had stood on the same site, but it was renovated in the 1980s. It used to be the New German Theatre, the second largest German-language stage in Prague, and was not entirely without its problems

If you walk down Wenceslas Square, the main shopping area of Prague begins around Jindřišská and Vodičkova streets, with a series of early 20th-century

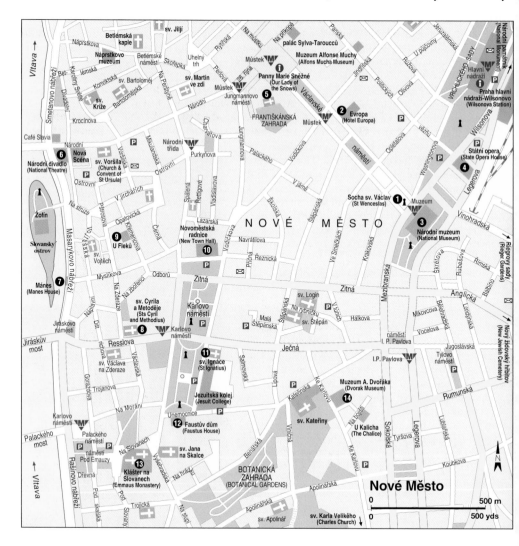

Nové Město

0   500 m
0   500 yds

shopping arcades (*pasáže*). The city's more expensive shops and bookshops, as well as the city's largest music store, can be found around the pedestrian precinct Na Příkopě and 28. října, branching off from the slopes of Wenceslas Square.

Map on page 190

Mustek to Narodni

The name of the Metro station, Můstek, at the end of Wenceslas Square, is a reminder that a little bridge (*most* or *můstek*) which led to the Old Town once stood on this site. Remains of the bridge can be seen in the Metro station. The pedestrian precinct of Na Příkopě ("on the moat") follows the course of the old fortifications towards the Powder Tower (*see page 169*). The most interesting buildings in this street are No. 12, the palác Sylva-Taroucců (Sylva-Tarouca Palace), built in 1670 and extensively altered in 1748, and No. 22, which dates from the 18th century and is now called the Slovanský dům (Slavonic House), currently undergoing renovation.

Immediately opposite, on Náměstí Republiky – where the Old Town meets the New – is the Art Nouveau Obcebni dům, or Municipal House (*see page 169*). The passage from Na Příkopě 11 is an attractive street to wander down. Panská, on which the **Alfons Mucha Museum** is located at No. 7, also leads off Na Příkopě (open daily; entrance fee). Mucha was one of the finest Art Nouveau artists of his time, and fans of the period should definitely take a look.

On the other side of Na můstku, 28. října leads to the Jungmannovo náměstí, with a memorial to the Czech linguist Josef Jungmann (1773–1847). Here, visitors to Prague should take a moment to go through the gate of the Franciscan rectory and admire the Gothic **Kostel Panny Marie Sněžné (Church of Our Lady of the Snows) ❺**, which had been planned as a massive building

Art Nouveau images can be seen all over the New Town.

BELOW: casino in Wenceslas Square.

in the 14th century. Today, all that is visible is the choir. Our Lady of the Snows was planned as a coronation church by Charles IV in 1347. The plans envisaged a three-aisled Gothic cathedral church, comparable to St Vitus' Cathedral, which was to be the tallest building in Prague. However, shortage of money and the start of the Hussite wars saw to it that the plans were never fulfiled. This is why the proportions of the church look rather odd. Inside, the 16th-century altar and the font dating from 1459 are worth special attention. You can get a good view of the church from the peaceful little park Františkánská zahrada, which leads to an arcade and on to Wenceslas Square.

The Národní třída (National Avenue) leads off Jungmannovo náměstí and on to the Vltava and the most Legií (Legions' Bridge). Notable are the glass façade of the New Theatre, now called Laterna Magika, as well as the Národní divadlo (National Theatre), but just before you get there, you will pass the Baroque Ursuline Convent and **Kostel sv Voršily (St Ursula's Church)**, dating from 1672. The church has been restored, and in front of it is a group of statues. Best-known is St John Nepomuk surrounded by cherubs, by Ignaz Platzer, dating from 1746–47. Nowadays the former convent building is a school, but on the ground floor there is an excellent wine bar, the Klášterní vinárna (Národní 8; tel: 290596).

National Theatre

The **Národní divadlo (National Theatre)** ❻ is the symbol of the Czech nation. In 1845 the Estates, with their German majority, turned down the request for a Czech theatre. In response, money was collected on a voluntary basis, and the building of a Czech theatre declared a national duty. In 1852 the site was bought, and the foundation stone was laid in 1868. The building, designed by

Josef Zítek in a style reminiscent of the Italian Renaissance, was opened in 1881 with a performance of Smetana's *Libuše*. In August 1881, only two months after the opening, the theatre burned down. Under Josef Schulz's direction, using many notable artists, and more public subscriptions, it was rebuilt and re-opened in 1883.

The auditorium is only open to the public during performances, but it is well worth a look, and tickets are relatively cheap, although most performances are in Czech. (Box office open daily; tel: 2490 1448.)

Next door to the National Theatre is the controversial modern (1983) glass construction of **Nová Scéna**, designed by Karel Prager and now the permanent home of Laterna Magika (*see page 96*).

En route to Charles Square

From the Legions' Bridge, which, as the second oldest bridge in Prague, has often had to change its name, take a look up the Vltava, and you will see the Slovanský ostrov (Slavonic Island), near which is the **Mánes house** of visual arts, a Bauhaus-style building with changing exhibitions and its own pleasant café (open Tues–Sun; entrance fee).

The starting point for many boat tours on the Vltava lies between the bridges Jiráskův most and Palackého most (*see page 158*). At the upper end of the Slavonic Island, near the Jirásek Bridge, is the street Resslova, on which lies the Orthodox **Kostel sv Cyrila a Metoděje (Church of SS Cyril and Methodius)** , which is now best known for its tragic history of World War II resistance. You can get into the (usually closed) church through the former sacristy. Today a number of photographs, documents and a plaque are displayed in the crypt which serves

Map on page 190

TIP

The Café Slavia is opposite the National Theatre and has a long tradition as a meeting place of Prague's literati (*see page 92*).

BELOW: memorial in Wenceslas Square.

REINHARD HEYDRICH

On 17 May 1942 three Czech men who had been plotting in England assassinated Reinhard Heydrich by throwing a bomb at his open-top car. Heydrich, the brutal Nazi governor (*Reichsprotektor*) of Bohemia and Moravia, had been on his way to his office in Hradčany.

After the murder, the assassins and four other members of the resistance movement barricaded themselves into the crypt of SS Cyril and Methodius. Their hiding place was discovered on 18 June and they shot themselves rather than surrender to the SS.

The plan had been hatched without the approval of the Czech resistance movement in Prague and proved disastrous. The Nazis exacted cruel revenge for the assassination: after Heydrich was given a grand funeral, the cortège pointedly moving down Wenceslas Square, his successor ordered the village of Lidice, some 25 km (16 miles) from Prague, to be burned to the ground (*see page 222*). This was done on 10 June 1942. All the men in the village were shot. The women were deported to concentration camps where many of them ultimately died in the gas chambers. Some of the children were dispersed around Germany to be raised as Germans, while others also perished in the camps.

The dark beer of U Fleku on Kremencova is sold in large quantities.

as a memorial to these seven brave men who single-handedly took on the Nazi SS (open Tues–Sun; entrance fee).

U Fleku

If you turn off from Resslova into Na Zderaze and then into Na zbořenci, you will come straight to Křemencova, which boasts at No. 11 one of the oldest and most famous of Prague's beer halls, **U Fleků ❾**. This brewery and small restaurant serves its own special dark beer (*černé pivo*), something not to be missed by any beer-lover. U Fleků and U Kalicha (*see page 67*), are the beer halls most visited by tourists throughout the year in Prague, and it is therefore usually difficult to find a seat. Every room here has a different name. For instance, you not only find the Velký sál (Great Hall), but also the Jitrnice, which means "liver sausage". The shady beer garden is extremely popular in summer, and in the evenings a small brass band adds to the atmosphere.

Charles Square

Your route through the New Town district of Prague continues from Resslova to **Karlovo náměstí (Charles Square)**. This, too, was part of Charles IV's building project for the New Town and was laid out in 1348. Charles Square was the biggest market in the city and, until 1848, was known as the Cattle Market. Its present appearance as attractive, landscaped parkland is due to 19th-century rebuilding. The monuments in the park portray numerous famous Czech scientists, scholars and literary figures.

BELOW: pub life at U Fleků brewery.

More interesting than the square itself is the **Novoměstská radnice (New Town Hall) ❿** situated at the northern end. It was built in several stages

between 1348 and 1418, after the founding of the New Town. Alterations to the south wing followed about a hundred years later, in 1520, and the tower was rebuilt in 1722. The extensive renovations carried out in 1906 restored the building to its original splendour. This is the site of the first Defenestration of Prague which took place in 1419, initiating the Hussite Wars which lasted for 15 years (*see page 29*). Today the building is used for social functions and is closed to the public.

In the middle of Charles Square, on the eastern side, is the Baroque **Kostel sv. Ignáce (Church of St Ignatius)** ⓫. This is where the Jesuits built their second college after the Clementinum in 1659 (*see page 172*). The college was dissolved in 1770 and since then the large complex has served as a hospital. The church, which was built between 1665 and 1670 by Carlo Lurago, was extended in 1679–99, with a pillared hall and arcade designed by Paul Ignaz Bayer. Inside, among other works of art, is a beautiful altarpiece *Christ in Prison* by Karel Škréta (1610–74).

A walk through the New Town doesn't offer nearly as much variety as a tour of Malá Strana or the Old Town, and if you want to see interesting buildings and sights here you'll need good, durable shoes. The façades of the New Town apartment houses are not, on the whole, very exciting, but they have been cleaned up and redecorated in recent years.

Large-scale renovations, like those in Charles Alley, for instance, are not in evidence here, but the present-day pharmacy which achieved fame as the **Faustův dům (Faust House)** ⓬, has been well renovated; the interior, however, is not open to the public. On this site in the 14th century an occult priest once lived. Then, in this Renaissance-style building, at the bottom end of Charles

Map on page 190

BELOW: a bat Trabant in the New Town.

Square, the alchemists Edward Kelley, in the 16th century, and Ferdinand Antonín Mladota, in the 18th century, conducted their experiments. The latter also entertained his guests with a series of conjuring tricks and magic lantern shows. In Prague, a city sensitive to such activities, that provided reason enough to give the house its peculiar name.

Two centuries earlier, Kelley, an Englishman whose ears had been cut off in his own country as a punishment for fraud, was no more a serious scholar than Mladota. However, he was given the task of discovering the Philosopher's Stone for Emperor Rudolf II, and to try and turn metal into gold. The search for the stone probably lasted too long for Rudolf's liking, and he had Kelley thrown into a cell, where he died of poisoning after two attempts at escape.

Emmaus Monastery

There are fewer legends surrounding the **Kostel sv. Jana na skalce (Church of St John on the Rock)** on Vyšehradská, just around the corner. It is a pity that it is so difficult to get into this beautiful Baroque church, designed by Kilián Ignaz Dientzenhofer, which, like many churches in Prague, is locked when services are not being held.

Immediately opposite, the grounds of the **Klášter na Slovanech** (Slavonic Monastery) **13**, also called the **Emmaus Monastery**, have been opened to the public. This establishment was founded by Charles IV in 1347 for Croatian Benedictines, but was destroyed by wartime bombs in 1945. To replace the towers, two sail-shaped buttresses were added in 1967. They can be counted among the few examples of originality in modern architecture in Prague. Unfortunately the whole structure is an illusion. The concrete additions of František Černý cover an unhappy ruin, although in the cloisters next door are some remarkable Gothic frescoes dating from the 14th century. The Emmaus Monastery became most famous as a medieval scriptorium producing Slavonic manuscripts. Today, since Emmaus is a working monastery, the frescoes can be admired by the public only during normal office hours.

Only a few steps away from the monastery lie the **Botanická zahrada (Botanical Gardens)**, first set out in 1897, and one of the few stretches of greenery in the area. They are highlighted by beautiful pre-war greenhouses and a collection of rare plants, including a giant water lily (open daily; entrance free).

Other New Town churches

If you keep following Vyšehradská, past the Botanical Gardens, it turns into Na slupi, and you come to another important (but often locked) church, **Zvestovaní Panny Marie Na slupi**. This former convent church of the nuns of the Elizabethan is also a rare example of a Gothic church supported by a central pillar.

If you go up the Albertov steps, you reach another building that's well worth seeing, **Kostel Panny sv. Karla Velikého (Church of the Virgin Mary and Charlemagne)**. The former Augustinian monastery is surrounded by university buildings, and you enter it

BELOW: sculpture in front of metro station Národní Třída.

through a plain gate. It is evident just by looking at the exterior that it is an unusual building, having an octagonal ground plan and a central dome. Founded in 1350 by Charles IV and dedicated to Charlemagne in 1377, it is reminiscent of the imposing Imperial Chapel in Aachen.

The church lies right on the edge of the descent into the Nusle valley, and only a few yards away from its surrounding wall the Nuselský most (Nusle Bridge) arches across the valley, over the apartment houses that lie beneath it. At 500 metres (1,640 ft) it is the second longest bridge in Prague. There are two modern glass palaces at the end of the bridge. One is the Hotel Forum skyscraper, completed in 1988, and on the other side is the **Congress Centre**, the former Palác kultury (Palace of Culture) and unfortunately one of the most unattractive of Prague's modern buildings. It was opened in 1981 and is an important venue for Prague's trade fairs and the occasional large-scale concert.

Villa Amerika

If you walk slowly back down Ke Karlovu and past the Church, of the Virgin Mary and Charlemagne you will see on the right-hand side the Villa Amerika, now housing the **Antonín Dvořák Museum** , one of the Czech Republic's greatest composers (*see page 85*). This charming little building, designed by Kilian Ignaz Dientzenhofer, was constructed in 1717–20 as a summer palace for the Michna family. Amid the rather dreary university buildings the little villa, named after a 19th-century inn, provides a pleasant change for the eyes. Inside, the museum contains various Dvořák memorabilia and musical scores, while music by the great man is played in the background (open Tues–Sun; entrance fee).

The **Kostel sv. Kateřiny (St Catherine's Church)**, which can be reached by following Kateřinská, is, however, much less attractive. The church goes back to a foundation laid by Charles IV in 1355, but was largely destroyed during the Hussite Wars (*see page 29*). The Gothic octagonal tower is all that remains of the original medieval building. The present-day church is the result of work undertaken in 1737.

New Town literati

Close to the Villa Amerika and St Catherine's, in the unassuming street Na bojišti, is one of the most famous restaurants in Prague, **U Kalicha (The Chalice)**. The tour buses parked in front of it are a sign that something special is going on here.

This is where the Prague author Jaroslav Hašek frequently used to drink, and it is his novel *The Good Soldier Švejk* which has made The Chalice famous (*see page 92*). "When the war's over, come and visit me. You'll find me in The Chalice every evening at six," Švejk says to his friend. Today, the inn has become a place of pilgrimage for fans of the book. The walls are covered with paintings and quotes, the waiters are dressed up in World War I costumes – almost everything here seems familiar from the book or the film. However, there is one drawback to U Kalicha – the countless coachloads of tourists which arrive constantly, and virtually no local feel at all. If you want to continue on the trail of the Bohemian

Map on page 190

TIP

If you have time to spare, the Police Museum near the Church of Virgin Mary and Charlemagne on Ke Karlovu is worth a visit. It concentrates on police activity over the years, including tales of murder, intrigue and forensic science.

BELOW: the Dvořák Museum in Villa Amerika.

Map on page 190

BELOW: Jan Zizka monument, Vitkov.
RIGHT: interior of Prague's main railway station.

(in both senses) Jaroslav Hašek, you can visit the house where he was born. It is also in the New Town on Školská, which branches off from Vodičkova about 1 mile (2 km) north of U Kalicha.

Another famous author who lived in the New Town is the Austrian writer Franz Werfel, who lived near the City Park and whose father owned a glove factory on Washingtonova behind the former Hotel Esplanade at No. 19. The famous Café Arco was the meeting place of the "Arconauts" – Franz Werfel, the "roving reporter" Egon Erwin Kisch, Franz Kafka, Max Brod and the editors of the German-language paper *Prager Zeitung*. The café lay in the northern half of the New Town, at Hybernská 16, in the days when Werfel, Kisch, Kafka and Brod dominated the intellectual life of Prague, but the original café closed down a long time ago.

For more devoted followers of Franz Kafka (*see page 95*), his grave is in the **Nový židovský hřbitov (New Jewish Cemetery)**, and a visit here can be combined easily with a tour of the New Town. You should take the Metro Line A to Želivského station. The route to the grave is marked on a tablet near the entrance to the cemetery. But make sure you don't go on a Saturday when the cemetery is closed to visitors. (Vinohradská at Jana Želivského; open Sun–Thur; entrance free).

Hlavní nádraží (Wilsonova Station), Prague's main railway terminus on the eastern edge of the New Town, has become quite sleazy in atmosphere of late, but its architecture is well worth a look. An Art Nouveau structure, it does have more nondescript additions, but the ornate façade and the domed and decorative entrance hall remain very attractive.

Beyond the New Town

Not far away, but actually in the district of Vinohrady (which gets its name from the vineyards that once thrived here), is the Riegrovy sady, a large, well laid-out park along the slopes of the hill, which offers a beautiful view across the whole city right up to Hradčany and the castle (*see page 123*). Numerous neighbourhood pubs with cheery ambience and good basic food and beer can be found alongside the park.

A little out of the way, no longer in Nové Město but in the district of Žižkov, is the **Národní památník (National Monument)**, an immense granite-faced cube containing the Tomb of the Unknown Soldier (closed to the public). In front of it stands one of the biggest equestrian statues in the world – the monument to the Hussite leader Jan Žižka. The heroic, Žižka, whose military experience included fighting for the British at Agincourt in 1415, was the chosen leader of the popular movement after the Hussite uprising on 30 July 1419. Having conquered Emperor Sigismund's army and captured Prague after the battle of Vítkov Hill in 1421, he erected the fortress at Tábor, from which the radical Táborites get their name. Despite losing both eyes in battle, Žižka went on to secure religious liberty for the Hussites.

Only the Stalin monument, which had dominated the Letná Hill until it was demolished in 1963, was bigger than that of Žižka. ❏

THE ROYAL WAY

Map on page 202

The once-grand coronation processions that took place in Prague until the early 19th century covered a route that takes visitors past many of the city's major sights

The last coronation in Prague took place on 7 September 1836, when Ferdinand I, the emperor of Austria, became the last crowned king of Bohemia. In 1848, the year of revolutions, Ferdinand abdicated in favour of his nephew Franz Joseph, but the latter was never to be crowned. And Charles, the last Habsburg emperor, had a sumptuous coronation in 1916, in spite of the war – but it was held in Vienna, much to the annoyance and upset of the people of Prague.

After all, even though the imperial seat had been moved from Prague to Vienna, all new monarchs had come to Prague to have the crown of Bohemia placed on their heads. And all of them had followed the route that is rightly called the Royal Way: from the Powder Tower to Celetná across Old Town Square, along Karlova, across the Charles Bridge and through Malostranské Square, up Nerudova and into Prague Castle. Even today, this route is still officially designated the Royal Way.

It is not so difficult to imagine, even today, the carriages with four or sometimes six pairs of horses, plus riders and runners, proceeding through the streets. The streets now have a very different appearance, but one can still imagine them as a Royal Way. The buildings along the route were for a long time subject to damage from the vibrations of modern traffic, until they were turned into pedestrian precincts. Today they are largely dominated by shops and restaurants dotted intermittently with historic buildings, by constant crowds of tourists and local families out for a stroll. But what did it look like in earlier years? What did the people of Prague see when they lined the narrow streets of the Royal Way in celebration?

Beginning the procession

Let's try to recreate the atmosphere of one of those processions, to follow it step-by-step and discover exactly where each salutation took place, how long the procession stopped, and where the cheering crowds would have gathered.

One of the most extravagant and celebrated coronations to take place in Prague was that of Empress Maria Theresa in 1743. According to one contemporary account there were "... on both sides many thousand people of both sexes, all filled with joy, who continually cried 'Long live Maria Theresa, our most gracious Queen!' to give utterance to their rejoicing." Maria Theresa was a popular Empress, known as "the mother of the nation", and who is said to have remarked, among other things, that she never had servants, only friends.

On 29 April 1743, on account of the "sudden inclement and windy weather", the Empress had to

LEFT: Maria Theresa.
BELOW: dressed as Charles IV.

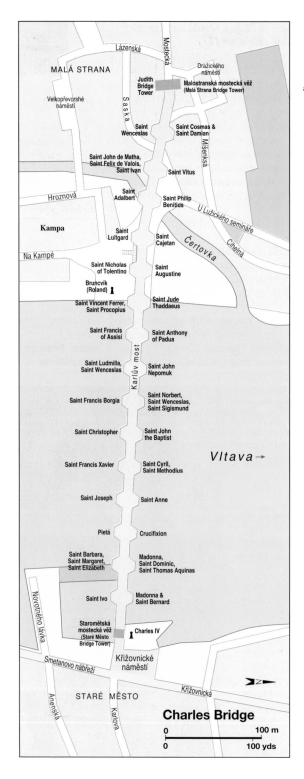

MALÁ STRANA

Lázenská

Mostecká

Drážického náměstí

Judith Bridge Tower

Malostranská mostecká věž (Malá Strana Bridge Tower)

Velkopřevorské náměstí

Saska

Saint Wenceslas

Saint Cosmas & Saint Damian

Míšenská

Saint John de Matha, Saint Felix de Valois, Saint Ivan

Saint Vitus

Hroznová

Saint Adalbert

Saint Philip Benitius

U Lužického semináře

Kampa

Saint Luitgard

Saint Cajetan

Čertovka

Cihelná

Na Kampě

Saint Nicholas of Tolentino

Saint Augustine

Bruncvík (Roland)

Saint Vincent Ferrer, Saint Procopius

Saint Jude Thaddaeus

Saint Francis of Assisi

Saint Anthony of Padua

Karlův most

Saint Ludmilla, Saint Wenceslas

Saint John Nepomuk

Saint Francis Borgia

Saint Norbert, Saint Wenceslas, Saint Sigismund

Saint Christopher

Saint John the Baptist

Vltava →

Saint Francis Xavier

Saint Cyril, Saint Methodius

Saint Joseph

Saint Anne

Pietá

Crucifixion

Saint Barbara, Saint Margaret, Saint Elizabeth

Madonna, Saint Dominic, Saint Thomas Aquinas

Novotného lávka

Saint Ivo

Madonna & Saint Bernard

Staroměstská mostecká věž (Staré Město Bridge Tower)

Charles IV

Smetanovo nábřeží

Křižovnické náměstí

Anenská

STARÉ MĚSTO

Karlova

Křižovnická

N

Charles Bridge

0 — 100 m

0 — 100 yds

travel in a closed carriage, drawn by six dark brown Neapolitan mares, strong and handsome creatures. To the left of Maria Theresa sat her husband Francis Stephen of Lorraine, who was himself soon to become Emperor Francis I.

In those days the Horse Gate at the end of the Horse Market, now known as Wenceslas Square, was still standing. A great tent would have been erected in front of it, into which the empress could withdraw for a short while. In the meantime, imagine the procession forming outside, all 22 groups of it. All were on horseback, in sparkling new uniforms, the ladies in splendid coaches, accompanied by various musical bands of drummers and trumpeters.

Into the Old Town

After crossing the New Town in a wide curve, via Charles Square and Na Příkopě, the procession would come to the Powder Tower and the entrance of the Old Town. From here on it went through the street of Celetná, where the Jewish community of Josefov greeted the monarch. It then passed what was once the most exclusive hotel in the Old Town of Prague, the Golden Angel, and the Týn Church with the peaceful courtyard behind it, which was at that time a hostel for travelling merchants.

When the royal procession reached this focal point, they would have assembled in front of the Týn Church for the deputation of all four faculties of *Alma Mater Pragensis*, when each nobleman or woman was greeted with a fine, well-turned speech of loyalty – in Latin, of course.

Once the ceremonies of the Old Town Square were over, the procession would continue past the magnificent houses, several storeys high, that lined the route, before entering the narrow Jesuit Alley (Karlova – or "Charles" street – today), which winds around a number of bends until it meets the Crusader Knights' Square. All along the route the citizens of Prague would be lining the streets, cheering and waving, to welcome their new ruler. The clergymen of Prague would have greeted the empress from the steps of the Clementinum (*see page 172*).

The last third of the Royal Way, once past the Clementinum and St Saviour's Church, took the procession on its way to the Old Town Bridge Tower. In spite of its slender form, the tower was originally designed for defensive purposes, proving its worth in 1648 when the Swedes spent two weeks vainly trying to conquer the Old Town, during the Thirty Years' War. The west side of the tower was destroyed, but on the Old Town side the gallery of sculptures survived. Charles IV still wears the imperial crown and the shield at his side bears the imperial eagle. At his side is the figure of his son, Wenceslas IV, wearing the crown of his saintly patron and bearing the imperial regalia in his hand. Between them, standing on a model of the bridge, is St Vitus, the patron saint of the city. The heraldic shields, lined up as if in greeting, display the crests of the countries that were once ruled by the King of Bohemia.

Across the Charles Bridge

The saints' statues which line the **Charles Bridge**, and which seem to be offering sound moral advice to passers-by, would have been witnesses as the coronation procession made its way over the bridge and into the Malá Strana (*see page 137*). Among the many saints who would have gazed down on later rulers are St John Nepomuk, whose body was thrown from this bridge on the orders of Wenceslas IV St Adalbert, first bishop of Prague; another Bohemian patron saint, St Procopius; the Jesuit missionary St Francis Xavier carved by Brokof; and St Luitgard, the blind Cistercian nun finely sculpted by the young Matthias Braun in 1710.

Map on page 202

Karl IV overlooking Charles Bridge.

BELOW: statues on Charles Bridge.

Map on page 194

Through Malá Strana

Watched by these saints, the procession would then have entered the Mostecká (or "Bridge" street) between the Malá Strana Bridge Towers. At this stage, the city's mayor handed the keys to the new monarch. High above the proceedings rises the dome of the great St Nicholas' Church which dominates Malostranské Square. The bells of the church would ring out through the air in celebration.

The procession would then have passed along the south side of the church, the symbol of the Malá Strana and the most spectacular example of the Prague Baroque style. Here the last part of the Royal Way began, the ascent up the steep street that is now called **Nerudova** (named after the 19th-century writer Jan Neruda who lived in the House of the Two Suns at Nerudova No. 47). This precipitous street would have demanded all the attention of the coach drivers and riders. It was particularly important to manage the great curve into Hradčany Square smoothly and to keep the horses moving at an even pace that would not jolt the royal occupants out of the carriages.

The royal procession would have passed many houses with delightful names to illustrate the professions of the occupants: The Three Violins and The Golden Horseshoe, as well as The Two Suns, among many others, the signs above their gates visible for quite a distance. Two Baroque palaces were also squeezed into this small stretch of road, which has been built on for more than a thousand years. The first was commissioned in 1715 by the wealthy Morzin family from the famous architect Giovanni Santini-Aichel, with sculptures by Ferdinand Maximilian Brokof, and is now home to the Romanian Embassy. The second, the Thun-Hohenstein Palace, was built by Matthias Bernard Braun, also in the first part of the 18th century.

BELOW:
St Vitus rooster at Prague Castle.
RIGHT:
wild vines on the Old Castle steps.

Reaching Hradcany

From here, it took the royal procession only a few more steps to reach Hradčany and the imposing triumphal arch of the Mathias Gate at the entrance to the castle. Within St Vitus' Cathedral is where the heir to the throne was officially presented to the people of Prague and Bohemia, in a ceremony that lent the occasion something of the spirit of an election, although quite falsely, for the candidate's actual succession had long before been established by the laws of inheritance.

Reliving the route

Walking the 2.5 km (1½ miles) along the Royal Way is not only a pleasurable stroll, but will take visitors past most of the central sights and areas described throughout this guide. There are numerous resting places along the route, including a number of good cafés and restaurants.

For those less willing or able to follow the route on foot, the Metro line A covers the distance in a matter of minutes, beginning with the station Můstek, and ending at the Hradčanska Metro (accentona) station not far from the castle. Not as quick, but with a view of many noteworthy sights, is tram 22 which passes through Malostranké Square before ascending to the castle's north entrance. ❑

VYSEHRAD

Map on page 208

The first royal region of Prague, Vyšehrad has now been given over to parkland, preserving its ancient sites. Also here is a cemetery devoted to the Czech Republic's finest artists and writers

The River Vltava flows down from the Bohemian forest and reaches Prague by the rock fortress of Vyšehrad (literally meaning "High Castle"). This is where, according to legend the rule of the wise women, skilled in magic, was replaced by the rule of men. The marriage of the Princess Libuše to the ploughman Přemysl brought this change about, and their successors ruled over the Czech people until the year 1306, when Wenceslas III, the last of the Přemyslid dynasty, was killed during his Polish campaign (*see page 25*). It was here on this rock, where the couple are supposed to have lived in a magnificent palace, that Princess Libuše experienced the vision in which she prophesied the future greatness and glory of the new capital, when "two olive trees will grow in this city ... they will shine throughout the world through signs and wonders".

Not until the 19th century did the Vyšehrad legend re-enter into the newly revived national consciousness. Then it was imaginatively embroidered and Vyšehrad became once more the seat of Libuše and the cradle of Czech history. Many poets and painters, musicians and sculptors, historians and architects worked on the Vyšehrad site, creating a memorial which says a lot about this nation living in the centre of Europe – Slavs, surrounded by German tribes, involved in complex relationships with their neighbours, yet very different in character and language.

LEFT: Vyšehrad, overlooking the Vltava.
BELOW: portal of St Martin's rotunda.

Vysehrad's churches

On the corner of K rotundě is a structure called the Devil's Column, said to have been put there by Satan after he lost a bet with a priest. It is just one of the myths that surround this ancient area of Prague.

The oldest building in Vyšehrad is **Rotunda sv. Martina (St Martin's Rotunda) ❶**, a tiny Romanesque church dating from the 11th century, restored in the 1870s, and one of the oldest Christian churches in the country. There are other Romanesque churches in various parts of Prague, such as St George's Basilica in Hradčany (*see page 132*), the Holy Rood Rotunda in the Old Town and St Longinus in the New. They are all that remains of cores of old individual settlements.

Much more is known about the vast, twin-spired **Kostel sv. Petra a Pavla (Church of Sts Peter and Paul) ❷**, which can be seen in its present Neo-Gothic form, dating from the mid-1880s. Archaeologists have been kept busy examining the walls of its predecessor on the same site, as there has been a church here since the 11th century, but which was destroyed by fire in the 13th century. Vyšehrad used to be a place of pilgrimage, and here, in this sandstone church, the votive tablet popularly known as the *Madonna of the Rains* was kept, along with the tomb of St Longinus. It is

now in the St George's convent collection in Hradčany. Many finds by archaeologists working in the area have now been put on display in the Vyšehrad Museum on K rotundě.

Vysehrad Cemetery

The redundant fortress on Vyšehrad Rock was finally demolished in the 19th century, for it had long lost its strategic importance. But in 1870 the **Vyšehradský hřbitov (Vyšehrad Cemetery) ❸** was created solely to be the final resting place for the country's most revered musicians, writers and artists (open daily; entrance free).

Dominating the cemetery is its last addition, dating from 1890, the tomb of honour known as the Slavín Monument, at the end of the main avenue. This communal grave of artists such as Mucha and Gočár is topped by a statue representing Genius.

Many of the graves within the cemetery are still regularly decorated with flowers, for the works of these artists live on in the memory of the nation. The most visited graves are those of the two best-known Czech composers, Bedřich Smetana and Antonín Dvořák (*see page 85*). Smetana's *Bartered Bride* has been performed in Prague more than five thousand times alone, and the performance of his opera *Libuše* at the newly-opened National Theatre in 1883 symbolised the fervent nationalist aspirations of the Czech people in the 19th century. Dvořák's grave is among the most extravagant in the complex. But these two composers are not the only musicians buried here. There are also great performers, members of the Prague Conservatory, such as the violinist Jan Kubelík (1880–1940).

The vast complex of buildings that can be seen to the south of Vyšehrad belongs to Podolská porodnice, considered one of the Czech Republic's finest maternity hospitals.

BELOW:
Dvořák's tomb.

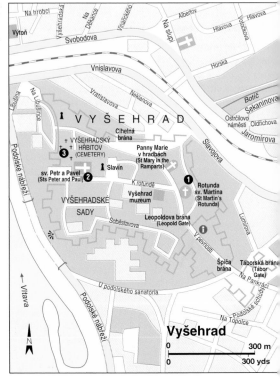

Vyšehrad

Also buried here is the 19th-century author of tales of life in the Malá Strana, Jan Neruda (*see page 143*). His stories chronicle the world of the lower middle classes, living in the Malá Strana in the shadow of the great palaces. They feature old women and their books of dreams, moonstruck students, grumbling caretakers, and a number of curious characters who inhabit the yards and alleyways. Other writers of Neruda's generation who are buried here include Svatopluk Čech, Jaroslav Vrchlický and Karel Hynek Mácha, whose romantic poem *Máj (May)* is known to every Bohemian. It was at Mácha's grave that the November 1989 demonstration began which sparked the revolution. A little more recently, the Czech poet, journalist and dramatist Karel Čapek (1890–1938) has joined his famous compatriots in death.

Visual artists and painters are represented by the sculptor Josef Myslbek (1848–1929), who created the impressive group of statues, including those of Přemysl and Libuše, which now stand in the western part of Vyšehrad, but he is perhaps best known as sculptor of the Wenceslas Monument in Wenceslas Square (*see page 189*); and by Alfons Mucha, who is best known outside the Czech Republic for his Art Nouveau posters, some of which featured the French actress Sarah Bernhardt.

Getting to Vysehrad

Vyšehrad can be reached easily from the Metro station of the same name, passing the gigantic Congress Centre, (*see page 197*). However, you can also get to it on foot along a pleasant path from Čiklova street or from the Vltava embankment through the wooded park to the castle. From the remains of the old fortifications there is a beautiful view over the city. ❏

Map on page 208

BELOW: cemetery for Czech national artists and heroes.

PRAGUE'S PARKS AND GARDENS

Prague is not just a city of architecture and urban style; its ancient parkland and lovingly designed gardens are all part of the city's charm

One of Prague's many benefits is its abundance of green spaces in which to get away from it all, even in the bustling heart of the city's main districts.

Amid the narrow winding streets of the romantic Malá Strana district lies a great concentration of gardens. Several of these, which were originally attached to palaces built for noble families, are modelled on Italian Baroque gardens and are now open to the public. At the top of the list is the Valdštejnská (Waldstein) gardens, set behind a tall wall on the street of the same name. With their triple-arched loggia (*sala terrena*) painted with frescoes, aviary motifs, artificial stalagmites and stalactites, the Waldstein Gardens offer not only a quiet place to unwind, but also a feast for the eyes. In the summertime, public classical music concerts are often held in the gardens. Other attractive green spots around the Malá Strana district are the peaceful Vojanovy sady (Vojan Park) and Kampa Park, on the small island just off the Charles Bridge.

HILL-TOP VIEWS

Why not combine a stroll in the park with a stunning view? In addition to Petřín Hill in the heart of Prague, Letenské sady (Letná Park) hovers over the river and affords striking views of the Old Town from its beer garden. A little further afield, but well worth the trip, is the sprawling park that is Vyšehrad. Located on the hill that claims its place in history as the mythical founding place of Prague, walkers can follow the perimeter of the fortification wall for a 360° view of the city. Inside the Vyšehrad complex itself are, among other sites, the national cemetery, where many of the country's pre-eminent artists and intellectuals are buried.

On a beautiful Sunday afternoon, a promenade in one of these parks is a favourite pastime of Prague residents and, of course, their dogs.

▷ **A QUIET SPOT**
Vojanovy sady (Vojan Park) in Malá Strana, the city's oldest park, is a peaceful place to relax before forging ahead to other sights in the area.

△ **BEAT THE DRUM**
An impromptu bongo concert is just one of the many musical interludes you may happen upon by buskers while strolling in one of Prague's parks.

△ **FORMAL BEAUTY**
The Waldstein Gardens, with formal hedges, statues and peacocks, are a very popular place in Malá Strana.

▽ **SNOW QUEEN**
The Church of Our Lady of the Snows towers above the secluded Františkánská (Franciscan) Gardens, near Wenceslas Square.

PETRIN HILL: THE HEART OF PRAGUE

Of all Prague's parks and gardens, perhaps the one most beloved is Petřín Hill. Actually five separate parks, including the Strahov, Kinský and Rose gardens, Petřín offers something for everyone.

Those unwilling to make the steep climb on foot can take a funicular railway (*lanovka*) up the hill. Halfway up is the Nebozízek restaurant with a wonderful view of the city. At the top are several amusements that were built for the 1891 Jubilee Exhibition, including a 60-metre (200-ft) scale model of the Eiffel Tower (one-fifth the size of the original), which visitors can climb, and a mirror maze that is great fun for children. In the summer there are pony rides near the funicular station.

On a spring afternoon, with lilacs in bloom and the city beginning to re-awaken, Petřín becomes a magical place.

△ **URBAN SPRAWL**
Karlovo náměstí (Charles Square) is Europe's largest square. Once the city cattle market, the square is now bisected by a street zooming with traffic.

▷ **AMAZING GRACE**
Statues abound in Prague's parks, but modern works are less common. This fountain of the Three Graces is in Františkánská Gardens.

Die Franzensbader Mineral-Wässer

und der

Eisenmineral-Moor

soweit dieselben als Heilmittel, entfernt vom Curorte, in Anwendung kommen.

VERLAG

DER

STADT EGERER BRUNNEN-VERSENDUNG

IN FRANZENSBAD A. M. PICK.

THE BEST OF BOHEMIA

Within an hour of central Prague is the Bohemian countryside. The open spaces are dotted with castles, forests and relaxing spa towns

Most travellers to the Czech Republic somehow never manage to venture outside of Prague. If you have only a couple of days to spend in the country, it makes sense to limit your stay to the beautiful capital.

But if you're lucky enough to have more time for leisurely excursions, it's well worth exploring the dramatic, and frequently gorgeous sites beyond the country's most famous city. In Bohemia, of which Prague is the cultural, geographical, economic and political centre, you'll find hundreds of castles, châteaux and other fascinating historical sites, only a fraction of which can be touched on in the chapters to follow.

Prague sits in the middle of what is a geographical bowl: in Bohemia, the region in which Prague lies, you'll find peaceful rolling countryside peppered by small towns and villages. As the ring extends outward, towards the edge of Bohemia which nudges Austria in the south, Germany in the west, the former East Germany with present-day Poland in the north, and Moravia in the east, the land gradually becomes more and more hilly, and, eventually distinctly mountainous.

The excursions detailed in the *Castles and Villages* chapter can all be recommended as ideal day-trips from the capital. You will find them described in a circular fashion, as destinations almost as spokes on a wheel, with Prague as your starting point. The Gothic castle Karlštejn, for instance, less than an hour from Prague, is one of the country's most famous sights and makes an unforgettable picture, surrounded as it is by massive walls and rocky cliffs. Travellers who would prefer to avoid crowds of tourists – which admittedly can be oppressive at better-known castles such as this – should check out the tidy, former silver-mining town of Kutná Hora, about one-and-a-half hours east of Prague.

Those looking for 19th-century elegance and relaxation should journey further, to the lovely spa towns of Western Bohemia. The two main spas – Karlovy Vary (Karlsbad) and Mariánské Lázně (Marienbad) – have hosted everyone from Peter the Great to Karl Marx.

These and other places recommended in the following chapters make it apparent that in Bohemia there's something to please just about every visitor. ❏

PRECEDING PAGES: transporting beer around the country; the former church of St Jost in Krumlov.
LEFT: a spa poster from 1890.

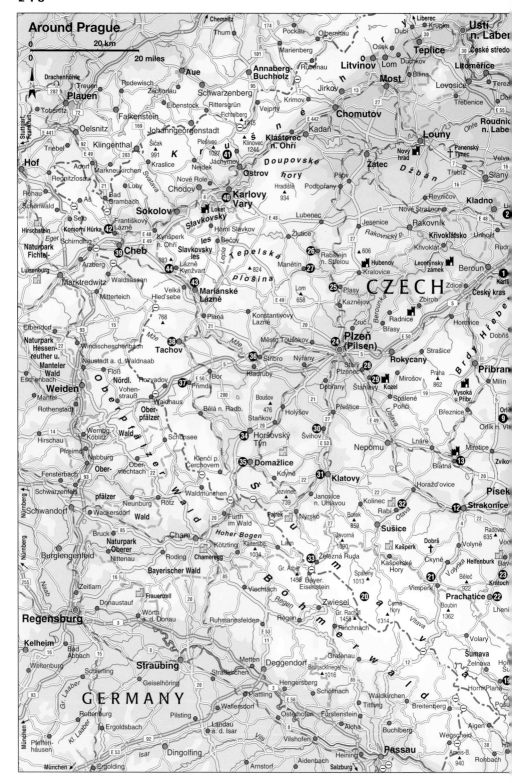

Around Prague

0   20 km
0   20 miles

Česká Lípa
vaře
15
Mimoň
Frýdštejn
Mruby Rohozec
Turnov
35
Železný Brod
Vrchlabí
Jilemnice
14
Mladé Buky
Broumov
Nowa Ruda
Starý Berštejn
Doksy
38
Mnichovo Hradiště
9
Dubá
Bezdězem
Kokořínsko
Slavín
Mšeno
Český ráj
Trosky
Sobotka
Jičín
Lomnice n. Popelkou
Semily
Nová Paka
Studenec
Hostinné
Trutnov
Úpice
Police n. Metuji
Radków
Hronov
Červený Kostelec
Klodzko
Kudowa Zdroj
E 67
Železnice
Miletín
Kuks
Ostroměř
Hořice
Česká Skalice
E 67
Nachod
Nové Město n. Met.
POLAND
Bystrzyca Klodzka
dek
tětí
3
Mělník
16
Byšice-Liblice
Liběchov
Neratovice
E 65
Brandýs n. L.
Stará Boleslav
Rozkoky
tava
upy
10
Mladá Boleslav
Jabkenice
Benátky n. Jizerou
38
Lysá n. Lab.
Nymburk
Čolákovice
E 67
Kopidlno
32
Městec Králové
Poděbrady
35
Nový Bydžov
Chlumec n. Cidlinou
25
Jaroměř
Dobruška
Hradec Králové
E 67
Třebechovice p. Orebem
Opočno
14
Orlické hory
Neratov
992
Rychnov n. Kněžnou
11
Kostelec n. Orlicí
Borohrádek
Vamberk
Žamberk
Letohrad
Praha (Prague)
řád.
Úvaly
Český Brod
12
Kolín
33
Chvaletice
Přelouč
Sezemice
36
Holice
Choceň
14
Lanšperk
Ústí n. Orlicí
Říčany
Šember
Kostelec nad Černými Lesy
Kutná Hora
4
Jakub
Čáslav
Vrdy
Chrudim
17
Heřmanův Městec
Hrochův Tynec
Luže
Skuteč
Chrast
Litomyšl
Mendryka
Česká Třebová
Mnichovice
Vysoká
Uhlířské Janovice
17
25
Tremošnice
Golčův Jeníkov
Oheb
37
Proseč
Dolní Újezd
E 442
Svitavy
Jílové u Prahy
E 55
Týnec n. Sáz.
3
Konopiště
5
Benešov
E 50
E 65
Český Šternberk
33
Štipoklasy
Zruč n. Sáz.
Chotěboř
Železné hory
Hlinsko
34
Žďárské vrchy
Ždírec
37
Devětska
836
Polička
E 461
Bměnec
43
Neveklov
Bystřice
Vlašim
Ledeč n. Sázavou
Světlá n. Sázavou
34
Sv. Anna
Přibyslav
18
Nové Město na Moravě
Blanických rytířů
Kunšat
E P U B L I C
Dublovice
Dubovice
18
Braník
Vysoký Chlumec
Sedlec-Prčice
Šelmberk
Čáslavsko
Strážiště
744
Havlíčkův Brod
Humpolec
E 65
Blažkov
694
Polná
38
Žďár n. Sáz.
18
Bystřice n. Pernštejnem
Svratka
Černá Hora
vice
Zvěřinec
Mladá Vožice
Pacov
34
Milevsko
Opařany
6
Tábor
19
7
Pelhřimov
19
Jihlava
Luka n. Jihlavou
37
Předklášteří
Tišnov
Velké Meziříčí
Velká Bíteš
Kuřim
Brno
33
Sezimovo Ústí
Kozí Hrádek
Černovice
E 55
Kamenice n. Lipou
E 551
Horní Cerekev
Pokštejn
Třešť
Střeliště
Okříšky
23
Náměšť n. Oslavou
8
Bechyně
Soběslav
837
Šternberk
Studená
Telč
Třebíč
Zbýšov
Oslavany
Ivančice
Strelice
Týn n. Vltavou
Veselí n. Lužnicí
23
Kardašova Řečice
Strmilov
Kunžak
E 59
Jaroměřice n. Rokytnou
Dukovany
Rouchovany
Moravský Krumlov
Jindřichův Hradec
3
Lomnice n. Lužnicí
Číměř
Dačice
Moravské Budějovice
421
vín
Skopojed
527
Sevětín
Lišov
Hluboká
34
Třeboňsko
15
Rudolfov
Třeboň
Chlum u Třeboně
Nová Bystřice
Landštejn
Jemnice
Slavonice
Bítov
Cornštejn
Jevišovka
54
Lechovice
České Budějovice
14
Ledenice
E 49
Grametten
Litschau
128
Hardegg
Znojmo
ský les
Zlatá Koruna
16
Rímov
Trhové Sviny
150
Heidenreichstein
Waidhofen a. d. Thaya
Raabs
Geras
Retz
38
Jaroslavice
Laa
17
Český Krumlov
Větřní
Žumberk
Beneškov Černou
Nové Hrady
České Velenice
Gmünd
303
Schrems
5
Weitra
Allentsteig
Horn
Maria Dreieichen
Eggenburg
E 49
Leiser Berge
Emsbrunn
Kaplice
Novohradské hory
1015
41
Nebelstein
Weitra
Greillenstein
Waldviertel
Manharts-B.
536
Hollabrunn
Vyšší Brod
125
Vich-Berg
1111
Rosenhof
Groß-Gerungs
38
36
Zwettl
37
AUSTRIA
Kamp
Gföhl
Langenlois
Schönburg
4
303
Linz
Freistadt
Liebenau
Albrechtsberg
Wien

CASTLES AND VILLAGES

The area around Prague has long been important historically as a link between the capital and the rest of Bohemia, and many beautiful old castles and fortresses dominate the landscape

Map on pages 218–19

I n an almost circular route, emanating out from Prague at a distance of about 50 km (30 miles), north, south, east and west, are a number of towns, villages and architectural wonders that are certainly worth a day-trip after you have had your fill of the city. The trips are described in a circular fashion with Prague as the starting point. Road and train networks are easy to navigate and most destinations can be reached within a couple of hours at most.

Karlstejn Castle

Every year, **Karlštejn Castle ❶**, lying some 30 km (19 miles) southwest of Prague on the railway line to Plzeň (Pilsen), is stormed by thousands of tourists. They achieve what their ancestors never managed, for the fortress, protected by massive walls and protruding cliffs, was impregnable to attackers.

But Charles IV did not have Karlštejn built as a military stronghold – strategically speaking, it would have served no useful purpose. It was planned solely to safeguard the holy relics and coronation insignia of the kingdom. In medieval times these relics were of immense significance: they included what are said to be two thorns from Jesus's crown, a fragment of the sponge soaked in vinegar offered to him on the Cross, a tooth of St John the Baptist and the arm of St Anne. To possess such treasures was seen as a sign of God's favour, a blessing for the emperor and his subjects. Even if Charles felt no regard for this legacy personally, it would have been regarded as an unpardonable sin if they had not been used to further the glory of the Holy Roman Empire. The collection of relics was presented twice a year for public worship: on the Friday after Easter, the Day of the Holy Relics, and on 29 November, the anniversary of Charles IV's death, the people flocked to Karlštejn. Mass is still celebrated in the Chapel of the Cross, where the precious items are preserved.

You can reach the castle by road along the Berounka Valley, or – best of all – by one of the frequent slow trains (*osobní vlak*) from Prague's Smíchov Station (Metro line B). From Karlštejn Station the castle is a pleasant stroll across the river, through the village and uphill through the castle grounds.

Visitors to Karlštejn Castle must join one of the guided tours, which are conducted in various languages. (Castle tours 9am–3pm, Nov–Mar; 9am–4pm, Apr–Oct; 9am–5pm, May, Jun and Sept; 9am–6pm, Jul–Aug; entrance fee; tel: 0311 681617/ 681695.) This may restrict your freedom, but it teaches you a lot about the castle's history. It was built in the 14th century by Matthew of Arras and Peter Parler, but much of what we see today is a reconstruction, dating from the 19th century. The

LEFT: Cěský Krumlov is dominated by its castle.
BELOW: at a folk festival in Jihlava.

tours explore the Gothic interiors of the castle and include an exposition about the life and works of Charles IV.

The palace, which includes the Great Hall, the Audience Chamber and the private apartments of the emperor and his wife, are lavishly appointed. The ornamentation of the rooms housing the relics, however, is almost beyond imagination. In the Church of Our Lady, Charles's court painter, Nikolaus Wurmser, portrayed the emperor with the relics of the Passion beneath a heaven filled with an angelic host. The St Catherine Chapel, adorned with semi-precious stones, is where Charles IV spent time in meditation. Above the door is a portrait of the emperor with his second wife, Anna von Schweidnitz.

The Chapel of the Cross itself – which unfortunately is rarely open to the public – is decorated with over 2,000 semi-precious stones. It is divided into two sections by a golden railing; the precious relics were preserved in the sanctuary, which only the emperor or the priests were allowed to enter. The walls are covered with over 100 paintings by Master Theodoric, dating from the mid-14th century; more relics are set into the picture frames. The themes of these paintings include the heavenly host of apostles and saints.

After so much splendour, a walk in the castle grounds provides a welcome contrast. The Bohemian limestone (*karst*) on which it is built is the setting for a number of lakes nestling in forests inhabited by wildlife. The nearby caves of Koněprusy were used in medieval times as workshops by counterfeiters.

At the end of World War II, many countries around the world renamed villages Lidice as a symbol of resistance to Nazi destruction. Towns as far afield as Mexico bear this Czech name.

Massacre at Lidice

Twenty-five km (16 miles) to the west of Prague is **Lidice** ❷, the site of a World War II massacre carried out by the SS in retaliation for the assassination of *Reichsprotektor* Reinhard Heydrich by the Czech resistance (*see page 193*).

It is believed that the SS received false information that Lidice had harboured the assassins, so on the night of 9 June the 95 village houses were burned to the ground. All 192 adult male occupants were shot; the women were taken to Ravensbrück concentration camp, where many of them were tortured to death. The 105 children were transported to Lódź, and many of them died in the gas chambers. After the war, a new village was built next to the ruins of the old. A rose garden was planted and the site became a memorial to the dead. The little museum to the left of the entrance shows films of the destruction and reconstruction of Lidice (open daily; entrance fee).

Terezin

The former Nazi concentration camp of **Terezín** (Theresianstadt), northwest from Lidice, makes for another sombre journey. Originally a garrison town established by Empress Maria Theresa (hence its name), it was used during World War II as a detention centre for Jews, political prisoners and prisoners of war. Although not an official extermination camp, those who did not die here of disease or starvation were doomed to be sent off to more lethal camps such as Auschwitz. Some 140,000 people passed through Terezín. The camp also had the bizarre distinction of

BELOW: Bohemians like their music.

being used by the Nazis for propaganda in 1942 as a "model concentration camp" which fooled even the Red Cross.

Visitors today can see numerous exhibits documenting Terezín's sad past. Especially illuminating is the **Muzeum Ghetta (Ghetto Museum)** just off the main town square (tel: 0416-782168; open daily; entrance fee). More authentic still is a tour of the Malá pevnost (Small Fortress) 2 km (1 mile) south of town, which contained the prison (tel: 0416-92225; open daily; entrance fee).

Map on pages 218–19

Melnik and its château

During the 9th century the Slavic Psovan dynasty constructed their castle, **Mělník ❸**, where the Vltava flows into the Labe (Elbe), about 32 km (20 miles) north of Prague. Although at first this dynasty was the rival of the Přemyslids in Prague, the marriage of heiress Ludmila with the Přemyslid prince Bořivoj united the twin territories. Thereafter the castle served as a dowager residence for the princesses of Bohemia. The settlement flourished as a trading centre; in 1274 Otakar II granted it royal privileges under the Decree of Magdeburg.

In the Holy Cross chapel at Karlštejn.

Under the direction of Charles IV vineyards were established on the slopes above the Elbe, after he returned as Duke of Burgundy in 1365 with vines and vintners. Not only was the red Burgundy-type wine popular at the imperial court, but it also brought considerable revenues to the town. And as the hosts to three national Utraquist conferences between 1438 and 1442, the town enjoyed the special favour of George of Poděbrady, who rose to the position of King of Bohemia. Fortunes declined when his widow died in Mělník.

Under a succession of further rulers the castle was rebuilt, fell into decay again and during the Baroque era acquired its current character as a château.

BELOW: grapes grow on the slopes around Mělník.

Baroque details of Mělník château.

The prestige it enjoyed in the Middle Ages never returned, however, for the new owners, the Princes of Lobkowitz, preferred to live in Prague. The town's growth stagnated, although the viticulture continued to provide a good income.

The architecture of the château reflects its historical development – each of the three main wings is characterised by a different style. In the west wing the Gothic influence is dominant; in the north, the Renaissance is evident in the arcaded walks and ornamental façades, and in the south, the opulent Baroque style unfolds. (Tours daily Mar–Sept; entrance fee; tel. 0206-622121.)

The centre of Mělník is quite picturesque, although much of it is, sadly, in need of renovation and repair. The market place, with its fountain commemorating the grape harvest, is framed by a curving arc of arcaded town houses. The clock tower on the Town Hall and the Church of the Fourteen Auxiliary Saints complete the harmonious effect. On the far side of the square, a busy street leads down to the Prague Gate and the remains of the town fortifications.

Kutna Hora

BELOW: the cathedral of St Barbara in Kutna Hora.

The quiet little town of **Kutná Hora** , located 70 km (45 miles) east of Prague, gained fame in the Middle Ages as a centre of silver mining, and many remnants from that era have been painstakingly preserved. The mammoth Gothic Chrám sv. Barbory (Cathedral of St. Barbara) is considered one of the most beautiful churches in the Czech Republic; it doubled for the Notre Dame in the 1998 film *Les Misérables*. Work on the cathedral began in 1388 under the patronage of the local miners, and it was designed by Jan Parler, son of Peter Parler (*see page 126*). A stroll inside the cathedral (open daily; entrance fee) is a must in order to appreciate its magnificent vaulting, with coats of arms painted on the

ceiling. The Miners' Chapel displays Gothic frescoes. Visitors should also explore the town's winding lanes, which reveal boutiques of local handicrafts.

Of more lurid fascination is Kutná Hora's ossuary (*kostnice*), or "bone church", actually located a short walk from the town, in the district of Sedlec. Not for the squeamish, the bone church features "sculptures" from 40,000 bones which were removed from a nearby graveyard, all put together in eye-catching styles, such as chandeliers and coats of arms (open daily; entrance fee).

Map on pages 218–19

Konopiste Castle

About 40 km (25 miles) southeast of Prague is **Konopiště Castle ❺**, dating from the 13th century. In 1423, in the midst of war, the two Hussite factions negotiated over liturgical details here. After plundering by the Swedish army during the Thirty Years' War, the complex – originally built in Gothic style – was rebuilt as a Baroque residence. However, it was Archduke Franz Ferdinand, the heir to the Habsburg throne who was assassinated in Sarajevo in 1914, who converted it into a fine private palace, which he embellished with an extravagant collection of art.

Visitors are greeted by a Baroque gateway in front of the moat; the high walls are dominated by the East Tower. Worth particular note is the banqueting hall, with two Gobelin tapestries from Paris and sketches made for Cervantes' *Don Quixote*. The smoking room and the library, as well as the hunting trophies adorning the corridors, bear witness to the pleasures of the lord of the castle. The castle grounds feature rose gardens and ponds. (Tours Tues–Sun; entrance fee; tel. 0301-24271.)

Tabor – bastion of the Hussites

In **Tábor ❻**, some 90 km (55 miles) south of Prague, every stone recalls the

BELOW: a room in Konopiště Castle.

Stone carving in Tábor.

BELOW: the market place and town hall of Tábor.

Hussite era. The town is easily reached on the E55 trunk road towards Ceské Budějovice (Budweis) and Linz.

According to the Bible, Christ's Transfiguration took place on Mount Tábor. The Hussites had this in mind when, in 1420, they gathered in their thousands near Kotnov Castle. It was five years after the execution of their teacher, Jan Hus (*see page 29*), and a few months after their rebellion in Prague. Men, women and children gathered to take up arms against Catholic bigotry. The camp required fortifications, and from it grew the new town of Tábor. It was the start of a long campaign which culminated in the victories at Vítkov in 1420 and Deutsch-Brod in 1422. However, after their leader, Jan Žižka, fell in 1424, the movement broke in two – the moderate Utraquists and the radical Táborites. Divided, their strength waned. A defeat for the Táborites at Lipany in 1434 put an end to their hopes and allowed George of Poděbrady to take power.

After the war Tábor grew into a busy town. All Christian sects, including Catholics, were tolerated and the inhabitants co-existed peacefully as Bohemian Brethren, Waldensians and Utraquists. The spirit of rebellion was still alive, however, and when Bohemia revolted against serfdom, the Táborite flag would be seen fluttering among the rebel ranks. After losing the Battle of White Mountain in 1620, they were forced to honour the Habsburgs.

Nonetheless, the town still offers a fascinating glimpse of life in this stormy era. From the ruined castle you can visit the Round Tower and the Bechin Gate, which houses a small historical exhibition. The streets were deliberately made narrow and winding for defensive purposes. They climb up to Žižka Square, which, like much of the town, has cellars and subterranean passages, sentry posts and storage areas. Since the Czech Nationalist movement in the 19th cen-

tury discovered its precursors in the proud Táborites, the square has been dominated by a monumental statue of the leader of the Hussite legions.

The lofty tower of the Church of the Transfiguration dates from Hussite times. It soars above the former Town Hall with its municipal coat of arms and a two-storey council chamber, now a museum to the Hussite movement (open Tues–Sun, Apr, Oct; Mon–Fri, Nov–Mar; daily May–Sept; entrance fee).

The street Pražská has a number of attractive Renaissance houses. During the past few years the side streets have undergone their own miniature renaissance; artists have established studios here, and a number of galleries, antiques shops and bookshops have opened.

The architecture of **Pacov** (**Patzau**) blends with the mountain scenery. Where a stronghold and later a fortress once stood you can now see a Renaissance palace, its former defensive walls transformed into a magnificent promenade.

Pelhřimov (Pilgram) ❼ nestles by the River Bělá. The heart of the old town is lined with Renaissance and Baroque buildings (early-Gothic traces are still found under the façades). Just south of Road No. 19 lies the village of Včelnice, with a glass foundry famous for the red glass known as Bohemian Garnet (*see page 78–79*). Another attraction is the narrow-gauge railway, which replaced an earlier horse-drawn tram through the forest, linking the towns of Kamenice nad Lipou, Obratan and Jindřichův Hradec.

Southwest of Tabor

The spa town of **Bechyně** ❽ has a pottery-making tradition which goes back to the 15th century and is the basis of today's ceramics industry. Since 1884 it has been home to a College of Ceramics, from which many artists have graduated.

Following the River Lužnice the route returns to the Vltava and the 60-km (37-mile) Orlík barrage. Dominating the central section of the lake is **Orlík Castle** ❾. Originally a Gothic fortress, the castle was rebuilt on a number of occasions. Surrounded by an attractive garden, the castle contains furniture and memorabilia dating from the Napoleonic Wars (open Tues–Sun, Apr–Oct; entrance fee; tel. 0362-841178).

Another popular castle is that at **Zvíkov** ❿, further south at the confluence of the Otava and the Vltava rivers (open Sat–Sun, Apr–Oct; entrance fee; tel. 0362-899676). **Písek** ⓫, 20 km (12 miles) south of Zvíkov, has a colourful history. A stone bridge dating from 1265, the oldest in Bohemia, crosses the Otava here. It formed part of the Golden Path, the trading route to Bavaria. The settlement prospered on the gold-rich sands of the river bed.

Strakonice ⓬ is often wrongly described as an exclusively industrial town. In fact, it has preserved many attractive medieval buildings and is the traditional setting for an International Bagpipe Festival.

To the north of the town is the moated castle of **Blatná** ⓭, an architectural jewel constructed in the late 14th century. Visitors can see a selection of salons, including an "Oriental" salon and a "Hunter's" salon, as well as historical costumes and other items (open Tues–Sun; entrance fee; tel. 0344-2934). The town is famous for its rose plantations. ❏

Map on pages 218–19

TIP

A motorcycle museum is housed in Kámen Castle, halfway to Pelhřimov, from Tábor. The International Motorcycle Federation was formed in 1904 in Pacov, and in 1906 the first ever Motorcycle World Championships were held here.

BELOW: a promising pub sign.

SOUTHERN BOHEMIA

Map
on pages
218–219

Bohemian noblemen built fortresses and houses along the medieval trading routes to the rest of Europe. Many of these still remain and are worth a visit for a glimpse of a long-gone way of life

T o the south of Prague, towards the borders of Austria and Germany, the landscape of the Czech Republic gives way to the beautiful woodland of the Bohemian Forest, mountain ranges and lakes. Dotted throughout this countryside are exquisite villages and historic castles that enhance rather than hinder their natural surroundings.

Ceske Budejovice

The 19th-century Czech writer Jan Neruda eloquently described the town of **České Budějovice (Budweis)**  at the confluence of the Vltava and the Malše as "Bohemia's Florence".

In 1265 the village, established by German settlers, received its town charter from Přemysl Otakar II, and in 1358 Charles IV granted it staple rights. The discovery of silver deposits during the 16th century increased the wealth of the community and made it the economic and cultural centre of Southern Bohemia. The old town was laid out on the rectangular grid pattern typical of German settlements; the site of the original walls and moat is now a broad belt of parkland. At the centre lies Přemysl Otakar II Square, with the main streets radiating from its four corners. In spite of damage over the centuries, its medieval origins are still apparent: the arcaded houses bordering the square have been restored and, only a few steps from the octagonal fountain graced by a statue of Samson the lion-tamer, one of the paving stones (distinguished by a cross) marks the spot where, in 1478, 10 men who murdered the mayor were executed. Legend has it that anyone who steps on the "madmen's stone" (*bludný kámen*) after 9pm will be led to hell.

Within the town itself, it is hard for visitors to lose their way. In the southwest, beyond the Baroque Town Hall and the Bishop's Palace, are the ruins of the town fortifications. In the west, the former **Dominican Monastery** lies on the defunct arm of the Vltava; it was founded by the King of Bohemia in 1265 and completed during the 14th century in Gothic style along with the Church of Our Lady of Sacrifice. Also nearby is the former arsenal, built in 1531, and the **Salt Gate**, the façade of which is liberally decorated with masks. On Kanovická is Kneisl House in the northwest corner and the Baroque **St Nicholas' Church**. Finally, you can climb the 225 steps of the **Cerná věž (Black Tower)**, a free-standing belfry which soars above the rooftops.

The view unfolds as far as **Hluboká château** some 10 km (6 miles) away. The 13th-century former royal stronghold rises majestically from its rocky perch above the River Vltava. Its design has changed numerous times over the years; today it is reminiscent

LEFT: the smoking room in Hluboká Castle, north of České Budějovice. **BELOW:** canoeing through the Bohemian Forest.

of Windsor Castle. It is one of the country's most visited castles and is worth seeing for the collections of woodcarvings, porcelain, tapestries, paintings and furniture amassed by the imperial princes of Schwarzenberg (tours: Tues–Sun, Apr–Jun, Sept–Oct; daily Jun–Jul; entrance fee; tel: 0389-65045). The castle riding school and the conservatory form the Southern Bohemian Gallery of Art, housing an exhibition of Bohemian Gothic and 16th- and 17th-century Flemish paintings. The permanent display is supplemented by travelling exhibitions of high standard. The Baroque **Lovecký zámek (hunting lodge)** contains a small zoo in its grounds.

Trebon

Woodland, meadows, canals and lakes are characteristic of the countryside surrounding the pretty town of **Třeboň** . Many of the lakes were dug in the 16th century; the largest, covering more than 500 hectares (1,200 acres), is Rožmberk Lake to the north of Třeboň. The lakes made Třeboň the fishery centre of Bohemia; local carp are considered a delicacy and are eaten by almost every Czech family on Christmas Eve. Every three years, a carp angling competition is held over a period of three days. To the north of Rožmberk Lake is Svět Lake, where you can take a trip on a steamer. The healing powers of the peat moors were exploited during the 19th century in medicinal baths and sanatoria. The town fortifications, including the old town walls, enclose a medieval centre where many houses date from Gothic and Renaissance times.

Třeboň château, sections of which date back to the 14th century, is one of the largest chateaux in the country. Visitors can join 45-minute guided tours of the château and see examples of Renaissance furniture and paintings, as well as

a 19th-century apartment which belonged to the ruling Schwarzenberg family (open Tues–Sun, Apr–Oct, December; entrance fee; tel: 0333-721193).

Chlum to Nove Hrady

The village of **Chlum** near Třeboň is famous for its glass-making; the blown and cut-glass products are exported all over the world. The little town of **Jindřichův Hradec** is also worth visiting, since attractive religious buildings and a large number of late-Gothic, Renaissance and Baroque houses have been preserved. The medieval castle and château were enlarged in Renaissance style by Italian architects in the 16th century. The Gothic chapel of St George contains a circle of frescoes depicting the slaying of the dragon. Here, too, the skills of an ancient handicraft are practiced: a local workshop still produces hand-made Gobelin tapestries. (open Tues–Sun, Apr–Oct; entrance fee; tel. 0331-22132).

The route from Ceské Budějovice leads in a southeasterly direction along the Malše to **Trocnov**, the native town of the Hussite leader Jan Žižka. The former gamekeeper's house has been turned into a museum. A few miles further on lies the village of **Římov ⑯**, surrounded by a Way of the Cross marked with 25 little chapels decorated with exquisite woodcarvings and sculptures. Near the village the valley has been dammed to create a reservoir serving two-thirds of Southern Bohemia. No bathing is allowed here, and the prohibition is accepted without demur as the area offers a large number of attractive alternatives.

Žumberk Fortress, southeast of Trhové Sviny, containing original furniture, provides an evocative picture of what life must have been like in these ancient castles, when pinewood torches were the only light and open fires the only heat (tours Tues–Sun, May–Sept; Sat–Sun, Apr, Oct: entrance fee; tel. 0335-92124).

Map on pages 218–19

Legend has it that the linden tree in front of the Zlatá Koruna monastery produces leaves in the shape of a hood, recalling the unfortunate Cistercian monks whom Žižka hanged from its branches after he had set fire to the monastery.

BELOW: Bohemian crystal is produced in Chlum.

The village of **Nové Hrady**, near the Austrian border, was built during the 13th century. Particularly interesting is the exhibition of black glass, known as hyalite, which was produced in the surrounding foundries.

Following Route 156 west from Nové Hrady, the **Zlatá Koruna (Golden Crown) Monastery** lies a few miles north of Český Krumlov. Attractions are the large library and the 14th-century triple-naved basilica. Otakar II founded the religious community here in 1263 in order to protect his royal interests in the region against the incursions of the noble Vítkovci (Wittigo) family.

Cesky Krumlov

Český Krumlov (Krumau) has retained its medieval character better than any other town in Southern Bohemia, and it is now protected by UNESCO as a World Heritage Site. Every alley and hidden corner is an invitation to explore, although restoration is slow, and some treasures are crying out for renovation.

In 1240, the Vítkovci dynasty built their castle overlooking the Vltava. They were followed by three families of German nobles: the Rosenbergs (1302–1611), Eggenbergs (1622–1717) and Schwarzenbergs (1717–1945). The fortress was rebuilt as an aristocratic palace from which the lords administered their interests throughout Southern Bohemia. German colonists settled on the far side of the Vltava and were awarded a town charter in 1274. Silver deposits in the Bohemian Forest brought wealth to the rulers and burghers; even when the mines were exhausted in the 16th century, the town retained its prosperous air.

In the middle of the Old Town lies the Ring, bordered by Renaissance houses and the richly decorated Town Hall. To the south and west you can see sections of the original fortifications, topped by the tower of **St Vitus' Church**, which

BELOW: Bohemian marionettes.

contains Gothic wall paintings and an elaborate early Baroque altar. Of interest in the east of the town are the **Curate's House** and the **Town Museum**.

In the suburb of **Latrán** on the other side of the Vltava a long-established brewery occupies a 16th-century arsenal. The attractive **castle** sprawls high above the town; its moat is now home to a rather lethargic bear. The Upper Castle was designed as a feudal residence. The Hall of Masques is decorated with wall paintings and the Chinese Cabinet contains a collection of exquisite porcelain from the Chang Dynasty. The massive tower belongs to the earliest period of the medieval castle, although the cap and arcade were not added until 1590. A bridge flanked with statues of saints leads across to the Baroque Castle Theatre, built in 1767. The castle gardens contain an open-air theatre with a revolving stage which hosts a wide range of imaginative productions during the summer (castle tours Tues–Sun, Apr–Oct; entrance fee; tel: 0337-711465).

The variety of manuscripts and books in the archives of **Rožmberk Castle**, 17 km (10½ miles) southeast of Český Krumlov on Route 160, has made them well-known throughout the world. Paintings and weapons are also on display (tours Tues–Sun, May–Sept; Sat–Sun, Apr, Oct; entrance fee; tel: 0337-749838.)

From the Lipno Reservoir

The road to the Lipno Dam on the Vltava passes through **Hořice na Šumavě** ⓲. This village was traditionally famous for its Passion Plays, performed by the local residents (largely of German extraction), which continued to be staged throughout the war years. The tradition broke down after the Germans were expelled, but now the community is endeavouring to revive it. The little medieval town of **Horní Planá (Oberplan)** ⓳ lies directly on the shores of the

Map on pages 218–19

Český Krumlov's castle overlooks the Vltava.

BELOW: Cěský Krumlov is a World Heritage Site.

lake. It is the birthplace of the poet and painter Adalbert Stifter (1805–68). The house where he was born now contains a small museum.

Lipno Reservoir is 44 km (27 miles) long and 16 km (10 miles) wide in places. A steamer links the lakeshore communities of Lipno, Frymburk, Černá v Pošumaví and Horní Planá. During the Cold War, a considerable stretch of the land between the lake and the Czech–Austrian border was fenced off with barbed wire, which saved much of its wildlife. A footpath leads from Nová Pec to Plešné Lake, above which a monument to Stifter stands on a high cliff.

Village character.

Unspoilt nature in the Bohemian Forest

The **Šumava (Bohemian Forest)** [20], especially the sections adjoining Germany and Austria, offer a peaceful stay in unspoilt natural surroundings. The Schwarzenberg Canal is a construction dating from the end of the 18th century. In times past it served as a means of transporting felled logs; today it links the sleepy villages and isolated farmsteads of the Bohemian Forest.

The Iron Curtain tolled the death-knell of the border regions. Now, with the creation of a national park spanning the frontiers, new life is blossoming in the area. For some years now it has attracted country lovers keen to save the old farmhouses from decay. Thanks to them a number of the 17th-century wooden cottages are still standing, and the wooden chapel on the hillside near Stožec has been faithfully restored. In the Upper Vltava Valley you will notice signs of careful tourist development designed to attract visitors. Here you can wander at leisure through the forests (though some sections of nature in the Bohemian Forest are under strict protection and not accessible to tourists). South of Vimperk, at the foot of Mount Boubín (1,362 metres/4,358 ft), lies the **Boubínský**

BELOW: deep in the Bohemian Forest.

prales forest, a conservation area since 1933. Some of the trees here are 400 years old, and the rare flora and fauna attract botanists and zoologists.

Vimperk ㉑ is the gateway to the Bohemian Forest. In 1264 Přemysl Otakar built a fortress above the Volynka Valley to protect the trading route. The town is noted for its printing works, founded in 1484. It produced elaborately decorated missals, copies of the Koran and other books. Fine examples are on display in the municipal museum and the Bohemian Forest Gallery in the castle, along with an exhibition of cut-glass characteristic of the region. Above Vimperk, the cross-country ski tracks leads to Zadov and Churáňov, the winter sports centres of the Bohemian Forest.

The town of **Prachatice ㉒** is where goods, cloth and weapons were stored until their sale or onward transport had been arranged. The most important trading commodity was salt; until the 17th century the town was the biggest salt repository in Bohemia. When the Habsburgs diverted the salt routes through Ceské Budějovice and Gmünd, Prachatice's fortunes declined, but remains of the 14th-century town walls and a Gothic church housing a number of treasures are still standing. The Town Hall (1570) was reconstructed during the 19th century with elaborate sgraffito decorations. The grammar school was where Jan Hus, a native of neighbouring Husinec, was educated.

At the end of the 16th century, Wilhelm von Rosenberg (Rožmberk) commissioned the Renaissance **Kratochvíle Castle ㉓**, some 20 km (12 miles) from Prachatice. His brother, Peter Vok, embellished the property with a park, surrounded by a wall and bastion. Today the castle serves as an exhibition centre for Czech animated films (open Tues–Sun, May–Sept; Sat–Sun, Apr–Oct; entrance fee; tel: 0338-324380). ❑

Map on pages 218–19

A yellowing postcard outside a wooden chapel near the forest border states: "This was once the flourishing village of Schwendreut, now gone with the wind. It was built upon a hill which used to be covered with dense forest and which the forest will now reclaim once more."

BELOW:
Sumava in winter.

WESTERN BOHEMIA

Maps:
Area 218
City 238

This area is dominated by the important town of Plzeň, home to the famous Czech beer. But other villages, bordering Germany, bear traditions and history that make them worth a visit

The historical and cultural development of Bohemia mirrors that of its capital, Prague. The area has always been subject to both Slavic and Germanic influences and this is particularly true of Western Bohemia. A journey through this scenically attractive region can be combined conveniently with a tour of the world-famous spa towns described in the next chapter.

Plzen: a beer drinker's paradise

With a population of 180,000 **Plzeň (Pilsen)** ㉔ is the second-largest town in Bohemia. It is famous as the home town of Prazdroj, or Pilsner lager (*see page 68*). Plzeň rose to international importance soon after receiving its charter from King Wenceslas II in 1295. Lying at the confluence of four rivers – the Mže, the Radbuza, the Úhlava and the Úslava – and at the crossroads of four long-distance trading routes, the town rapidly established itself as a trading centre. In addition, the locally mined raw materials (kaolin, mineral ores and hard coal) helped to make it a flourishing centre for crafts and industry.

It was in Plzeň that the first Czech book, the *Kronika Trojánská*, was printed and published in 1468. From 1420, following the voluntary departure from the city of the Hussite military leader Jan Žižka, Plzeň was loyal to the Catholic emperors. To show his thanks, Emperor Sigismund relieved the town of all feudal dues; Plzeň thus acquired the privileges of a tax haven and entered a new era of economic prosperity. In 1599, when the plague was rampant in Prague, Emperor Rudolf II moved his official residence here for nine months. The entire court and all foreign representatives followed suit, and once more the town boomed.

The stormy period of industrialisation during the 19th century was accompanied by the expansion of Plzeň to a cultural centre for the surrounding region. The first theatre opened here in 1832, and today Plzeň has three major dramatic stages, including a Children's Theatre and a Marionette Theatre where Josef Skupa, the creator of the legendary puppets Špejbl and Hurvínek, once worked.

Plzeň is also the home of the famous Škoda Works, founded by the engineer and industrialist Emil von Škoda at the end of the 19th century. The enterprise grew from the modest base of a small machine factory to become one of Europe's greatest industrial complexes, known for its arms production in both world wars. The company was for decades the town's largest employer, and would probably have continued to expand according to the values of western capitalism had the American troops under General Patton, who liberated the town in 1945, not withdrawn in accordance with an agreement with the Soviet Red Army.

LEFT: Plzeň houses on Market Square.
BELOW: golden statue in Market Square.

Inside the Church of St Bartholomew.

Central Plzen

The Gothic heart of the city takes the form of a rectangular chessboard, with a large square, known today as the Námèsti Republiky (Square of the Republic), in the centre. The middle of the square is occupied by the early Gothic parish **Kostel sv Bartoloměje (Church of St Bartholomew) Ⓐ**, whose 100-metre (330-ft) spire is the tallest in the Czech Republic. The interior is decorated with murals dating from before 1400. Dominating the high altar is a Gothic statue, the Plzeň Madonna, completed in about 1390. With its flying buttresses and pendant keystone, the Šternberg Chapel on the southern side of the chancel is a typical example of late-Gothic architecture.

The **Radnice (Town Hall) Ⓑ**, built in the Renaissance style between 1554–58, is decorated with sgraffito ornaments, making it the most conspicuous building in the square. When Rudolf II came to the city, he resided in the Emperor's House next door.

House No. 234, opposite the entrance to the church, dates from the Middle Ages. Since its renovation in 1770 it has been considered one of the finest Baroque buildings in Bohemia. The architectural magnificence continues around the square and along the narrow alleys of the Old Town, where the façades of the houses are decorated with fine frescoes and sgraffito, the work of Mikuláš Aleš, an esteemed Czech artist of the 19th century. In the midst of all this splendour, only the solitary **Morový sloup (Plague Column) Ⓒ**, erected in 1681, is a reminder that the residents of Plzeň did not escape the dreadful pestilence.

In the southeastern corner, Františkánská street leads to the former **Františkánský klášter (Franciscan Monastery) Ⓓ** with its pretty Chapel of St Barbara and its late-Gothic frescoes illustrating the lives of the saints. In the

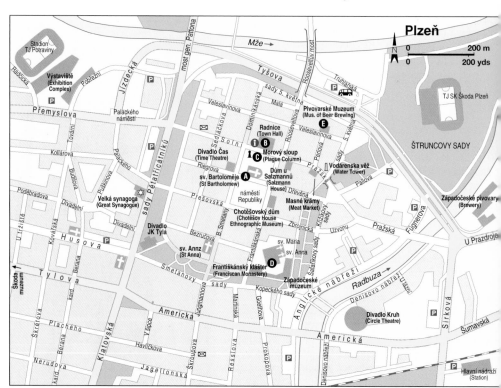

Plzeň

northeast of the Old Town, by Perlova, are the former butchers' stalls, recently converted into an exhibition hall and concert auditorium. The water tower nearby is 450 years old. A few yards further on, at No. 6 Veleslavínova, the **Pivovarské muzeum (Museum of Beer Brewing)** 🅔 is also worth a visit, particularly as it is the only such museum in the country (open Tues–Sun, Sept–May; daily, Jun–Aug; tel: 019-723 5574).

Around Plzen

During the Middle Ages a Cistercian monk communiuty settled near **Plasy** 🅭, some 15 km (9 miles) north of Plzeň. They built a vast monastery complex, one of the largest in Bohemia. The most impressive building is the convent itself, which was constructed on oak stilts because of the marshy conditions. The two-storey Royal Chapel is a fine example of the Gothic masons' art.

Following the course of the Střela in an upstream direction, you will reach **Rabštejn nad Střelou** 🅮, the smallest town in Central Europe, with only 40 inhabitants. It perches on a rock above the river, which is spanned by a magnificent Gothic bridge. From the 13th century onwards a fortified castle protected this important crossing on the long-distance trading route to Saxony and Northern Europe; the remains of the stronghold can still be seen.

The little town of **Manětín** 🅯 lives up to its reputation as the best place to see Baroque architecture in Western Bohemia. It lies 30 km (19 miles) from Plzeň. During the 18th century, Manětín was given a facelift. Surrounding the palace – the work of the Italian architect Giovanni Santini – are numerous examples of Baroque sculpture. Also worth noting are the paintings by the Czech Baroque master, Petr Brandl, which hang in the town's churches.

Some 9 km (5 miles) southeast of Plzeň lie the ruins of the former castle, mentioned in records as early as AD 976. After the foundation of the town of New Pilsen, the site of the fortress was rechristened Old Pilsen, later known as **Starý Plzenec** 🅲. The castle was built by the Přemyslid dynasty as a cultural and administrative centre. Its fortifications included a 10-metre (32-ft) wall, a section of which is still standing today, and the oldest intact monument in the Czech Republic, the **Rotunda of St Peter**, which dates from the late 10th century.

A few miles further on, on a hillside to the east of **Štáhlavy** 🅳, stands **Kozel château**. This Classical building nestles in magnificent woodland; the main section was completed from 1784–89. Several years later a number of additions were made, following plans drawn up by the master architect Ignác Palliardi. The palace houses an exhibition of 18th- and 19th-century art (tours Tues–Sun, May–Sept; Sat–Sun, Apr, Oct; entrance fee; tel: 019-796 9039).

Plzen to the German border

The E53 from Plzeň leads south to the little town of **Švihov** 🅴, where there is a magnificent moated castle built in a mixture of Gothic and Renaissance styles. It houses a comprehensive collection of medieval weapons (tours Tues–Sun, May–Sept; Sat–Sun, Apr, Oct; entrance fee; tel: 0186-693378).

Maps:
Area 218
City 238

TIP

Plzeň is, of course, home to the famous Czech beer Pilsner Lager. The Prazdorj Brewery, at ul Prazdroje, runs tours, in English and German, of its plant at, at 12.30pm daily. Telephone 019 706 1111 for details.

BELOW: decorative eggs for sale in Plzeň.

The town of **Klatovy (Klattau)** ㉛ is known as the gateway to the Bohemian Forest. It is also famous as a cultivation centre of carnations. The Black Tower soars to a height of almost 80 metres (256 ft) above the Renaissance-style market square. Its gallery affords a fine view of the historic town walls and the surrounding hills. Those with a liking for the macabre can gaze at the mummified corpses of Jesuits in the catacombs beneath the early Baroque **Church of St Ignatius**. Visitors should also take a look inside the former chemist's shop *(lékárna)* on the Town Square, which contains its original Baroque shop fittings. It is listed in the UNESCO catalogue of historic monuments.

The beautiful countryside of the central Bohemian Forest (Šumava) also deserves protection. Particularly attractive is the valley of the Vydra torrent, which is 7 km (4 miles) long, and lies a few miles southeast of Klatovy. Beyond Sušice, where the river flows more quietly, stand the ruins of **Rabí Castle** ㉜, built in the 14th century to protect the local gold-panning industry. The castle was captured twice during the Hussite rebellions; it was later destroyed by fire and finally abandoned (tours Tues–Sun, Apr–Oct; entrance fee; tel. 0187-96235).

To the west of the Bohemian Forest is **Železná Ruda** ㉝. The most interesting sight in this small town is a little church topped by the onion-shaped domes typical of high Baroque architecture in the region. In the vicinity is a ski circuit as well as a cable car to the 1,214-metre (3,885-ft) summit of Mount Pancíř.

The Chodsko region

Shortly before the German border, the ancient trading road turns in a southwesterly direction towards the Bavarian towns of Furth im Wald and Regensburg, cutting through the Chodsko region. The Chods – the name is

BELOW: the Chods celebrate their annual festival in Domažlice every August.

derived from the Slavic word for "patrols" – are a Slavic ethnic group whom the rulers of Bohemia allowed to settle in the district some 1,000 years ago. Their task was to defend the border and to offer protection to travellers and traders. They accomplished this with such efficiency that they were awarded special privileges, which they continued to enjoy until the region came under the rule of the Habsburgs after the Battle of White Mountain in 1620.

To this day, on the weekend after 10 August, the Chods make their annual pilgrimage to the Svatý Vavřinček mountain, where they take part in an age-old festival of song, dance and bagpipe music, dressed in their traditional costumes.

The town of **Horšovský Týn ❸** is another Chod settlement. It was protected by a mighty fortress, built during the second half of the 13th century. Some parts of the early Gothic castle are still standing. Following a devastating fire in the mid-16th century, the fortress was rebuilt in the style of a Renaissance palace. It is surrounded by an extensive landscaped park.

Domažlice (Taus) ❸, the capital of the Chodsko region, lies only a few miles from the German border crossing at Furth im Wald. The town was established around 1260 as a customs post. The fortifications are still visible in places; the **Dolní brána (Lower Gate)** leads directly on to the long, narrow market square of this pretty little town, fringed by attractive arcaded houses of various periods. A massive belfry rises up above the deanery church. Every evening, an ancient Chod trumpet melody rings out from its panoramic viewing platform.

The castle itself was built during the 13th century; it was later completely destroyed by fire and rebuilt in 1728. Of the original fortress, only the Round Tower remains today; it houses collections from the **Chodsko Regional Museum**. The **Muzeum Jindřicha Jindřicha (Jindřich Museum)** (open daily except Mon-

Map on pages 218–19

Map on pages 218–19

TIP

If visiting the Chodsko region, look out for the exquisite handicrafts, in particular pottery and woodcarving.

BELOW: a bubbling stream deep in the Bohemian Forest.

Statue in Cheb town square.

days; tel: 0189-722974) , named after the well-known composer and expert in Chod folklore, provides an introduction to the particular character of the customs and culture of the area. There is also an interesting and comprehensive display illustrating the traditional craft of glass painting.

Visitors wishing to learn more about Chod life and folklore should pay a visit to the surrounding villages. Draženov, Mrákov and Újezd are typical of the local architectural style; particularly attractive in all these villages are the traditional Chod log cabins.

There is plenty to see on the E50, which runs in a westerly direction from Plzeň (most drivers move too fast to appreciate the sights and villages). The first town along the route is **Stříbro** ❸, founded in 1240 in the vicinity of a silver mine. Parts of the late-Gothic fortifications are still visible, including a Gothic bridge with a Renaissance tower, and Renaissance-style houses – including the town hall – surrounding the market place. It is also worth making a short detour to the south to visit the important monastery at **Kladruby**; its cathedral is the work of the 18th-century architect Giovanni Santini.

A few miles before the border stands **Přimda** ❼, originally built in Romanesque style during the 12th century as a lookout fortress. The little township nestling beneath the castle used to be inhabited by Chods. **Tachov** ❽, a former royal town, is considered to be the centre of the region. Remains of the medieval town wall and a number of old houses testify to its past.

Cheb – a town with a turbulent history

BELOW: fine houses line the marketplace in Cheb.

From Stříbro you can turn north along the main road leading up to Cheb, a route which provides access to the Bohemian spa towns (*see page 245*).

Cheb (Eger) ❾, a lovely town on the bend in the river, always lay right in the firing line of two opposing cultures. The town bears traces of a turbulent history, originating in the 10th century when the Slavs built a stronghold on the rock overlooking the ford. Soon afterwards, German merchants settled around the fortress, founding the town of Egire which acquired market privileges in 1149. A young Swabian duke carried off and married Adelheid, the fair maid of the castle. In 1167, as the Emperor Frederick Barbarossa, he became ruler of the fortress and township, and embarked upon an ambitious scheme to enlarge its base. He held court here on three occasions; his son often celebrated Christmas here, and even his grandson, Emperor Frederick II, despite his preference for Apulia, summoned his vassals to this imperial palace on several occasions. Cheb Castle, therefore, is not only the oldest well-preserved building in the Czech Republic, it has also served as a stage for European history on various occasions.

The town has one more claim to fame – or notoriety. During the period when the country was subject to Habsburg rule, it fell into the hands of the Bohemians. Albrecht von Waldstein (*see page 143*) stationed his troops in Cheb during the Thirty Years' War. In the interests of a united Germany, with himself as its supreme authority, he was considering the possibility of negotiating peace with Sweden – a course of

Map on pages 218–19

action which would have saved many hundreds of thousands of lives and prevented the devastation of vast tracts of land. He demanded that his officers, who were under an oath of loyalty to the emperor, swear allegiance to him personally. The emperor naturally saw this as an act of high treason and declared the general an outlaw. The Irish cavalry officer Walter Devereux led an attack on Waldstein in February 1634; the general's troops were overpowered and Waldstein himself was assassinated in his house by the market square.

Cheb today is a much quieter place. The market square is the focal point of this little town of some 20,000 inhabitants. Surrounding the square (named after King George of Poděbrady, the first Hussite sovereign of Bohemia), beneath the arcades of the half-timbered houses, are a number of pretty shops and cafés. Some of the buildings are particularly striking: the former **Stará Radnice (Town Hall)**, a splendid example of Baroque architecture, dominates the eastern side of the square. The **Metternichův dům (Schiller House)** next door was where the famous German dramatist (1759–1805) stayed whilst researching his Waldstein trilogy.

The broad market place is graced by the Roland Fountain on the south side and the Hercules Fountain to the north. In the centre is the **Spalíček**, a collection of market stalls (formerly constructed of wood, which could be extended as required). Of special interest are the Schirnding House behind, with a high gable, and the Gabler House, which was originally Gothic in style. Tucked away at the top of the square is the **Chebské muzeum (Cheb Museum)** – the house in which Waldstein was assassinated (Náměstí Krále Jiřího z Poděbrad; open Tues–Sun; entrance fee; tel: 0166-422386).

On the southwestern and northern periphery of the Old Town, comfortably reached on foot through the picturesque alleyways, lie five interesting churches. All were built by religious communities which took up residence in the town during the 13th century. To the south lie the **Gothic Church of Our Lady of the Ascension** and the Baroque **Church of St Clare**; to the north are the churches of **St Wenceslas** and **St Nicholas**, the portal and towers of which display elements from the Romanesque period. The latter was substantially altered by the German Baroque master Johann Balthasar Neumann, who was born in Cheb in 1687 and went on to design many secular and religious Baroque buildings in southern Germany. **St Bartholomew's Church** lies directly on the River Ohře; from here it is only a few steps to the fortress.

The Black Tower, the massive keep of lava stone, overlooks the river and dominating the Romanesque castle complex. The showpiece of **Chebský hrad (Cheb Castle)** (open Tues–Sun, Apr–Oct; entrance fee; tel. 0166-22942) is the painstakingly restored two-storey Romanesque chapel. It looks unassuming enough from the outside, and the gloomy lower floor which housed the guards and servants confirms the initial impression. The airy upper floor, however, which was also reached by a wooden bridge from the palace proper, is a miniature gem of late-Romanesque architecture. Graceful columns support the elegant ribbed vaulting of the ceiling. ❑

BELOW: marketplace wares.

THE SPA TOWNS OF WESTERN BOHEMIA

The restorative natural spa waters that abound in the region towards the German border have made Bohemia internationally renowned since the 18th century

Map on pages 218–19

Nowhere else in the country will tourists find their needs better catered to than in the spa towns of Western Bohemia. Not even Prague has greater experience in dealing with the requirements of the more demanding guest. In the spas, visitors can still immerse themselves in an atmosphere belonging to the long-vanished era of the Austrian Empire. Since the Velvet Revolution of 1989, this has acquired even greater nostalgic value.

Sadly, the architectural sins of the more recent past are not so easily undone; here and there, grey concrete buildings characteristic of the Communist period rise between the faded "imperial yellow" of the residences and sanatoria.

Karlovy Vary

Formerly called Karlsbad (Charles' Spa) **Karlovy Vary** ⑩, is the oldest of the Bohemian spa towns. Legend has it that Emperor Charles IV discovered the healing spring on which it is centred quite by chance, whilst chasing a stag on a royal hunting expedition from his nearby castle of Loket. The exhausted animal sprang from a cliff straight into a bubbling hot spring, with the baying hounds close on its heels. Despite the scalding temperature of the spring, the emperor's personal physician declared that it possessed healing properties. In 1349 Charles founded a settlement here; and in 1370 he granted the town its municipal charter.

LEFT: the spa baths in Karlovy Vary.
BELOW: casino at the Karlovy Vary Grand Hotel.

But it wasn't until the latter part of the 17th century, following a period of devastating fires and damage during the period of Swedish occupation in the Thirty Years' War, that the town's golden age began. Under the generous patronage of the Habsburgs, Karlsbad rose to supremacy as the most elegant spa town in the world, offering every refinement essential for fashionable amusement at the time. Competitions and plays, gossip and political intrigue, exhibitionism and witty conversation were its hallmarks. Everyone wanted to be a part of the scene. The sins and vituperations of the nights of riotous drinking and extravagant parties were washed away by morning constitutionals and bathing in the healing waters.

Crowned heads, literary luminaries and great musicians were all attracted by this heady mixture. Peter the Great put in an appearance on two occasions – under the pretext of engaging in discussion with philosopher Gottfried Leibnizt over the progress of science and art in Russia. Among the visitors to the spa were great men of letters such as Gogol, Goethe and Schiller, and composers including Bach and Wagner, but Karlsbad also attracted the new tycoons of Europe, who tended to stay in the high-altitude Sanatorium Imperial. Aristocratic visitors preferred the plush Grand Hotel belonging to the former confectioner Johann Georg Pupp. Even Karl Marx took the waters here; in fact, the town provided him with inspiration for several chapters of *Das Kapital*.

World history was also made in Karlsbad. Matters reached a head in 1819, when the frenzied times of the French Revolution and the Napoleonic Wars gave way to the Congress of Vienna. The Austrian Chancellor, Prince von Metternich, invited representatives of those German states he considered to be "reliable" to join him in determining the Karlsbad Decrees. These represented a joint agreement to repress all attempts at greater civil liberty within Europe, an aim which would be achieved through the use of police informers and censorship. Metternich and his decrees were largely responsible for the tension that ultimately led to the European revolutions of 1848.

In the spa's heyday the journey to Karlsbad – by carriage through the Bohemian Forest and then down into the narrow Teplá Valley – was much more difficult than it is now. But at least there was no shortage of parking spaces, and the lords and ladies were not forced to abandon their carriages by the roadside. Today, vehicles are prohibited from the historic spa district itself. The easiest approach is from the south; if you are lucky you may be able to leave your car by the bend in the Teplá, or even on the promenade by the river.

Around the town

BELOW:
Karlsbad in 1905.

The row of stately buildings begins on the left bank of the river with the **Galerie uměni (Art Gallery)** and a magnificent **casino**. Together with the Parkhotel, the **Grand Hotel Pupp** is impossible to overlook as it extends across several

Karlsbad. Mühlbrunnquai u. Kreuzstrasse.

blocks along the esplanade. Its main entrance, much less conspicuous, is set back on a square where the Teplá takes a bend to the right. Behind the hotel, a cable car climbs some 200 metres (640 ft) to the Výšina přátelstvi **(**Friendship Heights**),** where there is an observation tower and the Restaurant Diana. The station halfway up is the starting point for a number of clearly marked walks such as the tranquil footpath to the Petrova Výšina (Peter's Heights) and the steep cliff known as Jelení skok (Stag's Leap), at the top of which a bronze chamois stands sentinel. From the numerous clearings in the woodland, the wanderer can enjoy a fine view of the town and the surrounding hills.

Returning to the valley, a favourite walk is along the **Stará louka** (Alte Wiese), an avenue containing the most elegant and expensive shops in town. Particularly tempting is a factory outlet selling locally-manufactured Moser glass and porcelain (*see page 78–9*); the factory's vases and dinner services are internationally known. Here, too, you can buy other typical souvenirs from Karlovy Vary, including Lázeňské oplatky (Karlsbader Oblaten) – wafers which have enjoyed popularity for over a century – and Becherovka, a brand of bitters prepared since 1805 from 19 different herbs, in accordance with a traditional recipe drawn up by the imperial count's personal physician, Dr Frobzig. The appropriate antidote in cases of excessive consumption is Karlsbad Salts, also locally produced and offered for sale in every shop in the town. Beware, though, they are a powerful laxative.

On the opposite bank of the river, which can be reached comfortably by one of the many little footbridges, stands another famous hotel, the **Kaiserbad,** which was built just before the turn of the 20th century by Viennese architects in French Renaissance style. Not far from the Kaiserbad is the **Municipal**

Map on pages 218–19

BELOW: drinking the curative waters.

Theatre, which was built in 1886 and carries on a strong theatrical tradition that has flourished in Karlovy Vary since 1602.

The promenade leads to the market place. It is to be hoped that future renovation work here will take into account the mistakes of the past, the most glaring examples of which are the hideous **Pump Rooms** opposite. The magnificent **Kostel sv. Maři Magdalény (Church of St Mary Magdalene)** is well worth a visit; completed in 1736 on the orders of the Knights of the Cross, it is another fine example of the work of the Bavarian architect Kilián Ignaz Dientzenhofer. It invites comparison with his famous church of St John on the Rock in Prague.

The focal point of the spa town is the **Mlýnská kolonáda (Mill Colonnade)**, built from 1871 to 1879 by Josef Zítek, who was also responsible for the National Theatre in Prague (*see page 192–3*). Here you can sample one of the four thermal springs upon which the town's reputation rests. There is no need to extend the tour to include the other spa and medicinal bath complexes further to the north, unless you want to indulge in long-term therapy in what is the largest balneological establishment in the country. Instead, take the left-hand fork, which leads to the **Russian Church**, completed at the end of the 19th century. By following the steep incline up the Sadová třída (Park Road), bordered by towering, ancient trees and attractive villas, you can quickly escape the noise and bustle of the promenade and look down over the spa quarter with its hotels and baths.

Spa treatments

The basis of the treatment at Karlovy Vary is its 12 thermal springs, each possessing a high mineral content. They gush out of the earth at high pressure, at a

BELOW LEFT:
summer rapture.
BELOW RIGHT:
Loket Castle.

rate of almost 3,000 litres (660 gallons) per minute. The best-known spring – Vřídlo, the "bubbly one" – produces more than 3 million litres (660,000 gallons) of water each day at a constant temperature of 73°C (163°F). The most important part of the cure is drinking the water, but the baths are also believed to be beneficial. In former times only baths were prescribed and the patients were obliged to lie in the water for two days and two nights without interruption. Today's cures are less rigorous, and treatments, whether they are for metabolic disorders, digestive complaints, chronic malfunction of the liver and gall bladder, infectious hepatitis, diabetes or gastric and duodenal ulcers, by no means preclude taking advantage of all the leisure facilities and attractions that this lively spa town provides. Karlovy Váry also has plenty to offer on the cultural side. As well as theatre and opera performances, exhibitions and promenade concerts, the summer film festival (*see page 99*) provides exciting variety.

Jachymov

Jáchymov (Joachimsthal) ❹ lies in the foothills of the Ore Mountains (Erzgebirge), a few miles north of Karlovy Vary on the road to Chemnitz in Germany. The first settlement was founded here in 1516 following the discovery of rich silver deposits; three years later, the town acquired a royal charter. The founder of Jáchymov, the Imperial Baron Schlick, was granted the privilege of minting the famous Joachimsthaler guilders, which were soon recognised as international currency, giving their name first to the *Thaler* – the silver coin formerly used throughout Germany and Austria – and ultimately to the leading monetary unit of the modern world, the dollar.

In the 16th century, Jáchymov, then with a population of some 20,000, was the

TIP

The Karlovy Vary International Film Festival has established a notable reputation as a stage for filmmakers from Central and Eastern Europe; as such, it attracts increasingly large audiences in July each year.

BELOW: Františkovy Lázně, near Karlovy Vary.

largest town in Bohemia, after Prague. At times, as many as 1,000 miners were employed underground. After just over a century of intensive exploitation, however, the silver seams were exhausted; by 1671, even the mint had to close down. The little town, having lost its *raison d'ŝtre*, was given a new lease on life by the worldwide industrial revolution. For a while, the people of Jáchymov eked out an existence manufacturing porcelain and glass. The coloured dyes were extracted from pitchblende, a waste product of silver mining.

But in 1896, the French physicist Antoine Becquerel discovered radioactivity in these mineral deposits. Shortly after, the physicists Marie and Pierre Curie demonstrated the existence of the elements polonium and radium, which they were able to isolate from the waste heaps. The town became the site of the first radium baths in the world. A baker was the first to open a bathing establishment. The next complex was more elaborate, and by 1906 Jáchymov was recognised as a medicinal spa town.

Today the little town's main source of income remains its medicinal baths and cures. The healing properties of the radioactive waters from the mines, which bubble forth from galleries more than 500 metres (1,600 ft) below the earth's surface at a pleasantly warm temperature, have been found efficacious in the case of disorders of the locomotive and nervous systems and cardiovascular disease.

The spa buildings are concentrated in the south of the town, surrounded by woodland some distance from the road. The **Radium Palace**, the magnificent spa rooms built in 1912 in the Secessionist style (also called of Art Nouveau, a style which began in Vienna and then spread to Bohemia), contains a concert hall and a number of elegant restaurants. In the nearby park stands a

BELOW: spa colonnade in Karlovy Váry.

monument to the scientific pioneer Marie Curie-Sklodowska, erected by the grateful citizens of Jáchymov. The modern spa rooms, the Akademik Běhounek, are named after one of Curie's pupils, and further testify to the town's economic expansion.

To the north, the **Stare Mesto (Old Town)** marks the historic centre of the mining community. Characterised by its octagonal tower and terraced gables, the late-Gothic **Radnice (Town Hall)** dominates the central square. The long, narrow market place is bordered by a number of distinguished, well-preserved houses in a mixture of Gothic and Renaissance styles. Despite frequent renovation, the parish **Kostel sv. Jachyma (Church of St Joachim)** is worth a visit. The former mint behind the town hall now houses a **Museum of Mining and Numismatics** and provides an interesting insight into local history. To gain the best overall view of the town, take the chair lift to the top of the **Klínovec**, at 1,244 metres (3,980 ft) the highest peak in the Ore Mountains and a spectacular vantage point.

Loket Castle

Some 10 km (6 miles) southwest of Karlovy Vary on a minor road to Cheb, **(Hrad Loket) Loket Castle** is a favourite destination for an outing and worth the detour. The royal fortress is built on a high cliff overlooking a bend in the River Ohře, which explains the appropriateness of its name: *loket* means elbow. The first documented reference to the stronghold was in 1239; the oldest section of the building still standing, a Romanesque-style rotunda, was probably built towards the end of the 12th century. The main tower is constructed of granite blocks; the gateways and the margrave's residence were added during the 14th century. Additional points of interest include an attractive collection of locally manufactured glass, porcelain and pewter. There is also the interesting **Goethe Museum**. Protected by the castle, the settlement has managed to survive until the present day, and the medieval houses grouped around the market square continue to charm visitors.

Frantiskovy Lazne

Františkovy Lázně (Franzensbad) ㊷, lying a few miles north of Cheb (*see pages 242–3*), is the odd one out among the spas of Western Bohemia, because the little town with its 24 icy mineral springs was conceived in a unified style at the end of the 18th century. Taking the waters here, or undergoing a course of baths in the radioactive moorland mud, is considered beneficial in treating coronary and rheumatic disease and a wide variety of gynaecological complaints. Because of these restorative qualities, Františkovy Lázně now has an international reputation.

The healing water comes from the Ohře, an acidic spring whose curative properties were well known even in the 16th century. It was a local physician, Dr Vinzenz Adler, who introduced the spa to an international public at the beginning of the 19th century. Emperor Franz I of Austria discovered the health benefits of the spring and gave his name to the newly-built town.

Map on pages 218–19

Interior details of Glauber spa in Franzensbad.

BELOW: marble elegance in the historic Grand Hotel Pupp.

The town centre is laid out on a regular grid pattern and surrounded by spacious parks, containing the springs, spa rooms and baths. The Národní třída, or National Street, is bordered along its entire length by attractive houses from the early 20th century, although the House of the Three Lilies at No. 10, one of the first boarding houses, is 100 years older. Standing off centre in the southwest corner is the main square (Náměstí Míru) with colonnade, meeting rooms, gas baths and the elegant **František Spring Pavilion**, which was built in 1832. Adjoining it on the west side, in **Dvořák Park** (named in honour of the great Czech composer), is the Bath House I and the massive wooden pavilion housing two further springs, the **Luisin pramen (Luisenquelle)** and the **Studený pramen (Kalter Sprudel)**.

In the vicinity are two Glauber's salt springs, the source of an efficacious laxative which, together with the spring water, constitutes one of the spa town's principal export commodities. The other springs are to the southeast near the **Hotel Imperial**, still one of the best addresses in town, which enjoys a splendid location and can be reached by a pleasant walk. To the north and east is the **Municipal Museum**, the theatre and the **Music Pavilion**, the setting for frequent promenade concerts.

Only 6 km (4 miles) from Františkovy Lázně lies a bizarre landscape. The peat moor of **Soos-Hájek** has been declared a nature conservation area. Poisonous carbon dioxide issues from funnel-shaped hollows; the bubbling mud, like a landscape in a science-fiction film, recalls the volcanic origins of the region. This is even more in evidence in the nearby **Komorní Hůrka Nature Reserve**, where traces of the region's last volcanic eruption during the Quaternary Period can still be seen.

BELOW:
ballroom dancing in
Mariánaské Lázně's
colonnade.

Marianske Lazne

Situated at a height of some 600 metres (1,920 ft) in a protective arc of wooded hills stretching to the north, west and east, **Mariánské Lázně ㊸**, (formerly called Marienbad), makes a good base for a tour through Western Bohemia, not only for its favourable geographical location but also for its very well-developed tourist infrastructure.

Map
on pages
218–19

One of Europe's most scenic spas, Mariánské Lázně, which has a long list of famous visitors includes Edward VII, king of England from 1901 to 1910. The town possesses more than 40 mineral springs, whose highly saline waters are used for the treatment of bladder disorders, respiratory problems, heart ailments, rheumatism and blood and skin diseases.

Typical spa vessel.

The Premonstratensian monks from nearby **Teplá** must have been aware of the healing properties of the water when they established the village of Auschowitz near the springs in 1341, creating a sort of *dépendance* of their abbey, which lay some 13 km (8 miles) to the east. In 1710 the abbot had a pilgrims' lodge built to provide shelter for the steadily growing band of invalids who came in search of a cure. At the same time, the springs were tapped; the monks decanted the water into barrels which they sold for a handsome profit to prosperous cities and noblemen's estates. In 1749 an inventive apothecary at the abbey found a convenient way of cutting the transport costs by evaporating the water and marketing the much more convenient Teplá Salt.

The mineral baths were added a few decades later. The water from the Stinking Spring (Stinkquelle) – named for its high hydrogen sulphide content which creates the odour – proved particularly efficacious, and thankful patients dedicated votive pictures to the Virgin Mary. The spring's name was changed to

BELOW: typical architecture in Františkovy Lázně.

Roadside flowers.

Mary's Spring (Marienquelle), and in 1818 it became known officially as the Spa Town of the Austrian Monarchy, although it did not officially receive its town charter until 1868.

Mariánské Lázně is full of fascinating stories. In 1820, at the age of 74, Goethe drove over by coach from Karlovy Vary. He returned the following year, the constant companion of the charming Baroness Ulrike Levetzov, who was only 19 years old. Their relationship developed into a passionate romance, but when the potential mother-in-law refused to give her consent to a marriage, Goethe withdrew and never visited the spas again.

Goethe was only the first of many writers and composers to be inspired by the springs of Mariánské Lázně. He was followed by Frédéric Chopin, Richard Wagner, Mark Twain and Henrik Ibsen. In 1833, the violinist Ludwig Spohr composed his romantic waltzes entitled *Memories of Marienbad*, and in the 1960s Alain Resnais made the film classic *Last Year at Marienbad*, which rapidly gained cult status.

Around the town

A popular venue for international congresses and symposia, Mariánské Lázně has developed into the most comfortable and modern of all the spas, expanding far beyond its modest origins. Today the southern approach leads through several miles of uninspiring modern suburbs before the elegant spa district unfolds. On the left-hand side, the central avenue, **Hlavní třída** (formerly Kaiserstrasse), is bordered by a variety of shops, attractive restaurants and several large hotels. The hotels include the Bohemia, which underwent renovation a few years ago and now combines Art Nouveau elegance with modern facilities and comfort.

BELOW:
the Rudolf spring in
Mariánaské Lázně.

On the right, the spa gardens extend towards the horizon across gentle hills. On its southern boundary stand two fine buildings dating from the turn of the 20th century – the Nové Lázně (New Baths) and the former pump rooms, now known as the **Casino** and used as a cultural centre. (The casino proper, with an excellent restaurant and bar, lies a good 300 metres – nearly 300 yards – further to the south, at the entrance to the spa district.) From here you pass the **Ambrožův prameny (Ambrosiusquelle)**, the Ustřední lázně (Central Baths), the Slatinné lázně (Mud Baths) and the Mariin pramen (Marienquelle).

Ascending the hill, the road passes the **Kostel Nanebevzetí Panny Marie (Church of the Assumption)** before reaching the spa promenade. The rotunda housing the Křížový pramen (Kreuzbrunnen) was built in 1818, when the town was first recognised as a spa. The cast-iron structure of the New Colonnade is fascinating both visually and technically. The filigree struts forming the framework of the finely proportioned Promenade Hall were produced by a Moravian foundry in 1884–89; they lend the open construction, with its lively ceiling frescoes, a wonderful light airiness. The computer-controlled Singing Fountains – a series of playful water sculptures immediately in front of the building which "make music" from the sound of the water and completed in 1988 – cannot really compete.

Climbing up to the next terrace, you reach the **Goethův dům (Goethe House)**. Today the Neo-Classical building serves as municipal museum. The square in front is dominated by the old-fashioned Hotel Kavkaz. Its rooms appeal to lovers of faded elegance who are prepared to ignore the dripping taps, musty carpets and warped window frames.

A stroll along the northern perimeter of the park will lead past a number of other hotels and bath houses and then back to the upper end of the Hlavní třída. Nature-lovers will also find plenty to enjoy in the immediate neighbourhood of the town. There are many delightful woodland walks along a total of 70 km (40 miles) of signposted paths.

Lázne Kynzvart

A few miles northwest of Mariánské Lázně lies **Lázně Kynžvart (Bad Königswart) ㊶**, another little spa town which is known for its therapeutic, iron-rich, acidic waters, and specialising in particular in the treatment of childhood illnesses.

The town, however, which came into the possession of the dukes of Metternich in 1630, is more notable for its massive castle, which dominates the view. In 1690, the dukes proceeded to erect a mighty Baroque palace over the old castle walls. Chancellor Metternich (1773–1859) then had the building elaborately renovated in the Empire style at the beginning of the 19th century.

Goethe and Beethoven both stayed in Lázně Kynžvart during the town's heyday. Today's visitors can enjoy the castle's valuable collections which include such diverse treasures as Egyptian mummies, and Oriental and Gothic paintings, as well as a display of curiosities. The castle is surrounded by an extensive, landscaped park. ❑

Map on pages 218–19

BELOW: holiday crowd at Marienbad in 1899.

INSIGHT GUIDES
TRAVEL TIPS

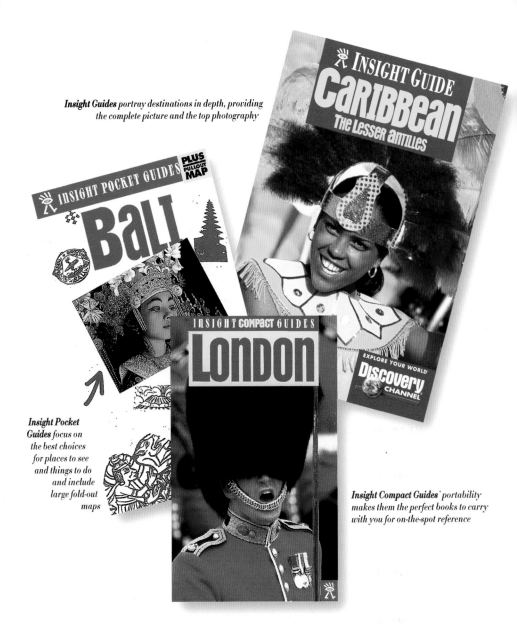

Insight Guides portray destinations in depth, providing the complete picture and the top photography

Insight Pocket Guides focus on the best choices for places to see and things to do and include large fold-out maps

Insight Compact Guides' portability makes them the perfect books to carry with you for on-the-spot reference

Three types of guide for all types of travel

INSIGHT GUIDES Different people need different kinds of information. Some want *background information* to help them prepare for the trip. Others seek *personal recommendations* from someone who knows the destination well. And others look for *compactly presented data* for on-the-spot reference. With three carefully designed series, Insight Guides offer readers the perfect choice. Insight Guides will turn your visit into an experience.

The world's largest collection of visual travel guides

CONTENTS

Getting Acquainted

Area: 497 sq km (190 sq miles).
Population: 1.2 million.
Language (everyday): Czech and some Slovak (both in the Slavonic language family, along with Russian and Polish).
Language (business): English and German.
Religion: Roman Catholic.
Time Zone: GMT plus 1 hour Oct–Mar; GMT plus 2 hours Apr–Sept.
Currency: Czech Koruna (Kč), called "crown" in English.
Weights & Measures: Metric.
Electricity: AC 220 volts. Two-pin plugs or adaptors are needed for British appliances.
International dialling code: 420 (Czech Republic) + 2 (Prague).

Geography

The capital of the Czech Republic is situated on the River Vltava (Moldau), spread out between seven hills. It lies between 175–400 metres (575–1,300 ft) above sea level, at 50° North and 14° East; about the same latitude as Frankfurt, Land's End and Vancouver. The historical part is made up of the Old Town (Staré Město), the New Town (Nové Město), Hradčany (Prague Castle) and the Lesser Quarter (Malá Strana). The city's parks cover a total area of 870 hectares (2,150 acres). Prague is divided into 56 districts which are administered from local town halls.

Climate

Thanks to its protected position, Prague's climate is particularly mild. The average annual temperature is 9.3°C (49°F). Summer averages are: June 17.3°C (63°F), July 19.2°C (66°F); winter averages: December 1.8°C (35°F), February 0.5°C (33°F). The average annual precipitation is 487 mm (19 inches). The least rain falls in February and the most in July.

Prague's position among hills means air can become trapped in the city, making it a bad place for winter smog. According to a report by the Organisation for Economic Cooperation and Development (OECD) released in 1999, the amount of nitrogen oxide in Prague is well above the European Union and OECD average. A rapid increase in traffic levels in Prague since the 1989 revolution has exacerbated a pollution problem – a legacy of wasteful economic planning during the Communist period. Air pollution overall in the Czech Republic, however, has decreased by 50 per cent since the 1980s, but there is still a long way to go.

The People

The city has a population of about 1.2 million. Nearly 70 per cent are Czech, around 20 per cent Slovak. German, Hungarian, Polish, and Ukrainian minorities make up the rest. Prague has also experienced an increase in the number of foreign residents since the 1989 revolution, but precise figures are hard to come by since the foreign population is quite transient.

Praguers tend to rise early and go to bed late. A normal workday starts at 8am or earlier (public transport can be jammed between 7am–8am) and ends at around 4pm. Like many other Europeans, Praguers' summer vacations can be for one month or sometimes longer.

Government

Prague was the capital city of Czechoslovakia until 31 December 1992, when the country split into the Czech and Slovak Republics. The Czech Republic came into being with a four-party coalition led by the dramatist Václav Havel as president and Václav Klaus as prime minister. Since 1998 the country has been ruled by a minority government of the left-of-centre **Czech Social Democratic Party**, with Miloš Zeman as prime minister, on the basis of an agreement with the opposition right-wing **Civic Democratic Party (ODS)**, headed by former prime minister Václav Klaus. Havel remains president.

Zeman has proven adept in pursuing his programme, which includes a minimum wage, higher pension payments, more social welfare and a stronger social network. Zeman has also attempted to rectify the corruption of the Czech Republic's privatisation programme.

Religion

There are more than 500 chapels and churches in the historic centre of Prague, many of which have undergone major restoration in recent years. Catholicism in the country is strong, but Bohemia's Protestant tradition, evoked by the figure of Jan Hus whose monument dominates the Old Town Square, remains important. Other, non-Christian religions have attracted a number of followers in the spiritual vacuum left by the departure of the old order.

Economy

Like all of Eastern Europe, the Czech Republic is coming to grips with capitalism slowly. What looked like phenomenal economic growth in the early 1990s had by March 1998 turned into recession, from which it has yet to recover. This has meant hardship for many, especially the elderly who are forced to live on fixed pensions, though the city has an air of prosperity. About 10 per cent of the republic's industry is based in and around the city. The inflation rate in February 1999 reached 8.9 per cent, but has been declining. The average salary for Czech citizens is around 11,500 Kč per month (approximately US$340).

Planning the Trip

When To Go

From a climatic point of view, the best times to visit Prague are the spring and autumn, when the weather is mild. In May, when the gardens and parks are in full bloom, the international classical music festival Prague Spring is held. The mild autumn with its stable weather offers the best prospects for extended strolls around town, and the brilliant foliage in Prague can be magnificent, especially near the Vltava river. Summer months mean that the main tourist areas, such as Golden Lane at Prague Castle and the streets off Old Town Square, can be unbearably crowded. The tourist season begins before Easter and extends through to September, with another huge increase over Christmas and New Year.

Visas & Passports

For citizens of the US, Canada and most European countries no visa is required for stays of less than 30 days. Nationals of other countries are advised to contact a Czech embassy or consulate for further information on visa requirements.

Customs

Czech customs controls are rigid. To avoid misunderstandings, check on anything you're unsure about beforehand. Upon entering the country, you'll be given a leaflet explaining the customs regulations.

Import

All items of personal use may be taken into the country duty free; any electronic, photographic and filming equipment should be listed, together with serial numbers, and presented to customs for confirmation. The list must be declared again upon departure. All items of personal use taken into the country must also be taken out.

You are allowed the following items for your own consumption (goods restricted to persons 18 years of age or older): 200 cigarettes, 50 cigars or 250 grams of tobacco, 2 litres of wine, 1 litre of spirits. Foreign visitors are permitted to take gifts into the country with a total value not exceeding 3,000 Kč. Hunting rifles require a special weapons' permit from the Czech authorities.

Export

Non-commercial items (i.e. not intended for resale) of unlimited value can be exported from the Czech Republic without an export permit. Valuable historic objects may not be exported. To export antiques and rare cultural objects, visitors need to get a special permit which can be very difficult to obtain.

Health and Insurance

While western medicines are becoming more and more available, it's always a good idea for visitors to bring along any medication that they require regularly. Before setting out, it is also advisable to take out international medical insurance. If you have to pay for treatment, make sure you get a receipt for money to be reimbursed, together with a certificate of the exchange rate at the time you pay.

No inoculations are required, and there are no diseases to be wary of. Tap water is drinkable, although most Praguers drink bottled water, and visitors may prefer to do the same.

Czech Embassies

Australia 38 Culgoa Circuit, O'Malley, Canberra ACT 2606 Tel: (612) 62 90 13 86.
Canada 541 Sussex Drive, Ottawa, Ontario, KIN 6Z6 Tel: (1613) 562 38 75.
Netherlands Paleesstraap 4, 2514 GA Den Haag Tel: (3170) 346 9712.
United Kingdom 26 Kensington Palace Gardens, London W8 4QY Tel: (44171) 243 1115.
United States 3900 Spring Freedom St. NW, Washington DC Tel: (1202) 274 9100.

Money Matters

Currency

The unit of currency is the crown (koruna or Kč), which is divided into 100 hellers (haléř). There are 20, 50, 100, 200, 500, 1,000, 2,000 and 5,000 crown notes and 1, 2, 5, 10 and 20 crown coins as well as 10, 20 and 50 heller coins. Czech crowns should not be taken in or out of the country.

It is no problem to change back your crowns into other major currencies at banks and exchange offices in Prague. Although in theory Czech currency is freely convertible in every country, in practice this is not always the case, thus visitors are strongly advised to make their conversions from crowns into other currencies while they are still inside the Czech Republic.

Cheques and Credit Cards

Travellers' cheques are only accepted by banks, but eurocheques can be exchanged in most places in the country and even on the border. Credit cards are accepted by many but not all shops, restaurants and hotels. Always check in advance to avoid embarrassment; signs of accepted cards are displayed on the door. When changing money and cheques, be careful: sometimes what looks like an exceptionally good rate may be accompanied by an inordinately high commission; this is especially true at Chequepoint Change kiosks.

Black Market

While it is possible to exchange money on the black market anywhere in Prague, it has no benefit since the rates on the street and in the banks are no longer different enough to warrant the hassle. The practice is officially forbidden and offenders will be prosecuted. Do not be tempted by offers, particularly as you might also be cheated: worthless Polish Złoty notes look conspicuously like crown notes.

Banks & Exchange Bureaux

In general most banks are open 8am–5pm Monday to Friday. Exchange bureaux are open from 8am until at least 7pm; some in the centre even remain open 24 hours a day. Most hotels will exchange money around the clock, but be aware that their rates are slightly higher than at a regular exchange bureau or bank.

To decide which outlet to use, enquire about the commission rate

Foreign Banks

Austria
Bank Austria Creditanstalt, Revoluční 15, Prague 1
Tel: 2489 2111.
Creditanstalt-Bankverein, Vienna, Široká 5, Prague 1
Tel: 2110 2111.
Belgium
Generale Bank Brusel, Josefská 6, Prague 1
Tel: 534759.
France
Société Générale, Pobřežní 3, Prague 8
Tel: 2483 2300.
Crédit Lyonnais, Ovocný trh 8, Prague 1
Tel: 2207 6111.
Germany
Landesbank AG, Berlin, Národní třída 10, Prague 1
Tel: 2491 3408.
Italy
Banca di Roma, Voršilská 10, Prague 1
Tel: 2491 0973.
United Kingdom
Barclays Bank, Na Příkopě 21, Prague 1
Tel: 2422 7994.
United States
Citibank NA, New York, Evropská 178, Prague 6
Tel: 2430 4111.

before you hand over your money as they can vary considerably. Czech banks along Na Příkopě and Wenceslas Square offer lower commissions than private exchange outlets.

Well-known international exchange outlets include:
Thomas Cook, Národní třída 28 and Karlova 3, both in Prague 1, Tel: 2110 5371 and 2110 5275. (Both open Mon–Sat, 9am–6pm; Sun 10am–6pm.)
American Express, Václavské nám. 56, Prague 1, Tel: 2280 0111, 2421 9992 (travel services: Mon–Fri, 9am–6pm, Sat–Sun, 9am–2pm; exchange services: daily including weekends 9am–7pm). There may be queues in summer.

Tipping

A ten per cent tip is a good idea unless the service is really atrocious. In pubs and cheaper establishments, it is customary to round up the bill by a few crowns.

Getting There

By Air

Prague's expanded, modernised Ruzyně airport lies about 20 km (13 miles) northwest of the city.

It is possible to book a flight to Prague from most European capitals and from New York, Montréal and Toronto. The flight from London takes about 2 hours.

The national airline is ČSA (České Aeroline), with several offices abroad, as follows:
Austria
Parkring 12, 1010 Vienna
Tel: 01-512 3805/512 98 86.
Canada
2020 rue Université, Montréal, Québec H3A 2A5
Tel: 514-844 42 00/844 63 76;
401 Bay Street, Suite 1510, Toronto, Ontario M5H 2Y4
Tel: 416-363 31 74/363 3175.
Germany
Baselerstrasse 46–48, 6000 Frankfurt/Main
Tel: 069-920 0350.
Switzerland
Sumatrastrasse 25, 8006 Zurich
Tel: 01-218 7010;

Airline Offices

Aeroflot Pařížská 5, Prague 1, tel: 232 33 33.
Airport: tel: 36 78 15.
Air Algerie Žitná 23, Prague 1, tel: 24 22 91 10.
Air France Václavské nám. 10, Prague 1, tel: 24 22 71 64.
Airport: tel: 2011 3737.
Alitalia Na Městku 9, Prague 1, tel: 2419 4150.
Airport: tel: 2011 3513.
Air Canada Revoluční 17, Prague 1, tel: 2489 2730.
British Airways Ovocný trh 8, Prague 1, tel: 2211 4444.
Airport: tel: 2011 3545.
British Midland Washingtonova 17, Prague 1, tel: 2423 9280.
Delta Národní třída 32, Prague 1, tel: 2494 6733.
Airport: tel: 2011 4384.
KLM, Na Příkopě 13, Prague 1, tel: 2421 6950.
Airport: tel: 2011 4139.
Lufthansa Pařížská 28, Prague 1, tel: 24 81 10 07.
Airport: tel: 2011 4456.
SAS, Rytífiská 13, Prague 1, tel: 24 21 47 49.
Swiss Air Pařížská 11, Prague 1, tel: 24 81 21 11.

334, Postfach 219, 1215;
Geneva Airport
Tel: 022-798 33 30.
United Kingdom
72 Margaret St., London W1N 7 HA
Tel: 0171-255 1898/255 1366.
United States
545 Fifth Avenue, New York, NY 10017
Tel: 212-765 6022/765 6545.

In Prague itself tickets, reservations and flight information are available from: V celnici 5, Prague 1, tel: 2010 4310/2011 3743. The office is open Monday to Friday 7am–6pm, Saturday 7am–3pm. The office is located near the metro station Náměstí Republiky (exit the metro either at Náměstí Republiky or Masarykovo nádraží).

Train

There are direct train connections to Prague from Germany and

Austria. From Stuttgart and Munich, the journey takes approximately 8 hours, from Frankfurt 10 hours, Berlin 6 hours, Hamburg 14 hours and Vienna 6 hours. Most trains from Southern Germany and Austria come in at the main Wilsonova Station (Hlavní nádraží). Trains from the west stop at Prague-Holešovice Station and many proceed on to Wilsonova. Other destinations in the country can be reached via Prague.

Travellers who do not have a ticket from the capital to their destination may purchase one at any of the railway stations in Prague. Domestic and international tickets can be purchased in Czech crowns, western currency or with credit cards at Čedok, Na Příkopě 18, Prague 1, or from the railway stations in crowns. Further information about rail travel can be obtained in English or German from the main station, tel: 2422 3887/4200.

Hlavní nádraží (Wilsonova Station) is clearly laid out on two floors. The lower end contains the counters for domestic tickets as well as the PIS (Prague Information Service) office, and shops. International tickets are purchased in the upper hall also has room booking agencies and exchange bureaux such as AVE, tel: 5731 2985, fax: 5731 5193, open daily 6am–11pm.

Two digital boards in the upper and lower halls show departures and arrivals. Toilets and left luggage are located beneath the main hall, together with the luggage lockers.

Bus & Coach
There is a wide choice of cheap and efficient coach tours from many European cities. Check with operators in your country for information.

Kingscourt Express operates buses between London and Prague (one-way and round trip). Departures in both directions are four times a week in low season, and six in high season (1 June–30 September).

Kingscourt Express
Havelská 8, Prague 1
Tel: 2423 4583/3334;
15 Balham High Road, London SW12
Tel: 0181 673 7500/6883
Both offices are open Mon–Fri, 9am–5pm; Sat, 9am–1pm.

CSAD, the state-run bus company, has offices in Hamburg and Münich as follows:
Deutsche Touring Buro
Adenaurallee 78, Hamburg,
Tel: 040-23 94 95;
Panorama Tours
Arnulfstrasse 8, Münich 2
Tel: 089-59 15 04;
Autobus Oberbayern
Lenbachplatz 1, Münich 2
Tel: 089-55 80 61.

The terminus is the Prague-Florenc bus station. Information regarding national connections can be obtained daily 6am–8pm from Florenc station on tel: 1034 (only Czech is spoken).

More gifted in languages are **Autoturist**, Náměstí Republiky 6, Prague 1, tel: 2423 7176 and **Bohemiatour**, Jungmannova 4, Prague 1, tel: 2421 6255.

Ferry
The Cologne-Düsseldorf passenger shipping line offers cruises from Berlin and Hamburg via Dresden to Prague. These last between 4 and 7 days. The Princess of Prussia does a one-day journey from Dresden.

In Prague itself river cruises are offered (see page 268).

Women Travellers

Women travelling in Prague and the Czech Republic should not expect to encounter any particular problems. If you are by yourself late at night, however, the usual rules of common sense apply. Keep in mind that pubs can be very male environments, and solo women will probably not feel comfortable.

Gay and Lesbian Travellers

The Czech Republic adheres to a live-and-let-live attitude toward gays and lesbians. Public displays of affection, however, might attract stares in Prague.

Travellers with Disabilities

Prague public transport was not designed with people with physical disabilities in mind. Most metro stations and all trams and buses involve climbing and descending what can be very steep steps. People in wheelchairs must be carried bodily on and off trams and buses, and pavement curbs do not often have ramps. But in general Praguers take a courteous view toward people with disabilities, and will make efforts to assist them.

Czech Tourist Offices

The largest Czech travel agency, Čedok, has these offices abroad:
Austria
Parkring 10, 1010 Vienna
Tel: 431/512 4372
Fax: 431/5124 37 285.
France
Čedok France S.a.r.l., Avenue de L'Opéra 32, 75002 Paris
Tel: 3301/4494 8750
Fax: 3301/4924 9946.
Germany
Čedok Reisen Berlin,
Leipzigerstrasse 60, 10117 Berlin
Tel: 4930/204 4644
Fax: 4930/204 4623.
Switzerland
Čedok Reisebüro AG,

Pelikanstrasse 38, 8001 Zürich
Tel: 411/221 3131
Fax: 411/221 3141.
United Kingdom
Čedok Travel Ltd, 53–54 Haymarket, London SW1Y 4RP
Tel: 0171/839 4414
Fax: 0171/839 0204.

Visitors from other countries should contact Čedok headquarters directly at:
Na Příkopě 18, 11135 Prague 1
Tel: 4202/2419 7111
Fax 4202/2421 6324
Website: www.cedok.cz
E-mail: overseas.incoming@cedok.cz

Practical Tips

Newspapers

Foreign news publications are readily available all over the centre of Prague, in English-language bookstores and in hotels. The PIS (Prague Information Service – see page 265) stocks event calendars, restaurant guides and general information brochures in a number of different languages.

The English-language weekly newspaper *The Prague Post* has articles on local news, culture and business as well a programme of events and extensive, up-to-date tips on restaurants, pubs, clubs and cafés. Both the weekly English-language *Prague Business Journal* and the monthly *Prague Tribune* focus on people and issues of interest to the business community.

Television and Radio

Radio is generally privatised, and television is heading in that direction thanks to competition from the private TV station NOVA, which has garnered the lion's share of the viewing audience with Czech-dubbed versions of (mainly) American fare.

On the radio, the **BBC World Service** can be picked up on 101.1 FM intermittently throughout the day and evening (with frequent BBC programmes in Czech and Slovak), as can local news in English on **Radio Prague**, on the same frequency.

The Czech state TV channel CT2 often shows high-quality foreign films by major directors, with Czech sub-titles. TV news programmes in English change frequently, but it's possible to see Euronews on week-days at noon and 7:15pm on CT2.

Numerous satellite channels are also available including CNN, HBO and Skynews.

Postal Services

The main Post Office, Hlavní pošta, Jindřišská 14, Prague 1, is open 24 hours a day. It is situated in a street off Wenceslas Square, in the southwest corner. The other post offices (marked with distinctive orange signs saying pošta) are open Mon–Fri 8am–6pm, and Sat 8am–noon; smaller branches are generally only open Mon–Fri 8am–5pm at the latest.

Postal Charges

Stamps can be bought in post offices or, if you're in luck, at newspaper kiosks. Enquire about current postal rates for letters and postcards once you're in the country, as they go up frequently. You'll find orange letter boxes just about everywhere you look.

Parcel Delivery Service

DHL, UPS and Federal Express (Fedex), the international parcel delivery services, offer a fast and reliable, but also expensive, means of sending important documents and parcels abroad. Employees speak English, and can arrange for courier pick-ups. DHL has a branch in the centre at Klimentská 46

DHL
Běžecká 1, Prague 6
Tel: 1030
UPS
Výtvarná 1023/4, Prague 6
Tel: 3300 3111
Federal Express
Olbrachtova 1, Prague 4
Tel: 4400 2200

Telecommunications

There are two different kinds of telephones in operation in the city (provided they are not out of order). The first kind only accepts 2-, 5- and 10-crown coins and is therefore only practical for making local calls. The phones are such that your coins will not be returned should the line be engaged or should no one answer the phone.

Most telephones, though, accept only phonecards which are available in unit sizes with a wide price range; these phones may have how-to-use information in English, but if not, simply insert the card where indicated, listen for a dial tone, and dial your number. Phonecards can be purchased in post offices or from newsagents.

If you want to make a long-distance call of more than minimal length your best bet is to dial from either a post office or hotel, but bear in mind that hotels will charge a 20–30 per cent commission for this service. The 24-hour phone centre at Prague's main post office (Jindřišská 14, Prague 1) is located around the corner in Politických vězňů. You must leave a deposit with one of the invariably grumpy attendants before you may dial. A series of phone books to Czech and foreign cities, none too drastically out of date, is also available here.
Directory enquiries (Prague and the Czech Republic) Tel: 120
International enquiries Tel: 0139 and 0149

Telegram, Fax & Computer Services

In most hotels you can both send and receive a fax or telegram. Faxes may also be sent from the main post office. In addition to this, almost all first-class hotels provide office services which include access to various computers and printers. Telegrams can be sent from every post office, or by phone: call 0127.

Photocopying is available at numerous establishments in Prague (look for signs marked Kopírování), including at **Copy General**, Senovážné nám. 26, Prague 1, tel: 24 23 00 20 (7am–10pm), and Milady Horákové 4, Prague 7, tel: 3337 0013 (7am–10pm).

Internet and e-mail

Internet cafés are popping up all over Prague, especially in the centre. Most charge by the hour for computer time; the fees are reasonable, and at least some degree of English is spoken by the personnel. Some good internet cafés to try include:

Terminal Bar
Soukenická 6, Prague 1
Tel: 2187 1711
Web site: www.terminal.cz
Open daily 11am–1am

Internet Lounge
Municipal House,
Náměstí Republiky 5, Prague 1
E-mail: kavarna@ctg.cz
Open daily 8am–11pm

Cybeteria
Štěpánská 18, Prague 1
Tel: 2223 0707/0703
Fax 2223 2227
E-mail: info@cybeteria.cz
Web site: www.cybeteria.cz
Open Mon–Fri 10am–8pm, Sat–Sun noon–6pm

Cafe.com
Na Poříčí 36, Prague 1
Tel: 0603/235 815
Web site: www.cafe-com.com
Open daily 11am–midnight

Internet Café Spika
Dlážděná 4, Prague 1
Tel: 2421 1521

Consulates/Embassies

Australia
Na Ořechovce 38, Prague 6
Tel: 2431 0743.

Austria
Victora Huga 10, Prague 5
Tel: 5732 1282.

Belgium
Valdštejnská 6, Prague 1
Tel: 5731 4434.

Canada
Mickiewiczova 6, Prague 6
Tel: 2431 1108.

France
Velkopřevorské nám. 2, Prague 1
Tel: 5732 0352.

Italy
Nerudova 20, Prague 1
Tel: 5732 0011.

Spain
Pevnostní 9, Prague 6
Tel: 24 31 14 41.

United Kingdom
Thunovská 14, Prague 1
Tel: 5732 0355, 5732 0496.

United States
Tržiště 15, Prague 1
Tel: 5732 0663.

Web site: www.netcafe.spika.cz
Open daily 10am–10pm.

Tourist Offices

The **Prague Information Service** (PIS) has an office at the Old Town Hall in Old Town Square, Prague 1. Here you can obtain information about Prague, including city maps and the free monthly booklet *Prague Cultural Events*, containing helpful information and addresses. For those who can read Czech, there are the more detailed *Přehled kulturních pořadů v Praze*, and *Kultura v Praze* (available in English as *Culture in Prague*), which list events according to venue; both are sold at news kiosks.

Travel Agencies

After a huge boom in the early 1990s, this business has levelled off dramatically since the economic recession began in 1998. However some of the main agencies have stayed the course, as follows:

Autoturist
Náměstí Republiky 6, Prague 1
Tel: 2423 7176.

AVE
Wilsonova station (Hlavní nádraží)
Tel: 5731 2985.

Balnea
Národní 28, Prague 1
Tel: 2110 5314.

Bohemiatour
Jungmannova 4, Prague 1
Tel: 2421 6255.

Čedok
Na Příkopě 18, Prague 1
Tel: 24 19 7111.

CKM
Jindřišská 28, Prague 1
Tel: 268623.
For young travellers

Fischer
Národní třída 10, Prague 1
Tel: 2495 2424.

GTS
Ve Smečkách 27, Prague 1 (off Wenceslas Square)
Tel: 9622 4300. (Discounts for student card holders.)

Prague Tourist Centre
Rytířská 12, Prague 1
Tel: 24 21 22 09.

Public Holidays

The dates of national holidays at present are as follows:
● **1 January:** New Year's Day
● **Easter Monday** – variable according to the Roman calendar
● **1 May:** Labour Day
● **8 May:** Day of Liberation from Fascism.
● **5 July:** Feast Day of SS Cyril and Methodius
● **6 July:** Anniversary of the death of Jan Hus
● **28 October:** Day of the origin of the independent Czechoslovakia
● **25–26 December:** Christmas
Various Christian holidays, for example the Feast of Corpus Christi and the Assumption of the Virgin Mary, are celebrated in different regions but are not considered national holidays.

Regius Tour
Vodičkova 41 (on the mezzanine inside the passage), Prague 1
Tel: 2494 8611. (Specialises in trips to Russia, Ukraine and Belarus.)

Sport-Turist
Národní 33, Prague 1
Tel: 2491 3102.

Wolff Travel
Václavské náměstí 57, Prague 1
Tel: 2166 2501.

Translation Services

The usual languages of business are English and German. The following agencies provide professional interpreting and translation services in all aspects of business and law for both individuals and conferences:

Artlingua Myslíkova 6, Prague 2
Tel: 29 37 41, 294198.

Kahlen Service Vlkova 24, Prague 3
Tel: 6719 5301.

Interlingua Servis Spálená 17, Prague 1
Tel: 2490 9250.

Media Market Truhlářská 16, Prague 1
Tel: 231 7951.

Presto Dlouhá 37, Prague 1
Tel: 231 1851, 231 3105.

Trint Malá Štupartská 5, Prague 1
Tel: 2482 7200.

Religious Services

The following churches have
services in English. Telephone for
details of times:
Anglican: St. Clement's Church,
Klimentská 18, Prague 1
Tel: 2162 2111.
Prague Christian Fellowship: Ječná
19, Prague 2
Tel: 5753 0020.
Evangelical Lutheran: St. Michael's
Church, V Jirchářích, Prague 1
Tel: 2097 0397.
Reform Jewish: Jewish Community
Centre, Maiselova 18, Prague 1
Tel: 2481 4162.
Roman Catholic: St. Thomas'
Church, Josefská 8, Prague 1
Tel: 530218.

Business Hours

Most grocery shops are open
weekdays 7am–6pm, with speciality
stores opening from 10am–6pm,
although those in the centre
catering to the tourist trade often
remain open late year-round.
Smaller shops may close their
doors for a couple of hours during
lunchtime. On Saturdays most
shops outside the centre close at
noon or 1pm, but shops in the
centre, especially the large department stores, may retain weekday
hours on Saturday and Sunday as
well. The main commercial streets
of Prague with dependably long

hours year round are Wenceslas
Square and Na Příkopě.

Medical Treatment

Western visitors now have a
number of options if they require
medical treatment. The **American
Medical Centre** at Janovského 48,
Prague 7, tel: 807756, 807757,
807758 has a 24-hour service, with
house calls available. All doctors
speak excellent English. There is
also a dentist, physical therapist
and psychotherapist on staff. Be
sure you have western health
insurance (BUPA and PPP are both
accepted) or the fees – which
otherwise must be paid in cash –
are very high.

The other hospital for foreigners
is **Na Homolce Hospital** (Nemocnice
Na Homolce), Roentgenova 2,
Prague 5, foreigners' department
tel: 52 92 2146. Staff physicians
speak reasonable English as well
as other foreign languages. It can
be reached by the metro station
Anděl on the yellow line B, then bus
167 to the last stop. Fees should
be paid in cash; you must then
arrange your own reimbursement.

Other hospitals include:
First Medical Clinic of Prague,
Vyšehradská 35, Prague 2
Tel: 292286.
24-hour emergency
Tel: 0601 225050.
Physicians speak English. Western
health insurance accepted.
**Charles University Medical School
and Hospital** (Fakultní nemocnice

Emergency Numbers

**General emergency and
ambulance:** tel: 155.
Fire Brigade: tel: 150.
Police: tel: 158.
Lost Property: tel: 2422 6133.
Lost or stolen credit cards:
• **American Express:** tel: 2421
9978.
• **Mastercard:** tel: 2442 3135.
• **Visa, Diner's Club:** tel: 2412
5353.

kliniky), Karlovo nám. 32, Prague 2
Tel: 2490 4347. English spoken.
For dental emergencies try the
clinics above, or call the dental
emergency hotline: tel: 1097.

Opticians
There are many shops now in the
centre of Prague offering optical
services, and western contact lens
solutions are readily available.
Some of the best are:
Eiffel Optic
Celetná 38, Prague 1
Tel: 2161 3301.
Attractive selection of glasses and
express service for glasses and
contact lenses. English spoken.
Open Monday to Friday.
Fokus Optik
Mostecká 3, Prague 1
Tel: 5731 3969. English spoken.
Open Monday–Saturday.
Grand Optical
Myslbek mall, Na Příkopě 19,
Prague 1
Tel: 2423 8371/4811.
All services, huge selection. Open
daily.

Chemists
Chemists (lekárna) are open during
normal business hours. In case of
an emergency after hours, you'll
find the address of the nearest
chemists on emergency duty posted
in the window. The following
chemists have extended hours:
Prague 1
Palackého 5 (near Wenceslas
Square)
Tel: 2494 6982.
Prague 3
Konĕvova 210

Weights & Measures

The Czech Republic uses the
metric system.

Temperatures
To convert Centigrade into
Fahrenheit, multiply by 1.8 and
then add 32; for Fahrenheit to
Centigrade, subtract 32 and
multiply by 0.55.

Metric to Imperial
1 cm	= 0.39 inch
1 metre	= 3.28 ft

1 km	= 0.62 miles
1 gram	= 0.035 oz
1 kg	= 2.21lbs
1 litre	= 0.22 Imp. gallons
1 litre	= 0.26 US gallons

Imperial to Metric
1 inch	= 2.54 cm
1 ft	= 0.30 metres
1 mile	= 1.61 km
1 oz	= 28.35 grams
1 lb	= 0.45 kg
1 US gallon	= 3.79 litres

Tel: 644 18 85.
Prague 4
Antala Staška 80
Tel: 42 78 32, 6100 6432;
A. Drabíkové 534
Tel: 791 2743. (24 hours.)
Prague 5
Štefánikova 6
Tel: 53 70 39. (24 hours.)
Prague 6
Evropská 55
Tel: 320212.
Prague 8
Heydukova 10
Tel: 6631 0899. (24 hours.)
Prague 9
Gen. Janouška 902
Tel: 8191 2525.
Prague 10
V Olšinách 41
Tel: 781 10 68.

Security and Crime

The violent crime rate in Prague is still lower than that of many western European cities. Since 1990 the incidence of offences such as robbery and fraud have increased dramatically; cases of visitors having their handbags or wallets snatched are increasingly common, as are car theft and robbery from cars. It's a good idea to deposit valuables in the hotel safe and, if possible, always park at a supervised car park. Stay alert to your surroundings, especially in crowds.

Particular hot spots for pickpocketing and other crimes against visitors include Old Town Square, Charles Bridge, any crowded areas at Prague Castle such as Golden Lane and St. Vitus' Cathedral, and Wenceslas Square. Jostling on metros and trams can be the work of pickpockets, particularly as you get on and off; trams to be especially careful on are Nos. 9 and 22, which cater to tourist routes.

In case of emergency either consult your hotel reception or contact the police directly by dialling 158. If you should have the misfortune to either lose your personal documents or have them stolen, get in touch immediately with your embassy representative.

Getting Around

Information Services

The **Prague Information Service** (PIS) is one of the best agencies to provide tourists with information relavant to travellers. Another agency to try is the former state-run (now privatised and professional) Čedok, which has information desks and an exchange bureau, and can book international tickets as well as tours and stays in the spa towns of Bohemia. Čedok also arranges accommodation in a network of castles and chateaux throughout the Czech Republic.

Prague Information Service (PIS)
Na Příkopě 20
Tel: 264020;
Old Town Hall, Staroměstské nám.
Tel: 2448 2018.
Čedok
Na Příkopě 18
Tel: 2419 7111.

To/From the Airport

There is a public bus service to the metro Dejvická (bus 119), as well as taxis and hire cars. A private minibus shuttle service, Čedaz, operates between the airport and Republic Square (Náměstí Republiky) with a stop at Dejvická metro station, every day between 6am and 9:30pm, and charges a nominal fee. This shuttle runs approximately every half hour, and a journey between the airport and Republic Square terminus or vice-versa takes from 1/2 hour to 45 minutes depending on traffic.

Taxis from the airport are controlled by a monopoly, **Bellinda**, which was granted exclusive rights by the city to carry passengers out of the airport, after years of intense and

dangerous competition among drivers and complaints by passengers about overcharging. (All other taxi services may bring passengers to the airport, however.) Bellinda taxis do not have meters; go to the Bellinda booth at the airport arrivals area, where the clerk will write the fee for your destination on a piece of paper, which you then show to the driver. Taxis are lined up outside the arrivals exit. Rates are still high, however: a ride to the centre will cost between 400 and 500 Kč (US$12–15), whereas a ride from the city to the airport by any other taxi carrier, with a meter, would be at least a third lower.

Tourist Passes

There is a special tourist pass which allows an unlimited number of journeys on all public transport within a set period from the time of issue, valid for 1, 3, 7 or 15 days. Visitors staying in Prague for a length of time might consider buying a one-month pass. Transport on the entire network is completely free for children under 6 and adults over 70. Children under 16 pay half fare. For ticket sales and further information contact the information office of the **Public Transport Executive**, Můstek metro station exit hall on Jungmannovo nám. 1, tel: 2264 6350 (7am–9pm daily).

City Transport

The various means of public transport in Prague are cheap and well synchronised. The network includes trams and buses, the metro and the funicular up the Petřín Hill.

Tickets can be purchased in shops, at the kiosks of the Prague Public Transport Executive, and at hotel receptions, as well as from the automatic ticket machines at some tram stops and in all metro stations. Travellers should stock up on tickets for the weekend if they don't have the necessary change to use the machines, as not all metro stations have attendants on duty at weekends. On all Prague public transport, a ticket allows you to travel for 60 minutes between 5am–8pm (for 90 minutes after 8pm) and to change as often as you like within that time among the various modes of transport.

Remember that bus and tram drivers do not sell tickets. Transport operates on a system of honour; each traveller must punch his or her ticket into a machine on the upper platform at the metro stations, or on the tram or bus (passengers may enter any door of trams and buses). Plain-clothes controllers carrying small identity badges make periodic checks; if you can't show that your ticket has been punched recently you could be faced with a large fine to be paid on the spot.

The Metro

The modern underground metro system links the city centre with the suburbs, and provides for convenient travel inside the city. It is a remarkably clean and fast means of public transport. The three lines have been developed with an eye towards expediency, and by transferring it is possible to reach just about all the important tourist attractions located within the city.

The lines intersect at three main stations. From Můstek station at the bottom of Wenceslas Square you can take the green line A over to the Lesser Quarter and Hradčany. The yellow line B runs south to Charles Square and to the Smíchovské nádraží station. The Florenc bus station and the northeast can be reached by travelling in the opposite direction. Line A intersects with the red line C at the Muzeum station at the upper end of Wenceslas Square. The latter runs north to the main station, then to the Florenc bus station where it intersects with line B before continuing to the terminus Nádraží Holešovice, the station for many of the trains on the Berlin-Budapest route. To the south it leads to Vyšehrad. Because of the

frequency of the trains (every 5–12 minutes), you don't need to plan for more than about 30 minutes even for journeys into the suburbs. The Metro operates from 5am–midnight.

Metro signs outside the stations are small and square and decidedly inconspicuous, with a white M on a green, yellow or red background, depending on which line the station is on. But inside, the stations, often beautifully designed, are clean and clearly laid out. Network plans are prominently located at all entrances and above the platforms; the station you are at is highlighted; the stations you can change at are marked with the colour of the intersecting line.

Funicular Railway

The funicular railway up Petřín Hill (Újezd, Prague 5) runs daily from 5am to midnight. It can be reached by taking trams 9, 12, 22 or 23 to the stop Újezd. Public transport system tickets are valid on the funicular.

Trams and Buses

Among the many tram and bus routes within Prague, line 22 is probably the most interesting for visitors. It runs from Náměstí Míru through Charles Square and along the Národní třída (National Avenue). It crosses the Vltava and then runs along Karmelitská in the Lesser Quarter to Lesser Quarter Square. From there it winds its way up the Castle Hill and on along the Keplerova to the starting point for Strahov and Petřín Hill. On line 22 it is possible to have an almost complete tour of the city for the price of a single ride. Prague has a comprehensive bus network: buses (*autobus*) run all day, particularly frequently in the suburbs, to connect with the metro.

Night trams on an abbreviated route arrive at intervals of 30 minutes to one hour, as do night buses. The numbers and schedules of night trams are visible at most tram stops.

Taxis

After midnight taxis constitute practically the sole form of transport if you want to get anywhere in a hurry and don't want to bother with night trams or night buses. You'll find a number of taxi stops in the city centre as well as in front of larger hotels.

Prague taxi drivers remain the shame of the city, however. Some taxis have a meter which, if it's running at all, is often rigged. During the day, when you're not desperately marooned on some street corner, you can attempt to bargain. At night this is difficult as prices are dictated by supply and demand and the driver knows the passenger is in the weakest position. Before setting foot in the cab, it pays to do a little bargaining until a mutually acceptable fixed price is reached. But unless your Czech skills are very convincing, it's better to stick to public transport.

Better still is to call for a radio cab. Two reputable firms with English-speaking dispatchers and reasonable rates are **AAA**, tel: 1080, and **Profi Taxi**, tel: 1035.

Taxi stands in the centre of Prague include:
Václavské náměstí (Wenceslas Square) almost anywhere in the square;
Národní třída (outside Tesco);
Municipal House (Obecní dům);
Wilsonova Station (follow the signs);
Old Town Square (near the corner of Pařížská street);
Malostranské nám;
Hradčany;
Malostranská metro station;
Karlovo nám. (Charles Square).
It is also possible to flag down a passing taxi.

Driving

Although there are not as many private cars yet as there are in western Europe, drivers on their way to Prague still have to reckon with delays. The main roads are generally in good condition comparable to other European countries, but the many lorries using them can make progress very slow, especially by day.

Even for drivers who know Prague, the city can be a traffic nightmare. Large sections of the Old Town and the Lesser Quarter have been completely closed to traffic. If you do manage to get through the maze of one-way streets and cul-de-sacs to find yourself in the centre, at Wenceslas Square or the Powder Tower, you'll probably be turned away by the police (or may even get a ticket) unless you can prove you are resident at one of the hotels nearby. It is therefore highly advisable to leave your car at one of the car parks and explore the city either on foot or by public transport.

Car Hire

Those wishing to hire cars with **Avis** or **Hertz** can book from home as this generally works out a lot cheaper. To rent a car in the Czech Republic you have to be at least 21 years of age and in possession of a valid drivers' licence that has been in effect for at least a year. Credit cards are accepted as payment. Rates change often and it's wise to shop around.

Pragocar, with its fleet of Škodas, offers reasonable terms. The ubiquitous Škodas (manufactured by Volkswagen) have two major advantages: Czech mechanics can repair them with ease, and they are also not the most desirable booty for car thieves. It may also be possible to pick up a car in one town and deposit it in another.

Alamo
Revoluční 25
Prague 1
Tel: 231 6947
Fax: 231 7100;
Ruzyně airport,
Tel: 2011 3676.
Avis
Klimentská 46
Tel: 2185 1225
Fax: 2185 1229;
Ruzyně airport
Tel: 316 6739.
Budget
Hotel Intercontinental

Tel: 302 5713
Fax 302 5711;
Ruzyně airport
Tel: 2011 3253
Tel/fax: 316 5214.
Europcar
Pařížská 28
Prague 1
Tel: 24 81 1290
Fax: 2481 0039;
Ruzyně airport
Tel: 3167 7849
Fax: 316 7920.
Hertz
Karlovo nám. 28; and
Ruzyně airport
Tel: for both: 290122
Fax: 297836.
Pragocar
Vršovická 5
Prague 10
Tel: 7174 5926
Fax: 7174 6056.

Rules of the Road

All drivers must be in possession of a valid driver's licence, car registration documents and a nationality sticker at all times, as well as an international green insurance card.

Drivers arriving in the Czech Republic by car must buy a road permit (800 Kč) for their vehicle at the border crossing, valid for the given calendar year, which is then displayed on their windscreen. If you are not using your own vehicle, you will have to provide written consent for use of the car from the vehicle's owner. Caravans, trailers and boats require no special customs documents. Be prepared for queues at crossings year round.

By and large, the international traffic regulations apply here. The maximum speed limit within city boundaries is 50 kph (35 mph); on country roads 90 kph (55 mph); and on motorways 130 kph (65 mph). (The 800 Kč mentioned allows you to drive on those motorways for which a permit is required). Exceeding the speed limit can result in a hefty fine.

Driving after drinking even small amounts of alcohol is absolutely prohibited in the Czech Republic.

Children under 12 years of age are not allowed to sit in the front

seat, and the wearing of seat belts is compulsory at all times.

Petrol Stations

All necessary kinds of petrol and fuel are commonly available at filling stations, which have been much improved in recent years. But if you're travelling by night make sure you have enough petrol, as it may be difficult to find a station open except on the major highways.

Twenty-four hour petrol stations can be found at: Prague 2: Svatoplukova; Prague 3: Olšanská, Kališnická; Prague 4, Újezd u Pruhonic; Prague 5: Motol, Plzeňská; Prague 7: Argentinská; Prague 8: Prosek, Ceskobrodská; Prague 9: Liberecká. Prague 10: Limuzská, Průmyslová.

Prague Car Parks

Car parks in the centre of Prague can be found at the following locations:
Platnéřská, Rytířská, Haštalská, Pařížská (outside the Hotel Intercontinental), Štepánská, Národní třída, Náměstí Jana Palacha (in front of the Rudolfinum), Senovážné náměstí, Opletalova (outside the main station), Politických vězňů, Malá Štepánská, Těšnov (outside Hotel Opera), Petrské náměstí (outside Petrská věž tower), Sázavská, Ibsenova, Škrétova, Tylovo náměstí (outside Hotel Beránek).

Parking

It is policy to keep the city centre as free of traffic as possible. To this end the centre has been divided into three zones: Zone A (Old Town), Zone B (New Town to the east of Wenceslas Square) and Zone C (to the west of Wenceslas Square). Within these zones parking spaces cost a nominal fee. Only guests staying in Wenceslas Square hotels have access to the square and the surrounding streets. Guests obtain a permit at reception, which must be visibly displayed on the dashboard and which enables them to park in special slots reserved for the hotels or in the hotel garages.

Police and traffic wardens are extremely vigilant and clamped cars are a common sight. Vehicles that have been towed away are kept in Hostivař, Cernokostelecká, 15 km (9 miles) from the centre.

Breakdown

Although there is an organised breakdown service including over 31 emergency aid vehicles in the country, it can be difficult to obtain the necessary spare parts for foreign vehicles. Therefore, it's a good idea to purchase international travel cover from your own auto-mobile association before starting your journey.

In case of breakdown ring the police, tel: 158 or the tow-away service **Yellow Angels** on tel: 123.

There are many garages which will repair foreign and domestic vehicles; one notable garage in the centre is:

Papoušek Autoservice
Opletalova 45
Tel: 2423 5485/7587

A non-stop service is **AAA Emergency Repair**: tel: 1044.

Members of the AA or other automobile associations can contact **Autoturist**: Náměstí Republiky 6, Prague 1, tel: 2423 7176.

Sightseeing Tours

Čedok agencies and PIS (see page 265) offer foreign language-speaking tour guides to travel

groups as well as to independent travellers, for both day excursions or trips lasting several days. They can also equip you with an inter-preter or translator upon request. It is not unusual in Prague to "rent" a tour guide to accompany you on foot through the city. The hourly rate for this service varies.

Three-hour city tours called "Historic Prague" and "Jewish Prague" are conducted by numer-ous establishments which have kiosks dotting Wenceslas Square, Na Příkopě and Old Town Square.

English-language tours of Prague Castle (Hradčany) or headphone sets are organised by:

Informační středisko pražského hradu (the information centre at Prague Castle), Third courtyard, Prague 1 (on the northern side of St Vitus' Cathedral). Tel: 2437 3368.

Vltava Cruises

The frequency of cruises on the River Vltava depends on the weather, but there are plenty to choose from during the summer. Some ticket prices include a meal on board. An evening cruise under the Charles Bridge is a particularly unforgettable experience.

Information on cruises can be obtained from the quayside on the Rašín embankment at the Palacký Bridge (Palackého most) or on the Na Františku embankment at the Čech Bridge (near the Hotel Inter-continental).

The following tour operators can also be contacted for cruise times:
Martin Tour
Štěpánská 61
Prague 1
Tel: 2421 2473
Also at kiosks in the city centre);
Orbis Link
Václavské nám. 48
Prague 1
Tel: 9622 4220
Thomas Cook
Národní 28
Prague 1
Tel: 2110 5371

Where to Stay

Finding a Hotel

Finding a hotel room in Prague is getting easier all the time, but if you'd like something cheap it's necessary to book far in advance. Due to the fact that hotel manage-ments often have fixed contracts with foreign tour agencies, rooms can be reserved for travel groups quite far in advance of the intended trip. Therefore, individual travellers will usually be told that the hotel is fully booked. A possible alternative to this often frustrating search is to reserve a room through a travel agency or stay in one of the many affordable, pleasant pensions that have now emerged to accommodate the needs of more free-spirited travellers (see page 270).

The more expensive hotels are a category unto themselves; facilities, decor and service conform to inter-national standards. The bill can usually be paid in Czech crowns, western currencies or major credit cards such as Eurocard/Master-card, American Express or Visa.

Hotel Listings

The following hotels are listed in alphabetical order within their price range.

Luxury
Grand Hotel Bohemia
Královdvorská 4
Prague 1
Tel: 2480 4111
Fax: 232 9545
Truly grand, this Art Nouveau gem under Austrian management rates as one of the most beautiful (as well as most expensive) luxury hotels in Prague, with sumptuous, spacious rooms decorated in soft

tones. Around the corner from the Powder Tower and less than five minutes' walk from Old Town Square, the hotel is also a practical choice for business travellers, since each room comes with an answering machine, fax and trouser press.

Hotel Savoy
Keplerova 6
Prague 1
Tel: 2430 2430
Fax: 2430 2128
The luxury choice near Prague Castle, lovingly renovated and painted a cheerful yellow. The good-sized rooms all come with substantial bathrooms. The Savoy is small by luxury hotel standards (55 rooms), which makes its service all the more personal.

Inter-Continental
Náměstí Curieových 5
Prague 1
Tel: 2488 1111
Fax: 2488 1118
Affording gorgeous views of Prague Castle (ask for a front-facing room), the Inter-Continental, with 365 rooms, offers all important hotel amenities. Its fitness centre and pool also win high marks. The hotel is only ten minutes' walk from Old Town Square, down elegant Pařížská, and only steps away from the Jewish Quarter.

Jalta
Václavské náměstí 45
Prague 1
Tel: 2422 9133
The Jalta is a large, boxy yet utterly professional hotel located near the bottom of Wenceslas Square. All rooms have the amenities expected for the price; there is also a Japanese restaurant and casino on site.

Palace
Panská 12
Prague 1
Tel: 2409 3120
Fax: 2422 1240
Dating from 1906, this classy Art Nouveau-style hotel one block from Wenceslas Square successfully uses muted shades of green in its spacious rooms. Bathrooms are luxurious, each even equipped with a telephone. Business travellers will also find a PC port for their computer. There is a non-smoking floor.

Two rooms (out of 114) have barrier-free facilities for travellers with physical disabilities.

Expensive
Best Western Meteor Plaza
Hybernská 6
Prague 1
Tel: 2419 2111
Fax: 2421 3005
A modernised, efficient hotel near Obecní dům; ask for a room that faces the courtyard, where it is quieter. The on-site wine cellar dates from the 14th century.

Diplomat
Evropská 15
Prague 6
Tel: 2439 4111
Fax: 2439 4215
An excellent choice for business travellers and those on the go, since this sizable hotel (369 rooms) is situated midway between the airport and the city centre. Facilities are clean and modern, but slightly lacking in local charm. There is a no-smoking floor.

Corinthian Towers Hotel
Kongresová 1
Prague 4
Tel: 6119 1111
Fax: 6119 1238
Comfortable facilities in a high-rise hotel; views from any side will not disappoint, but do request a room which faces the direction of Prague Castle. Rooms are not huge but have every facility: e-mail links, satellite channels on the TV, minibars, thick towels. There is a popular fitness centre on the upper floors, as well as a small but nice bowling alley. Five rooms (out of 531) are specially equipped for the physically disabled. The hotel is two metro stops from Wenceslas Square, and about 10 minutes' walk from Vyšehrad and Prague's Cubist houses.

Dům U Cerveného lva
Nerudova 41
Prague 1
Tel: 537239
Fax: 538193
The Red Lion is a lovely, small hotel on romantic though busy Nerudova, with rooms featuring dramatic beamed ceilings and parquet floors.

There are only 11 rooms, so book ahead. Prague Castle is a five-minute walk uphill.

Hotel Hoffmeister
Pod Bruskou 7
Prague 1
Tel: 5731 0942
Fax: 5732 0906
Comfortable, stylish Old-European style hotel in Malá Strana, near the Vltava. Film director Miloš Forman stays here when in Prague.

Kampa
Všehrdova 16
Prague 1
Tel: 5732 0508/0404
Fax: 5732 0262
A romantic hotel secreted on a quiet lane in Malá Strana, not far from its namesake Kampa Park, but also within easy reach, via several tram lines, of Prague Castle and Wenceslas Square. The 85 rooms, simply furnished, have the usual hotel amenities.

Price Guide

The following price categories are for the cost of a double room, including breakfast, in high season:
Luxury: more than US$200.
Expensive: US$100–200.
Moderate: US$60–100.
Budget: Less than US$60.

Maximilian
Haštalská 14
Prague 1
Tel: 2180 6111
Fax: 2180 6110
A luxurious choice on a serene square in the Old Town, not far from the heavenly shopping on Pařížská. Each room has a fax machine; pleasant service.

Prague Hilton Atrium
Pobřežní 1
Prague 8
Tel: 2484 1111
Fax: 2484 2036
The Atrium has all the facilities and standards one would expect from a Hilton hotel: its atrium foyer is stupendous, although the 788 rooms could be a bit larger. It is the largest hotel in the Czech Republic.

Price Guide

The following price categories are for the cost of a double room, including breakfast, in high season:
Luxury: more than US$200.
Expensive: US$100–200.
Moderate: US$60–100.
Budget: Less than US$60.

The location is a bit out of the centre, but only about 15 minutes' walk from Old Town Square. Fitness facilities (indoor tennis and squash courts, pool, work-out equipment) are among the best in Prague.
Renaissance Prague Hotel
V Celnici 7
Prague 1
Tel/fax: 2182 2100
A large, modern, well-equipped hotel near Obecní dům. All rooms are air-conditioned and have sealed windows, which is good because there is construction in constant progress in the neighbourhood.

Moderate

AXA
Na Poříčí 40
Prague 1
Tel: 2481 2580
Fax: 232 2172
A simple, well-kept hotel (with just over 100 rooms) near the centre, the Axa appeals to families and sports buffs due to its 50m (160 ft) swimming pool, sauna, and fitness centre. The rooms, refurbished in the late 1990s, are pleasant and functional; the foyer is a bit over-whelming, due to a plethora of chrome and mirror effects.
Bílá Labuť
Biskupská 9
Prague 1
Tel: 2481 1382
The White Swan is on a quiet side street within easy walking distance of the Old Town. The 54 rooms feature minibars and satellite TV in addition to clean, simple furnishings. Children up to age 12 stay for free in their parents' room.
City Hotel Moráň
Na Moráni 15
Prague 2

Tel: 2491 5208
Fax: 297533
Only two blocks from leafy Charles Square, the City Hotel is a bit off the beaten track, but upper-storey rooms offer fine views of Prague Castle. The 57 rooms are clean and pleasant, but without much character. This is a good choice for travellers who like being close to the centre (Wenceslas Square is less than 10 minutes away via tram or metro) without having to be in the thick of things.
Hotel U staré paní
Michalská 9
Prague 1
Tel: 267267, 264920
Fax: 267 9841, 267267
A small, comfortable hotel on a picturesque street in the Old Town, near Old Town Square. All 18 rooms are decorated with Scandinavian-style furnishings. There is also a popular (and soundproofed) jazz club in the basement.
Opera
Těšnov 13
Prague 1
Tel: 231 5609
Fax: 231 1477
This pink-and-white *fin-de-siècle* hotel has a certain old world appeal, partly thanks to its relative proximity to Old Town. The rooms are plain but perfectly functional; all were renovated in the late 1990s.

Budget

Apollo
Kubišova 23
Prague 8
Tel: 688 0628
Fax: 688 4570
Boxy hotel without much character. Still, the prices are decent, the service is fine, and public transport is ample, although the journey takes 25 minutes to the centre via bus.
Astra
Mukuřovská 1740/18
Prague 10
Tel: 781 3595
Fax: 781 0765
Convenient to the metro station Strašnická, which is reasonably convenient to the centre (15 minutes maximum to the Old Town), the 50 clean, large rooms. This

hotel offers a good choice for an inexpensive hotel.
Balkán
Svornosti 28, Prague 5
Tel: 540777
Fax: 540196
Clean, simple, no frills hotel with easy access via public transport to the major sites of Prague. A good budget choice; 24 rooms.
Central
Rybná 8
Prague 1
Tel: 2481 2041
Fax: 232 8404
The slightly shabby Central still offers affordable rooms only 5 minutes' walk from Old Town Square. There are 62 rooms, which go fast given the location; book far in advance.

Botels

Staying at one of the floating hotels along the Vltava in Prague can provide you with an experience you won't soon forget – nor will you forget the invariably cramped rooms! They do tend to be kept busy by coach tour operators, but it is worth trying the following:
Admirál
Hořejší nábřeží,
Prague 5 (near Palacký Bridge)
Tel: 5732 1302.
Albatros
Nábřeží Ludvíka Svobody,
Prague 1 (near Stvanice Island).
Tel: 2481 0547.
Fax: 2481 1214.
Botel Vodník
Strakonická street,
Prague 5.
Tel/fax: 5731 5667.

Hotel Olšanka
Táboritská 23
Prague 3
Tel: 6709 2202
Fax: 273 386
A huge boxy complex that offers basic, clean rooms and numerous hotel services (sauna, pool, several restaurants) that befit an establishment in a higher price range. Three tram lines connect in

front of the hotel; the main train station is only 10 minutes away via tram.

Mepro
Viktora Huga 3
Prague 5
Tel: 5721 5263
Fax: 527 343
Clean, with 26 simply furnished rooms. The location, near Petřín park with its mirror maze and little Eiffel Tower, should appeal to families travelling with children.

Petr
Drtinova 17
Prague 5
Tel: 5731 4068
Fax: 5731 4072
A basic but perfectly fine hotel not far from Malá Strana, on a quiet side street in the Smíchov residential neighbourhood. There is ample public transport close by, but there is no restaurant on site.

Pensions

If the choice is between a hotel and a *pension*, go with the *pension* every time. Usually privately owned and managed, the service is personal and their prices are reasonable. These are a few of the best:

Betlem Club Praha
Betlémské nám. 9
Prague 1
Tel: 2421 6872
Fax: 2421 8054
Prices in this *pension*, across from historic Bethlehem Chapel on a peaceful square in the Old Town, include breakfast in 12th-century Romanesque cellars. The 20 rooms are attractively furnished; each comes with toilet and shower or bath.

Penzion Digital
Na Petynce 143
Prague 6
Tel: 2431 3739
Full service *pension*; use of fax machine, as well as laundry services, babysitting, local tours – and they will even walk your dog!

Penzion Sprint
Cukrovárnická 62
Prague 6
Tel: 312 3338
Fax: 312 1797

Tiny bathrooms but pleasant management and 12 clean, simply furnished rooms make the Sprint a good place to stay. About midway between the airport and the centre; a tram line is two short blocks away.

Pension Unitas (The Prison)
Bartolomějská 9
Prague 1
Tel: 232 7700
Fax: 232 7709
Notorious as the former convent that was turned into a prison under Communism and even housed dissident Václav Havel. It is possible to stay in his former cell if you reserve far enough ahead. No en-suite rooms.

Motels

Motels offer a cheap alternative to hotels, particularly if you are travelling through the country and are only looking for one or two day-trips into the city.

Club Hotel Praha
E14 motorway towards Brno, Průhonice.
Tel: 67 75 08 68
Fax: 67 75 00 64
This 4-star hotel opened in 1991, with major sports facilities including tennis and squash courts, bowling alleys, swimming pools, fitness centre and much more. It is also situated adjacent to the Botanical Gardens and the grounds of Průhonice Castle.

Hotel Golf
Plzeňská 215a, Prague 5
Tel: 523251, 5721 5185
Fax: 5721 5213
Located on the E15 highway, the Hotel Golf has 129 rooms (with satellite TV) as well as excellent sports facilities.

Camping

Information regarding camping is available through automobile associations, or the headquarters of the Czech Automobile Association, Autoturist (*see page 263*).

As a rule, campsites in the Czech Republic are divided into three categories (all have cold running water and lavatory facilities). Those

Youth Hostels

For information about the many Prague youth hostels, most of which are open in summer only (except Travellers Hostel), contact:
Čedok
Na Příkopě 18, Prague 1.
Tel: 262904.
CKM
Jindřišská 28, Prague 1.
Tel: 268623.
Travellers Hostel
Dlouhá 33, Prague 1.
Tel: 231 1234.

falling into the third and simplest category "C" do not have access to electricity. In addition to plots reserved for caravans and tents, some campsites of the category "A" have holiday houses for rent.

Don't expect anything luxurious from this kind of accommodation. It does however present a reasonably clean and inexpensive alternative to staying in a hotel:

Apple Garden Caravan Camp
K Hrnčířům 72
Prague 4-Šeberov
Tel: 792 8529
Open May to October.

Autocamp Džbán-Aritma
Nad Lávkou 5
Prague 6-Vokovice
Tel: 369006
Open May to October.

Autocamp Trojská
Trojská 157
Prague 7-Troja
Tel: 688 6036
Open May to October.

Autocamp Žižkov
Koněvova 141a
Prague 3
Tel: 644 2061
Next to a public swimming pool and sports facilities and close to a tram stop with three lines. Summer only.

Caravancamp Motol
Plzeňská 256
Prague 5-Motol
Tel: 524714
Open May to October.

Dolní Chabry
Ustecká
Prague 8-Dolní Chabry

Tel: 688 1180
Open year round. Four-person cottages as well as space for tents and caravans.
Kotva
U ledáren 55, Prague 4-Braník
Tel: 4446 1712
Open May to October.

Private Lodgings

Private lodgings offer an inexpensive alternative to hotel rooms. There are a number of agencies through which you can book an apartment in the city with prices starting at about $20 per day, per person. It's usually possible to find rooms at the last minute.

People advertise private accommodation on street corners or at the exits to the motorways, and if you're arriving by train you may be accosted as soon as you arrive. Use your judgement: many people who offer lodgings without the benefit of an agency are perfectly reputable, but make sure that you confirm the location on a map before you accept their offer, or you may find yourself miles off the beaten track.

Private lodgings can also be booked through the following agencies, among a host of others:
AVE Offices in Wilsonova and Holešovice train stations
Tel: 2422 3226
City of Prague Accommodation Service
Haštalská 7, Prague 1
Tel: 231 6663
Hello Travel
Senovážné nám. 3, Prague 1
Tel: 2421 2647
Top Tour
Rybná 3, Prague 1
Tel: 231 4069

If you feel happier booking from England, the following are reputable agencies which arrange both self-catering and bed-and-breakfast accommodation in Prague:
Czechbook Agency
52 St John's Park, London SE3 7JP
Tel: 0181-853 1168
Czechdays
89 Valence Road
Lewes, Sussex BN7 ISJ
Tel: 01273 474738

Where to Eat

Finding a Restaurant

There is no single neighbourhood in Prague that is best for dining, and good restaurants can be found in virtually every district, although the finest and most expensive are generally scattered throughout Old Town and Malá Strana.

Visitors to Prague will find that the city is now home to a sophisticated mix of ethnic restaurants that offer a variety of cuisines, from Pakistani to French to Tex-Mex, as well as a number of vegetarian establishments. For those who want to sample more of the national flavour, however, a taste of the local cuisine should be on the itinerary.

A couple of Prague peculiarities worth noting are that in all but the loftiest establishments you may expect to share a table at peak times, and the background music will almost always be from whatever radio station the waiting staff is partial to.

What to Eat

Czech cooking is generally heavy on meat, most often pork or beef, which is often accompanied by knedlíky – sliced dumplings of either potato or bread. Goulash or roast pork with cabbage and dumplings are virtually national dishes.

A full-course meal starts with a bowl of soup, often meat-based; main meat dishes, whether pork, beef, goose or duck, can be very good. Beware, however, the ubiquitous smažený (fried) cutlet – usually a thickly breaded, unremarkable centrepiece for lower-budget meals.

Vegetables are, surprisingly, still not as plentiful here as in other European countries. The reliable

staples are cabbage, peppers, cucumbers and tomatoes, all of which seem to find their way into nearly every salad and garnish. Fresh vegetables such as spinach and broccoli seem to be in eternal short supply. Diners should be aware that vegetable side dishes are often of the defrosted variety, and lettuce is still a relatively rare participant in most salads. Vegetarians may have a hard time if they wish to stick to Czech cuisine, and may find themselves limited to fried mushrooms, fried cauliflower or fried cheese.

Czech desserts include a sweet pancake (palačinky), which is similar to a French crêpe, apple strudel, fruit or cheese-filled dumplings, and ice cream.

Fast food addicts can take advantage of the local snack options, usually in the form of hot-dogs and klobasa, or the greasy but frighteningly delicious fried bread with filling of your choice called langoš. There are also a number of McDonald's and KFC outlets for the less adventurous.

Restaurant Listings

The following is a list of selected establishments in different districts of the city that offer something special in terms of food and ambience. A few restaurants appear under more than one heading (e.g. International Specialities and city district) for easy reference.

Major credit cards such as Eurocard/Mastercard, American Express and Diners' Club are accepted in most restaurants in the Moderate and Expensive categories, but please confirm before placing your order.

THE LESSER QUARTER (MALÁ STRANA)

Bohemia Bagel
Újezd 16, Prague 1
Tel: 531002
Its bagels will not be confused with the real New World variety, but Bohemia Bagel makes an impres-

sive attempt to jazz up its wide assortment (including tomato-basil and poppyseed) with tasty cream-cheese, all served in an informal cafeteria style. Unlimited refills on designer coffee; weekend brunches are always popular. **$**

Circle Line Brasserie
Malostranské nám. 12, Prague 1
Tel: 5753 0021
An elegant yet cosy restaurant that offers world-class cuisine in the *nouvelle* style. The exquisite chocolate plate is a perfect dessert, almost too pretty to eat. Unfailingly terrific, discreet service. **$$$**

Kampa Park
Na Kampě 8b, Prague 1
Tel: 5731 3493
Nouvelle style cuisine served up on the banks of the Vltava. In fair weather, diners can enjoy a spectacular view of Charles Bridge. **$$$**

Malý Buddha
Úvoz 46, Prague 1 (near Prague Castle)
Tel: 2051 3894
A serene tea-house atmosphere is the setting for fresh and delicious Asian cuisine, such as spring rolls and glass noodles with vegetables, along with an impressive selection of exotic juices. **$**

Nebozízek (The Little Auger)
Petřínské sady 411, Prague 1
Tel: 53 79 05
The menu is less spectacular than the restaurant's location halfway up Petřín hill (take the funicular), with a gorgeous view over the city and the castle. Czech staples, including potato and garlic soups and meat dishes, are good. **$$**

Palffy palác
Valdštejnská 14, Prague 1
Tel: 5732 0570
An intimate space tucked away on the second floor of a Malá Strana palace; offers excellent Continental cuisine and a charming, faded elegance. **$$**

U Černého orla
Malostranské nám. 14, Prague 1
Tel: 53 63 73
Traditional Czech dishes, cheerfully served. **$$**

U Malířů (The Painters)

Maltézské nám. 11, Prague 1
Tel: 2451 0296
French restaurant since 1543 with an impressive *haute cuisine* menu; probably the most expensive restaurant in Prague. Its setting, in one of the city's quietest and most romantic squares, is superb. **$$$**

U Maltézských rytířů (The Maltese Knights)
Prokopská 10, Prague 1
Tel: 53 63 57, 53 66 50
A tiny cellar specialising in Czech cuisine and atmosphere. The homemade apple strudel alone is worth the visit. **$$$**

U Modré kachničky (The Blue Duck)
Nebovidská 6, Prague 1
Tel: 5732 0308
Delicious food, with game dishes a speciality. Elaborately decorated surroundings. **$$$**

U Patrona
Dražického nám. 4, Prague 1
Tel: 53 15 12; 53 14 97
A charming pocket-size restaurant near Charles Bridge which offers a small, high-quality menu of French inspired cuisine. **$$$**

U Tří houslíček (The Three Violins)
Nerudova 12, Prague 1
Tel: 535011
Elegant setting; classic Czech food. **$$$**

U Vladaře
Maltézské nám. 10, Prague 1
Tel: 53 81 28, 53 17 76
An ideal location for well-prepared Czech food. **$$$**

Price Guide

Prices are per person, including a glass of beer or wine.

$$$: 500 Kč and up
$$:   300–500 Kč
$:   up to 300 Kč

OLD TOWN

Amadé
U Milosrdných 10, Prague 1
Tel: 231 8867, 232 0101
Pleasant, well-lit wine cellar near St Agnes' Convent serves Czech specialities and maintains a small

but smart selection of fine wines. **$–$$**

Barock Bar & Café
Pařížská 24, Prague 1
Tel: 232 9221
Sushi and Thai food on one of the Old Town's most elegant streets. A place where the beautiful people go to see and be seen. **$$$**

Bellevue
Smetanovo nábř. 18, Prague 1
(near Charles Bridge)
Tel: 2222 1438
Fax: 2222 0453
Old world elegance with Continental cuisine and respectful presentation of Czech specialities (such as roast duck, brought to new heights with a delectable honey-lavender sauce). The name is fitting, since window tables afford views across the river to Prague Castle. **$$$**

Caffrey's Irish Bar
Staroměstské nám. 10, Prague 1
Tel: 2482 8031
One of Prague's growing population of Irish pubs, Caffrey's offers a more extensive menu than most, featuring items such as bangers and mash or a traditional Irish breakfast. **$$$**

Canadian Lobster
Husova 15, Prague 1
Tel: 2421 3530
Answering the question as to whether one can one get fresh lobster in a land-locked country with a very positive "yes". **$$$**

Chez Marcel
Haštalská 12, Prague 1
Tel: 231 5676
The bustling, informal charm of a French brasserie has been transplanted onto this quiet side street in the Old Town. Delicious fresh salads and hand-cut chips; daily specials such as *moules frites* or ratatouille. The crème brulée is consistently flawless. **$$**

Country Life
Melantrichova 15 (enter the courtyard), Prague 1
Tel: 2421 3366
Tasty all-vegetarian fare, served café style. The salad bar is extraordinarily bountiful by any standard. Table service begins at 6pm, and prices go up slightly. **$$**

Jewel of India
Pařížská 20, Prague 1
Tel: 2481 1010
An elaborately appointed cellar space offers genuine Indian cuisine such as Boti kabob (lamb) and Murgh maghani (chicken in a tomato-based sauce). **$$$**

Kožička Pivnice-Cafe Restaurant
Kozí 1, Prague 1
Tel: 231 0852
The Little Goat is a hip Czech pub-restaurant for the new generation; can get crowded. **$**

Obecní dům French Restaurant
Náměstí Republiky 5, Prague 1
Tel: 2200 2777
An unsurpassably sumptuous Art Nouveau setting for decent food at reasonable prices. **$$**

Red Hot and Blues
Jakubská 12, Prague 1
Tel: 231 46 39
Reasonably authentic New Orleans and Cajun-style cooking, with live jazz, blues or rockabilly most evenings. Full, hearty breakfasts served daily; the weekend brunches (with specialities such as Creole omelettes and spicy fried potatoes) are very popular. In pleasant weather the outdoor courtyard is a calming place to while away a couple of hours. **$$**

U Velryby
Jilská 24, Prague 1
Tel: 26 69 33
A Czech restaurant with trendy appeal to the young. **$$**

U Zlaté hrušky
Nový Svět 3, Prague 1
Tel: 2051 5356, 2051 4778
The Golden Pear is an elegant setting for traditional food. Some have described the service as a bit frosty, though. **$$$**

V Zátiší
Liliová 1, Prague 1
Tel: 2222 1155
Fax: 2423 1187
Delectable main courses of the *nouvelle* variety, glorious desserts and a warm, sophisticated atmosphere. Highly recommended, whether for a business-related dinner or a romantic *tête-à-tête*. **$$$**

Zlatá ulička (Golden Lane)
Masná 9, Prague 1

Tel: 232 08 84
Yugoslav specialities on offer in a tiny, friendly café. Try anything with veal in it. **$$**

Price Guide

Prices are per person, including a glass of beer or wine.

$$$: 500 Kč and up
$$: 300–500 Kč
$: up to 300 Kč

NEW TOWN

Buffalo Bill's
Vodičkova 9, Prague 1
Tel: 2494 8624
A wide variety of Tex-Mex favourites such as spicy burritos, tostadas and tortillas. **$$$**

Ceská restaurace
Krakovská 63, Prague 1
Tel: 2221 0204
Excellent, hearty Czech food and beer in a friendly atmosphere, right off Wenceslas Square. **$**

Dynamo
Pštrossova 221/29, Prague 1
Tel: 29 42 24
A few steps behind the National Theatre, Dynamo offers an imaginatively modern space and a menu filled with delicious options. Excellent pastas and big, fresh salads. The lunch specials are usually a great bargain. Pleasant service. **$$**

Fakhreldine
Klimentská 48, Prague 1
Tel: 232 79 70
Genuine, delicious Lebanese food from start to finish. **$$$**

Marco Polo
Masarykovo nábřeží 26, Prague 1
Tel: 2491 2900/3853
A wonderfully eclectic menu offers everything from meatballs to salmon, delicate homemade pastas and creative salads. Situated on the river (no views, however, as Marco Polo is several steps below street level) behind the National Theatre; an ideal locale for an after-dinner stroll. **$**

Pivovarský dům
Lípová 15, Prague 2

Tel: 9621 6666
Independent-minded microbrewery serves up delicious Czech food in a clean, relatively smoke-free environment. Try the wheat or champagne beers with an appetiser of *pivní sýr* (garlicky and salty "beer cheese" to spread on the accompanying rye bread). **$**

Rusalka
Na Struze 1/227, Prague 1
Tel: 24 91 58 76
Italian and Czech cuisines with pleasant atmosphere; behind the National Theatre. **$$**

U Kalicha (The Chalice)
Na Bojišti 14, Prague 2
Tel: 29 07 01
The great beerhall celebrated in Jaroslav Hašek's classic of Czech literature, *The Good Soldier Švejk*, frequented nowadays only by tourists. The Czech cuisine served is simple and hearty, but unfortunately not of tremendous quality. **$$$**

Universal
V Jirchářích 6, Prague 1
(off Národní třída).
Tel: 2491 8182
One of the best bargains in town. Tasty main courses with a French flair, dinner-sized salads, and desserts (such as the English Cream Dessert) as good as you'll find anywhere, at an unbelievably reasonable price. Reservations several days in advance are mandatory at peak hours. **$**

U Piráta
Vojtěšská 9, Prague 1
Tel: 29 10 40
Good, honest Czech food, with quirky additions to the menu, such as crocodile. **$**

U Zlatého soudku
Ostrovní 28, Prague 1
Tel: 2491 2202
Veritable meat feasts. Recommended are the potato pancake stuffed with pork, beef and cabbage, or the 400-gram Old Bohemian Dinner: a platter of pork, chicken and beef, potato and bread dumplings and cabbage. **$$**

Zlatý kohout
Karlovo nám. 24, Prague 1
Tel: 2223 2382
A terrific Continental selection, a

warm, elegant ambience and attentive service make this a gem worth seeking out, just across from the New Town Hall. Soothing jazz is usually the music of choice on the soundtrack. **$$$**

OTHER

Dolly Bell
Neklanova 20, Prague 2
Tel: 29 88 15
Yugoslav dishes in an imaginatively decorated restaurant. Veal ragout is a stand-out. **$$**

Hanavský pavilon
Letenské sady 173, Prague 7
Tel: 32 57 92.
Traditional Czech cuisine in one of Prague's main diplomatic quarters. **$$$**

Orso Bruno (Bruno the Bear)
Za Poříčskou bránou 16
Prague 8
Tel: 231 0178
Unpretentious Italian cuisine. Try the scaloppini with Gorgonzola cheese, chicken cacciatore, or penne melanzane. **$$**

Radost FX Café
Bělehradská 120, Prague 2
Tel: 2425 4776
This tiny restaurant is packed with eclectic style, and the menu is packed with imaginative dishes covering an international range – and all vegetarian. It's attached to a dance club of the same name (see page 282). The weekend brunch omelettes are enormous, and enormously good. **$**

Restaurace Ullmann
Letenský zámeček, Letenské sady 341, Prague 7
Tel: 37 16 78
Friendly restaurant in a very small château situated in Letná park, not far from Prague Castle. The beer garden is highly popular with locals in warm weather. **$**

U Bílé krávy (The White Cow)
Rubešova 10 (behind the National Museum), Prague 2
Tel: 2423 9570/9571
Connoisseur-quality steak with French variations: marinated in Cognac and served with garlic-herb sauce, for instance. **$$**

U Cedru
Na Hutích 13, Prague 6
Tel: 312 29 74
Authentic, delicious Lebanese food in a diplomatic district. **$$$**

U Počtů
Milady Horákové 47, Prague 7
Tel: 37 00 85
Off the beaten track, but the neighbourhood charm and old-fashioned decor make it worth a visit to sample traditional meals. **$$**

Velehradská vinárna
Velehradská 18, Prague 3
Tel: 627 6748
Unpretentious hideaway for well-prepared Czech food. The beefsteak with a dot of herb butter is tender and good. **$$**

Beer Halls

If you believe the statistics, each resident of Prague downs about 150 litres of beer per year. The usually over-crowded pubs and inns attest to the fact that not much of it is drunk in privacy at home.

Czech beer is probably the finest in the world. Its quality is largely due to the famous Bohemian hops, which have been cultivated in Bohemia since the Middle Ages. The hop centre is Žatec (Saaz), in western Bohemia.

In Prague both light (světlé) and dark (tmavé or černé) beer is poured. The degrees (°) do not refer to the alcohol content but rather to the percentage of malt in the wort, which is boiled with hops to make the brew. Light draught beer (10°) has an alcohol content of between three and four per cent; lager (12°) five per cent. The stronger, dark varieties (13° and more) are fairly comparable with strong German beers.

The most famous beers are Pilsener Urquell from Plzeň (Pilsen) and Budvar from Ceské Budějovice (Budweis). But the beer from Prague's Smíchov brewery is also good, and then there is the strong dark beer brewed on the premises at U Fleků. Another strong beer comes from the district of Braník.

A few of Prague's best beer halls are listed as follows:

Pub Etiquette

Always plan on sharing a table in a Prague beer hall. Before sitting down at an empty seat, first ask "Je tu volno?" (Is it free here?). Then put a coaster in front of you to indicate that you'd like a beer.

If you're not served immediately, don't stand up and wave. At worst you'll never be served and at best you'll be marked as a greenhorn.

When he serves you, the waiter ticks off each beer on a tab – he will probably keep bringing beers until you signal to stop! – then adds them up when you're ready to leave.

When you want to pay, say "Zaplatit". Leave a tip by giving a higher figure than the total bill or waving away part of the change. Tips in beer halls are low, and it is usual to just round up the bill to the nearest whole number.

Cerný orel (Black Eagle)
U Lužického semináře 40
Prague 1
No phone
Rustic neighbourhood pub serves Budvar and Regent, as well as fabulous fruit dumplings.

Malostranská hospoda
Karmelitská 25, Prague 1
Tel: 532076
A variety of beers are poured in a cheerful, clean and relatively tourist-free pub off Malá Strana Square.

Novoměstský pivovar (New Town Brewery)
Vodičkova 20
Prague 1
Tel: 2223 2448
A meandering set of rooms welcome visitors for beer and good pub food. The pub brews its own light and dark beer.

Pivnice Radegast
Templova 2
Prague 1
Tel: 232 8069
Beer hall in a gothic architecture-style near the Old Town Square serving a variety of delicious Radegast beers.

U Výstřeleného oka (The Shot Out Eye)
U božích bojovníků 3, Prague 3
Tel: 627 8714
A popular spot for hip young Czechs, named after the great one-eyed Hussite warrior Jan Žižka.

U Zlatého tygra (Golden Tiger)
Husova 17, Prague 1
Tel: 2422 9020
Pilsener Urquell beer; this pub was a haunt of the bohemian writer Bohumil Hrabal, who died in 1997.

Nad Královskou oborou (Above the Royal Enclosure)
Nad Královskou oborou 31
Prague 7
Tel: 374966
Czech and Irish beers consumed by a clientèle of art students from the nearby academy.

Molly Malones
U Obecního dvora 4, Prague 1
The city has many Irish pubs now; this is one of the best and cosiest, with a roaring fire in winter. Serves Guinness, naturally.

Pivovarský dům (Brewer House)
Lípová 15, Prague 2
Tel: 9621 6666
Pleasant, welcoming microbrewery with good food.

U Fleků
Křemencova 11, Prague 1
Tel: 2491 5118
The malthouse and brewery date from 1459. A traditional Prague whistle-stop for large tour groups.

U Medvídků (The Little Bears)
Na Perštýně 7, Prague 1
This traditional restaurant and pub (and former brewery) offers South

Bohemian and Old Czech specialities, accompanied by Budvar beer.

Na staré kovárně v Braníku (At the Old Metalworks)
Kamenická 17, Prague 7
Tel: 376911
Youthful owners serve up Braník beer in a friendly atmosphere.

U Milosrdných (At the Merciful)
U Milosrdných 12
Prague 1 (near St. Agnes Convent)
Tel: 232 7673
Gambrinus beer in one of the last great cheap pubs in the Old Town.

U Cerného vola (The Black Bull)
Loretánské nám. 1
Prague 1 (near Prague Castle)
Tel: 2051 3481
Popular light and dark beer from Velké Popovice.

Prague's Coffee Houses

Read, smoke, discuss, let the day go by; that's what Prague's coffee houses are all about. These institutions still offer more than simply coffee and cake, and remain an important element in the daily life of the city.

Kavárna Slavia
Národní třída at Smetanovo nábřeží, Prague 1.
Prague's most important café, with Art Deco decor, affords lovely views onto National Avenue and Prague Castle. Composer Bedřich Smetana and poet Jaroslav Seifert were former denizens. Nowadays the café caters to both Czechs and tourists. Service can be casual and the coffees and light meals are unremarkable, but there is no more beautiful café setting.

Evropa
Václavské nám. 29, Prague 1.
A classic of the old-world café genre, the Evropa (on the ground floor of Grand Hotel Evropa) offers faded Art Nouveau elegance. Drinks are on the ordinary side, but go to absorb the ambience.

Malostranská Kavárna
Malostranské nám., Prague 1.
Clean, simply furnished café in the heart of Malá Strana which draws an intellectual crowd and remains

one of the last bastions of neighbourhood life. Czech newspapers are available; coffee and cakes are rather ordinary.

Franz Kafka Café
Široká 12, Prague 1.
Chances are, Kafka would find this tasteful, old-Europe style café very inviting. The hot chocolate is excellent, and the old photos of the writer and his family lend interest. Incongruously, pop music is on the stereo system.

Globe Coffeehouse and Bookstore
Janovského 14, Prague 1.
The coffee house for Prague's European and American expats and a growing number of local Czechs, the Globe offers a light selection of food. Coffees and desserts are best. Settle in for the afternoon and read the news-papers provided.

Kavárna Archa
Na Poříčí 26, Prague 1.
Popular café, always packed with a hip clientèle of local artists and intellectuals. The café is on street level, attached to the theatre Divadlo Archa.

Le Patio Café
Národní 22, Prague 1.
Beautiful, airy café providing an oasis on National Avenue, and the

coffees are very good too. There's also an excellent albeit pricey menu of salads and snacks.

French Institute Café
Štěpánská 35, Prague 1.
A little taste of Paris in the centre of Prague, catering to Czech students of the French language and the local French community. Open Monday to Friday only.

Café Milena
Staroměstské nám. 22, Prague 1.
Named after Milena Jesenská, lover of Franz Kafka. Coffees and pastries are unremarkable, but where can you get a better view of the Old Town Clock?

St. Nicholas Café
Tržiště 10, Prague 1.
Highly trendy young café.

Kavárna Praha-Roma
V Jámě 5, Prague 1.
Tiny, elegant, old-style Italian café, serving appetising and unusual pastries and terrific coffee.

Vzpomínky na Afriku (Memories of Africa)
Rybná & Jakubská, Prague 1.
Whimsically decorated hole-in-the-wall (with only two tables) serves a vast number of speciality coffees and teas, and American snacks such as brownies and bagels.

Wine Bars

Every bit as popular as the pubs are the wine bars, known as *vinárna*, which serve predominantly Czech wines. The best wine comes from Žernoseky in the Elbe Valley, where the Mělník wines are also cultivated. Good wines are also produced in Southern Moravia, Mikulov, Hodonín, Znojmo and Valtice. At one time there were vineyards in Prague, recalled by the name of the district Vinohrady.

Snacks are served in wine bars and in recent years many *vinárna* have become expensive restaurants. Opening times vary, but most stay open until midnight.

Amadé
(*See page 274*)
Café El Centro
Maltézské nám. 9
Prague 1
Tel: 5731 2181
Intelligent selection of wines from a private cellar in Moravia.
Česká vinotéka
Anežská 3, Prague 1
No phone
Wide choice of Czech wines.
Paradiso Café-Bar
Týn 2 (in the courtyard)
Prague 1
Tel: 2489 5787
Elegant French wines and tasty appetisers, near Old Town Square.
U Kiliána
Všehrdova 13, Prague 1
Tel: 5731 0950
Unpretentious wine bar (with light meals), named after the Baroque architect Kilián Ignác Dientzenhofer, who lived in this building.
U Vinařů
Nosticova 1, Prague 1
Tel: 5731 2516
Czech and imported wines in a genteel yet comfortable setting.
Svatá Klára
U Trojského zámku 35/9, Prague 7
Tel: 688 0405
Exclusive cellar wine bar and restaurant near Troja château towards the outskirts of Prague.
Klášterní vinárna (Monastery Wine Bar)
Národní 8, Prague 1
Tel: 290596

In a former Ursuline Convent, serving wines from Moravia and Slovakia's Nitra region.
Lobkovická vinárna
Vlašska 17, Prague 1
Tel: 530185
A historic wine bar in the Lesser Quarter, belonging to the one of the Czech lands' oldest families; wines from the Mělník region are particularly good here.
Makarská
Malostranské nám. 2, Prague 1
Tel: 531573
Balkan wines and specialities.
U labutí
Hradčanské nám. 11, Prague 1
Tel: 2051 1191
Exclusive wine bar near the castle serving South Moravian wines.
U mecenáše (The Sponsor)
Malostranské nám. 10, Prague 1
Tel: 533881
There was an inn in the house at the sign of the Golden Lion as long ago as 1604.

Cocktail Bars

The cocktail bar is experiencing a renaissance in Prague, as many young people spurn the traditional, smoky pub life in favour of more sophisticated pleasures.
Bugsy's Bar
Kostečná 2 (off Pařížská), Prague 1.
Possibly the best cocktails in town, with an enormously extensive drinks list from which to choose.
Corona Bar Latino Café-Restaurant
Novotného lávka 9, Prague 1 (below Charles Bridge in the Old Town). Cocktails and socialising, all to sultry Latin music. Tasty *tapas* are served, too.
La Casa Blú
Kozí 15, Prague 1
Rum, coffee and tequila drinks in a fun joint with a hot soundtrack.
La Cubana Café Bar
Míšeňská 12, Prague 1
Imaginative rum drinks, to be sipped in time to a mambo beat.
Marquis de Sade
Templová 8, Prague 1
Trendy watering hole draws a mixed and occasionally dubious clientè le. Still, the cocktails are excellent.

ZanziBar
Lázeňská 6, Prague 1
Well shaken or stirred dry martinis, margaritas and other drink classics in a rambunctious setting, with pop and reggae on the soundtrack.
Žíznivý pes (Thirsty Dog)
Elišky Krásnohorské 5, Prague 1 (near the Hotel Intercontinental). Raucous drinking hole favoured by the young. The food (Tex-Mex, pasta) is surprisingly good for a bar.

Teahouses

Prague *Čajovny* (teahouses) have taken off in recent years as mellow venues for sipping exotic teas and speciality blends, in what is usually a calm, soothing (some might say soporific) atmosphere. Usually snacks (such as ginger cookies or homemade cakes) are available as well, and loose teas as well as tea accoutrements are for sale.

The following teahouses should provide an oasis in the middle of a hectic day of sightseeing.
Dobrá Čajovna
Boršov 2, Prague 1 (a blind alley off Karoliny Světlé)
Pull the velvet rope for entrance to this casbah-like quiet teahouse. About 50 different teas as well as flavoured tobacco for smoking in their hookah. Tasty humus and baba gannoush are served as well. Linger for as long as you like, which may be difficult because the low seats don't have backs.
Růžová cajovna (Rose Teahouse)
Růžová 8, Prague 1
Intimate, cosy spot in the chaos of New Town (near Wenceslas Square) with an impressive range of teas. This cheerful teahouse features three levels; the lowest level frequently offers live music on guitar or Andean flute. Charming ceramic cups and teapots can also be purchased.
U Zeleného Čaje
Nerudova 19, Prague 1
Easy to miss because it's right on the tourist trail leading up and down from Prague Castle, The Green Tea – a quiet, simple room with only six tables – has an excellent selection of international teas and light

snacks. Regulars rave about the apple strudel.

Zapomenutá Čajovna (Forgotten Teahouse)
Jánský vršek 8, Prague 1
This peaceful little oasis off Nerudova is rarely happened upon by tourists. It specialises in Ceylon and Chinese teas, and also sells incense, infusers and boxed teas.

Roxy Kuskuserie
Dlouhá 33, Prague 1
Downstairs in the Roxy club complex, this dimly lit, languorous café might well be in Marrakesh. A wide variety of exotic teas is available, as are simple North African treats.

Culture

Buying Tickets

To get tickets, we recommend going directly to the box office in order to get the best price, since ticket agencies may mark up prices significantly or charge a commission. You can also buy tickets through various tourist agencies, but expect to pay a hefty commission.

If you do need to go to a ticket agency, some of the best are:
Bohemia Ticket International
Malé nám. 13, Prague 1
Tel: 2422 7832
PIS (Prague Information Service)
Staroměstská radnice, Prague 1
Tel: 2448 2018.
Ticketpro
Salvátorská 10, Prague 1
Tel: 2481 4020
Fax: 2481 4021.
Top Theatre Tickets
Celetná 13, Prague 1
Tel: 232 2536.
The box offices for the **National Theatre** and **Laterna Magika** are situated in the glass buildings off Národní třída 2.

Dance

The National Theatre Ballet frequently performs ballet classics such as *Swan Lake* and *Coppélia*, but has been branching out in more adventurous directions in recent years by including choreographies by George Balanchine and Jiří Kylián. The usual venues for National Theatre Ballet performances are:
National Theatre (Národní divadlo)
Národní třída 2, Prague 1,
Tel: 2491 3437.
Estates Theatre (Stavovské divadlo)
Ovocný trh 6, Prague 1
Tel: 24 21 50 01.

Keep an eye out also for neo-Classical dance performances by the Prague Chamber Ballet, which changes venues during the season. The **Duncan Centre** (Branická 41, Prague 4, Tel: 4446 1810), named after Isadora Duncan, is a popular centre for the teaching and performance of modern dance, and often hosts visiting foreign artists.

Classical Music

High-quality concerts of classical music, emphasising Mozart, Vivaldi, Dvořák and Smetana, are held throughout the year in churches and many other venues far too numerous to list here. For schedules of current concerts, refer to entertainments listings. The **Czech Philharmonic** and the **Prague Symphony Orchestra** are two outstanding Czech orchestras. Their concert seasons run from September through to June. Other important venues for classical music are also listed below:

What's On

Prague has a very rich and varied cultural palette with something for everyone. To find out what's on during your visit, check posters around the city on billboards and kiosks, or buy a copy of the monthly booklet *Culture in Prague* or the weekly newspaper *The Prague Post*.

Czech Philharmonic
Rudolfinum, Alšovo nábřeží 12, Prague 1
Tel: 2489 3352
Prague Symphony Orchestra
Obecní dům (Municipal House), Prague 1
Tel: 2200 2336
Atrium
Čajkovského 12
Prague 3-Vinohrady
Tel: 627 0453
Classical recitals held in an appealing venue.
Bertramka
Mozartova 169
Prague 5

Tel: 54 38 93, 54 00 12
Mozart museum hosts concerts.
**House at the Stone Bell
(Dum U Kamenného zvonu)**
Staroměstské nám. 13
Prague 1
Tel: 2481 0036
Vocal and instrumental recitals.
Klementinum (Hall of Mirrors)
Karlova
Prague 1
Tel: 2166 3111
Daily concerts of classical music.
**Lichtenstein Palace
(Lichtenštejnský palác)**
Malostranské nám, 13
Prague 1. Main venue of the music
academy.
**Lobkowicz Palace
(Lobkovický palác)**
Jiřská 3
Prague Castle
Tel: 53 73 64

**St Agnes Monastery
(Anežský klášter)**
U milosrdných, 17
Prague 1
Spanish Hall (Španělský sál)
Prague Castle, off the Second
Courtyard.
Holds concerts of the Prague Spring
International Music Festival as well
as by important visiting performers.
**Spanish Synagogue
(Španělská synagóga)**
Vězeňská street
Prague 1
Tel: 2481 0099
Frequent recitals of Jewish music.

Theatre and Opera

The quality of Czech theatre and
opera is quite high. Most opera is
rendered in its original language,
with digitalised supertitles in Czech.

(Performances in Czech of works by
Dvořák and Smetana do not have
supertitles in foreign languages,
however.) The ensemble theatres
listed below usually perform in
Czech. If you're interested in
English-language theater, keep an
eye out for sporadic performances
by the local Black Box Theatre and
Misery Loves Company which both
provide interesting shows.
Prague's major theatrical and
operatic venues are:
**State Opera
(Státní opera)**
Wilsonova 4
Prague 1. Metro: Muzeum
Tel: 26 53 53
Nightly productions, usually of a
very high standard; the repertoire
provides a nice mix of romantic
classics (by Verdi, Puccini, etc) and
more daring contemporary works,

Prague's Annual Festivals

A visit to Prague and the Czech
Republic could be combined with a
visit to one of the countless
festivals or sporting events that
take place in the country throughout the year. The best time for
culture is from September through
to June. Here is a selection of only
a few annual highlights; however,
you can almost bank on at least
one festival of classical music
every day of the year in Prague.

November through May
Prague: AghaRTA Prague Jazz
Festival. A bit of a misnomer, since
this "festival" is actually a series
of high-quality concerts, usually
one per month, throughout the
winter–spring season. Concerts
are usually held at Lucerna Music
Bar (*see page 281*), but
occasionally they take over more
spacious venues. Performers in
recent years have included the Pat
Metheny Group, saxophonist
Joshua Redman, and fusion kings
Yellowjackets.
Prague: United Colors of Akropolis.
Held at Palác Akropolis a popular
series of concerts, also throughout
the winter–spring season, focusing

on exciting innovations in world
music.

Late March through early April
Brno: Easter Festival of Sacred
Music.

May
Prague: Spring International Music
Festival. (12 May–3 June.) Venues
include the Rudolfinum, Obecní
dům, the Spanish Hall and St.
Vitus' Cathedral.
Prague: International Marathon.

May and June
Ostrava: Janáček May International
Music Festival.

July
Strážnice/Southern Moravia:
International gathering of folk
groups in ethnic costume, with
traditional dancing and music.
Karlovy Vary: International Film
Festival. An excellent forum for
films from eastern Europe and new
European and American
productions in general.
Prague: Harp Congress.
International harp festival.
Český Krumlov: Piano Festival.

August
Domažlice/Western Bohemia:
Chode Festival. Festival of the
independent border people with
dancing, music and bagpipes.
**Mariánské Lázně/Western
Bohemia:** Chopin Music Festival.
Český Krumlov/South Bohemia:
International Music Festival.
České Budějovice: Emmy Destinn
Music Festival.
Brno: Motorcycle Grand Prix.

September
Žatec/Western Bohemia: Žatec
Hops Festival.
Brno: Autumn Music Festival.

October
Prague: Autumn International
Music Festival. A young festival,
not yet on a par with Prague Spring
although its reputation is growing.
Pardubice/Eastern Bohemia:
Velká Pardubická International
Steeplechase.

October and November
Prague: Musica Iudaica.
International festival of Jewish
music, held in the major concert
venues as well as in synagogues.

such as Philip Glass' *Fall of the House of Usher*.

**National Theatre
(Národní divadlo)**
Národní třída 2
Prague 1
Tel: 2491 3437
Opera, ballet and theatre by the National Theatre ensembles.

**Estates Theatre
(Stavovské divadlo)**
Ovocný trh 6
Prague 1
Tel: 24 21 50 01
Opera, dance, theatre; the première of Mozart's opera *Don Giovanni* was held here in 1787, conducted by Mozart himself. Part of the National Theatre network.

**Alfred Mime Theatre
(Divadlo Mimů Alfred ve dvoře)**
Františka Křížka 36
Prague 7
Tel: 2057 1584
Mime theatre that does not pander to tourist taste.

**Archa Theatre
(Divadlo Archa)**
Na Poříčí 26
Prague 1
Tel: 232 8800
Progressive theatre with emphasis on the avant-garde. Archa hosts groups from Prague and abroad: visiting ensembles have included the Royal Shakespeare Company.

**Fantastika Theatre
(Divadlo Ta Fantastika)**
Karlova 8
Prague 1
Tel: 2422 9078
One of Prague's best black light theatres.

Laterna magika – Nová scéna
Národní třída 4
Prague 1
Tel: 2421 2691
Prague's famous black-light theatre.

**National Marionette Theatre
(Národní divadlo marionet)**
Žatecká 1
Prague 1
Tel: 232 34 29
Puppetry for all ages, with an enjoyable, long-running *Don Giovanni*.

**Royal Route Theatre
(Divadlo na Královské cestě)**
Karlova 12
Prague 1

Tel: 2422 1604
The performance venue of the International Institute of Puppeteering.

**Theatre on the Balustrade
(Divadlo na Zábradlí)**
Anenské nám. 5
Prague 1
Tel: 2422 1933
Famous as the theatre where President Havel worked; his plays are still performed here.

Cinema

During the 1960s, Czech film achieved world renown, with excellent films such as Miloš Forman's *Loves of a Blonde* and the Academy-Award-winning *Closely Observed Trains*. As elsewhere, Prague cinemas are now filled with mainly Hollywood fare, usually in English with Czech subtitles. Box offices indicate dubbed films by posting a small sign which reads "*České znění*". Posters at the cinemas, as well as the English-language *The Prague Post*, are the best sources for up-to-date information.

Cinemas that show more daring English-language and foreign productions and cinema classics are:

Dlabačov
Bělohorská 24
Prague 6
Tel: 3335 9058

Aero
Biskupcova 31
Prague 3
Tel: 89 36 01

Evald
Národní třída 28
Prague 1
Tel: 2110 5225

MAT Studio
Karlovo nám. 19
Prague 2
Tel: 2491 5765

Prague Post Film Club
Tel: 2487 5000 for details and current venue.

Art Galleries

Prague is awash with a wide range of art galleries, but some of the best and the more unusual are as follows:

French Institute
Štěpánská 35
Prague 1
Mon–Fri 10am–6pm.
Rotating exhibits of contemporary French art in a stylish gallery.

**Galerie AVU
(Fine Arts Academy Gallery)**
U akademie 4
Prague 7
Mon–Fri 10am–6pm.
The new generation of artists.

Gallery of the City of Prague
House at the Stone Bell,
Staroměstské nám. 13
Prague 1
Tue–Sun 10am–6pm.
Invariably good exhibitions of Czech and international art.

Gallery of the City of Prague
Municipal Library (Městská knihovna)
Mariánské nám. 1 (entrance on Valentinská)
Prague 1
Tue–Sun 10am–6pm.
Rotating exhibitions.

Galerie Fronta
Spálená 53,
Prague 1
Tue–Sun 10–12.30, 2–5.30.
Popular contemporary Czech art.

Galerie Hollar
Smetanovo nábř. 6
Prague 1
Tue–Sun 10–1, 2–6.
Good graphics exhibitions.

Galerie Oskara Kokoschky
Jungmannovo nám. 18
Prague 1
Mon–Fri 10am–5pm.
Sponsored by the Prague Austrian Centre, highlights contemporary Austrian art, and works by Oskar Kokoschka.

Galerie Rudolfinum
Alšovo nábř. 12
Prague 1
Tue–Sun 10am–6pm.
Superb exhibitions, often by internationally recognised artists.

Galerie Václava Špály
Národní 30
Prague 1
Tue–Sun 10am–1pm, 2–6pm.
Challenging exhibits by some of the better Czech artists.

Karolinum
Ovocný trh 3
Prague 1

Daily 10am–6pm.
Excellent rotating exhibitions, relating to aspects of Czech history.
Mánes Gallery
Masarykovo nábř. 250
Prague 1
Tue–Sun 10am–6pm.
Rotating exhibitions by contemporary artists.
National Gallery Collection of Asian Art
Zámek, Zbraslav nad Vltavou
Prague 5
From Smíchovské station, take bus 129, 241, 243, 255 or 360 to Zbraslavské náměstí.
Tue–Sun 10am–6pm.
This Baroque mansion in a suburb of Prague houses 12,000 items of art from India, Tibet, China and southeast Asia.
**Obecní dům
(Municipal House)**
Nám. Republiky 5
Prague 1
Daily 10am–6pm.
Art Nouveau exhibits.
**Staroměstská radnice
(Old Town Hall)**
Old Town Square (entrance on Valentinská)
Prague 1
Tue–Sun 10am–6pm.
Rotating exhibitions, often of historical interest.
**Valdštejnská jízdárna
(Wallenstein Riding School)**
Valdštejnská 3
Prague 1 (at Malostranská metro station)
Tue–Sun 10am–6pm.
Rotating exhibitions.
**Veletržní palác
(National Gallery Centre for Modern and Contemporary Art)**
Dukelských hrdinů 47
Prague 7
Tue–Sun 10am–6pm (Thurs until 9pm).
Permanent collection of European (especially French) 19th- and 20th-century art, including Renoir, Van Gogh, Cézanne, Gauguin, Chagall and Picasso. Also rotating exhibitions by contemporary artists.

Nightlife

Prague is no Paris or Berlin, but it is endeavouring to hold its own against smaller European cities as far as nightlife is concerned. Hip bars and clubs compete with casinos and sleazy discos to beckon the night-owl, and live jazz music in particular is of a very high standard. Late-night cafés such as the Globe (*see page 276*) may appeal to those who aren't inclined to loud music and dancing.

Generally, it's a good idea to avoid the discos in the Wenceslas Square area, which tend to attract mobs of teenage tourists who don't know what else to do; most locals won't go near such places. The better clubs are sprinkled all over the city, and there is no one best area for nightlife. *Culture in Prague* and *The Prague Post* (*see page 278*) will also offer up-to-date information on what's on in the city.

Jazz Clubs

Prague is a jazz aficionado's dream, but it is worth noting that a lot of clubs now seem to cater to herds of tourists, who don't allow the music to get in the way of their conversations. If you'd like to go where actual Praguers go to hear jazz, **Jazz Club Železná** and **U Malého Glena** are the best venues. Other clubs worth visiting are as follows:
AghaRTA Jazz Centrum
Krakovská 5
Prague 1
Tel: 2221 1275
This intimate (some say cramped) cellar space off Wenceslas Square offers some of the top local jazz acts, beginning at 9pm each evening. The acoustics are excellent; be sure to arrive early, as

the best seats go fast. The on-site CD shop is Prague's best for jazz recordings.
Golem Club
Na Perštýně 18
Prague 1
A businessmen's club known colloquially as the "Millionaires' Club," this comfortable and relatively smoke-free venue hosts occasional jazz of a high standard.
Jazz club U Staré paní
Michalská 9
Prague 1
Tel: 26 49 20, 26 72 67
Popular jazz and supper club; occasional musicians from abroad.
Jazz Club Železná
Železná 16
Prague 1
Tel: 2423 9697
This performance space off Old Town Square presents a variety of adventurous musical acts, but focuses mainly on jazz and world music. The Sunday afternoon jamming sessions to accompany poetry readings in English and Czech are popular.
Malostranská beseda
Malostranské nám. 21
Prague 1
Tel: 53 90 24
A popular venue for some of the best in local blues, jazz and folk.
Metropolitan Jazz Club
Jungmannova 14
Prague 1
Tel: 2421 6025
Reliable locale for swing and Dixieland jazz.
Red Hot & Blues
Jakubská 12
Prague 1
Tel: 231 4639

Casinos

Prague has casinos galore, but it is hard to say which ones are the best since many tend to be operated by a disreputable, if not dangerous, underworld element. Visitors interested in slot machines only might want to duck into one of Prague's ubiquitous *herna* (gaming) bars and try their luck.

Cajun restaurant offers nightly rockabilly, blues and jazz standards.

Reduta
Národní třída 20
Prague 1
Tel: 2491 2246
Dark, increasingly shabby perennial with a tourist crowd. The same jazz groups may be enjoyed at better clubs elsewhere in Prague.

U Malého Glena
Karmelitská 23
Prague 1
Tel: 535 8115
Intimate basement club and a hip bar, with sterling acoustics and management.

Rock Venues

Palác Akropolis
Kubelíkova 27
Prague 3–Žižkov
Tel: 2271 2287
This converted theatre in a working-class neighbourhood is a relaxed venue for high-quality music of all kinds, especially Gypsy tunes and world-music acts. It is also the venue for major foreign bands who'd like to do a "small club date" while in Prague.

Rock Café
Národní třída 20
Prague 1
Tel: 2491 4414
Rock, rock and more rock; its location on National Avenue means, however, that the clientèle tends to be touristy and generally undiscriminating.

Roxy
Dlouhá třída 33
Prague 1
Tel: 2481 0951
Fun and adventurous programme of alternative rock and theatre, with occasional trance-music discos.

Klub Delta
Vlastina 887
Prague 6
Tel: 301 9222
Hard, gloomy rock; worth the trek to this distant Prague neighbourhood only for those who like their music loud and live.

Klub Hrob
Sokolovská 144
Prague 8–Karlín

Tel: 684 0263
"The Grave" offers live rock nightly, and throws in a popular once-a-week film screening along the lines of *Mad Max* or *A Clockwork Orange*.

Lucerna Music Bar
Štěpánská 61
Prague 1
Tel: 2421 7108
Big, shabby space off Wenceslas Square pulls in locals and tourists for a varied programme of rock, pop, jazz and/or blues. Occasional concerts by major performers on European tours are a draw throughout the year.

Nightclubs & Discos

Jo's Garáž
Malostranské nám. 7
Prague 1
Jo's "garage" is the consistently packed dance space of the expat institution Jo's Bar upstairs. A DJ spins pop hits until the wee hours

Klub Lávka
Novotného lávka 1
Prague 1
Tel: 2421 4797
Open 24 hours a day, seven days a week, this raucous entertainment complex near Charles Bridge attracts all kinds for dancing, drinking, food (Italian and American) and fun. The disco (house, pop, Latin-American) is on the lower level.

La Habana Club
Míšeňská 12
Prague 1
Tel: 5731 5104
Almost like a visit to Cuba, with hot salsa on the soundtrack and inventive rum concoctions to drink.

NASA Club
Konviktská 6, Prague 1

Fridays and Saturdays are "house party" nights starting at 9pm. The bar appears to have been fashioned from pieces of plane shrapnel and fuselage, and there are plenty of space-themed drinks for the young clientèle to choose from. The music leans towards spacey tunes as well.

Radost FX
Bělehradská 120
Prague 2

Tel: 25 69 98, 25 12 10
Still the king of dance clubs, with animal-print furniture, Prague's most attractive waiting staff, and top local and international DJs. Gay night "hot house" parties are held one night a week; call for details.

XT3
Pod plynojemem 5
Prague 8–Karlín
A small, not-so-well-kept secret catering to aficionados of electronic dance music, leaning towards drum'n'bass, break beat, cool jazz and trance.

Gay & Lesbian Venues

Favoured venues change fast and frequently, but the following are reliable in what is still a relatively new scene for Prague, and the patrons there can at least direct you to the latest dance clubs (see also Radost above). But be warned: denizens of the Prague gay night scene have described it as "just like San Francisco in the 1970s". Travellers who know better what decade they're in might want to keep this in mind.

"A" Klub
Milíčova 32
Prague 3
Mostly women; women only on Fridays. Otherwise, men are welcome provided they have a female escort. Comfortable, relaxed club for dancing, talking, flirting. The decor is by local female artists.

Piano Bar
Milešovská 10
Prague 3-Vinohrady
Tel: 627 5467
Gay and lesbian. Open only until 10pm. Eclectic clientèle enjoys drinks, snacks, good talk. Gay and lesbian reading material is also available for browsing through.

U Střelce
Karolíny Světlé 12
Prague 1
Mixed. Midnight "Travesty" (transvestite) cabaret every Friday and Saturday. Popular and most recent incarnation of the Střelec series of Prague gay clubs. Dancing and carousing.

Shopping

What to Buy

Shopaholics are bound to have a fabulous time in Prague: chic boutiques can be found everywhere in the centre. Shopping in Prague is increasingly on a par with western Europe, both in terms of quality and prices. **Bohemian glass and china** are held in high esteem throughout the world due to their exceptional quality and fair price, but now it's almost impossible to find a good deal in antique shops. **Antique** dealers have become wise to the foreign predilection for their wares and have altered their prices accordingly. **Arts and crafts** and **fashions** are also finding a ready market.

Street vendors – usually young people on Charles Bridge and Na Příkopě – sell handmade goods, such as **marionettes** and costume **jewellery**, as well as quirky gift items, such as refrigerator magnets depicting famous Prague sites like Charles Bridge!

Classical music buffs can look forward to acquiring good quality and fairly inexpensive **CDs** in Prague, with the best deals to be had on music recorded by contemporary Czech musicians.

If you're looking for something typically Bohemian to take home as a gift, a Prague ham is a nice idea, but despite the fact that butcher's shops are numerous in the capital, authentic Prague ham is quite hard to find. It may prove less troublesome to get a bottle of the herbal liqueur Becherovka or some Slivovice. Fruity wines from Bohemia and Moravia will also be appreciated. Wooden toys and puppets make excellent gift items for children. Huge Christmas and Easter markets, selling appealing,

Glass & Crystal

On the whole, visitors can expect excellent deals in the glass, porcelain and crystal shops. Bohemian glass and china are held in high esteem throughout the world due to their exceptional quality and fair price. The choice does not vary dramatically, but the following shops have impressive selections, and shop assistants speak at least some English. Almost all of these shops will also deal with the care and shipping of your new items, for a fee.

Sklo Bohemia
Na Příkopě 17, Prague 1.
Tel: 2421 0574.
Crystalex
Malé nám. 6, Prague 1.
Tel: 2422 8459.
Český Křišťál
Jilská 10, Prague 1.
Tel: 266262.
Cristallino
Celetná 12, Prague 1.
Tel: 261265.

hand-crafted items, are held in the Old Town Square in season. The Havelská fruit and vegetable market, open year round on Havelská near Old Town Square, also sells interesting gift items.

Visitors preparing to head out for an extensive round of shopping should bear in mind that such an excursion can turn out to be fairly time-consuming. Shopping can really turn into a test of patience, especially at weekends when both tourists and Prague natives hit the streets. Taking this into account, it's a good idea to get your errands and shopping accomplished during the week and to reserve the weekend for visiting the interesting sights that the city has to offer.

Whatever you can't find in the centre of Prague, you can be sure you won't be able to find in any of the other city districts either. The following list of some of the special retail shops located in the centre should be of help to you in finding exactly what you're looking for.

Opening Times

Most speciality stores are open from 10am–6pm, although those in the centre, catering largely to the tourist trade, often remain open late almost year round.

On Saturdays most shops outside the centre close at noon or 1pm; shops in the centre, especially the department stores, may retain weekday hours on Saturday and Sunday as well.

Shopping Areas

The main commercial streets of Prague with dependably long hours year round are Václavské náměstí (Wenceslas Square) and Na Příkopě, but they are notoriously crowded into the bargain.

Some little streets of the Old Town, such as V Kolkovně, Dušní, Týnská, and Panská, have a number of exciting and unusual boutiques. The Týn Courtyard near the Old Town Square also has numerous little shops with wonderful gift items which are well worth exploring.

Antiques

If you are in search of good antiques, look for signs marked *Starožitnosti*; but be warned that it may be difficult to find bargains. The best area for antiques is the Old Town:

JHB Starožitnosti
Panská 1, Prague 1
Tel: 261425
Specialising in old clocks and pocket watches.
Antik Art Gallery
Maiselova 9, Prague 1
Tel: 231 9816
Art et Decoration
Pařížská 21, Prague 1
Tel: 2481 2086
Alma
Valentinská 7, Prague 1
Tel: 232 5865
Papillio
Ungelt 1, Prague 1
Tel: 2489 5454
This is a wonderful all-purpose antique shop, with lovely antique glass.

Bookshops

Big Ben Bookshop
Malá Štupartská 5, Prague 1
Tel: 231 8021
A plethora of recent and classic paperbacks in English, with strong drama, poetry and central European history sections. English-language newspapers and magazines, and a selection of maps and guides to Prague. Very helpful service.

The Globe Bookstore and Coffeehouse
Janovského 14, Prague 7
Tel: 6671 2610
This bookstore and coffee house is the expat hangout (*see page 276*) and there's enough to occupy a visitor for the entire day. Books, both new and used, cover everything from fiction and history to gender studies. In the back of the shop on the notice board you can read all the news of the American/English community. Prices for the invariably dog-eared used books, however, are high.

Knikupectví Franze Kafky
Old Town Square 12, Prague 1
Tel: 232 1454
Appealing, modern bookstore located on premises which long ago were occupied by Kafka's father. There is a small exhibit of photographs of the author and his family commemorates this fact. Meanwhile, the bookstore holds an impressive, multilingual selection of art books, fiction and nonfiction, as well as unusual postcards of Prague which can't be found elsewhere in the city. It also has a good CD selection.

Jan Kanzelsberger Nakladatelství
Václavské nám. 42, Prague 1
Tel: 2421 7335
Excellent, three-level bookstore on Wenceslas Square that sells a large selection of English-language books on the lowest level, and a fine array of CDs (Czech and foreign classical, jazz and folk) on the uppermost. Visitors in search of maps, including speciality hiking maps, should have no trouble (head for the back, on the lowest level). Art books are also a speciality. Staff may not speak English.

Kiwi-Svět map and průvodců
Jungmannova 23, Prague 1
Tel: 2494 8455
The "world of maps" sells just that. Lots of maps of other Czech towns and cities in particular.

Knihkupectví Fišer
Kaprova 10, Prague 1
Tel: 232 0733
A literary institution (Czech authors always have their book-signings here), this is the best place to find Czech literature and poetry.

Mega Books
Mánesova 79, Prague 2
Tel: 627 7770
Off the beaten track in Prague's leafy Vinohrady district, this English-language bookshop stocks mostly academic books and teaching materials. Adjacent bistro.

Department Stores

The department stores with the largest selection of goods (including gifts, fabric, clothes, shoes, perfume, groceries, travel accessories, stationery, electrical goods, books, etc.) are: **Bílá Labut'**, Prague 1, Na Poříčí 23; **Tesco**, Národní třída 26, Prague 1; and **Kotva**, Nám. Republiky 8, Prague 1.

Most large department stores have a supermarket in the basement; the one at Tesco is very good. A delicatessen shop to be particularly recommended is **Fruits de France**, Jindřišska 9, Prague 1.

Boutiques

Prague's most exclusive boutiques line the street of Pařížská, and you will also find a Versace outlet on Celetná at Týnská. However, the following shops feature Czech designers:

A+G Flora
Štěpánská 61, Prague 1
Beautiful clothes by Prague's best local designer, Helena Fejková.

Piano Boutique
Vinohradská 47, Prague 2
Clothes and handbags by a variety of local designers.

Delmas
Vodičkova 36, Prague 1
Czech-made leather handbags look as good as any from Italy.

Cosmetics & Perfumes

Besides proffering their perfumes and cosmetics, the following well known shops also provide facials, and other beauty treatments:

Christian Dior
Pařížská 7, Prague 1
Tel: 232 7382

Lancôme
Jungmannovo nám. 20, Prague 1
Tel: 2421 7189

Institut Orlane
Rybná 13, Prague 1
Tel: 2481 8518

Boutique Nina Ricci
Pařížská 4, Prague 1
Tel: 2481 0905

Yves Rocher
Vodičkova 15, Prague 1
Tel: 2494 6843

Jewellery

Art Décoratif
U Obecního domu, Prague 1
Tel: 2200 2350
Multi-faceted shop sells, among other things, glass jewellery inspired by the renowned Art Nouveau artist and designer Alfons Mucha.

Granát
Dlouhá 30, Prague 1
Tel: 231 5612
Specialising in garnet jewellery of all kinds. The selection of delicate earrings is especially nice.

Hair Salons

English-speaking hairdresser services include:

James & Monika Salon
Malá Štupartská 9, Prague 1
Tel: 2482 7373

California Hair
Tel: 301 9905.

Hat Shops

Model Praha Družstvo
Mikulandská 2, Prague 1
Tel: 2491 5831.

Music

AghaRTA Jazz Centrum
Krakovská 5
Prague 1
Great selection of jazz CDs.
Popron Megastore
Jungmannova 30
Prague 1
Everything imaginable.
Supraphon
Jungmannova 20
Prague 1
High-quality CDs, mostly classical
works by Czech musicians.
Bontonland
Václavské nám. 1
Prague 1
The closest Prague has to a Virgin
Megastore, located at the foot of
Wenceslas Square.

Handmade Toys

Lidová Řemesla
Jilská 22 & Mostecká 17,
Prague 1.
These two folk art shops offer
adorable wooden toys, lovely
home textiles, as well as original
holiday season ornaments.

Sports Equipment

Hudy Sport
Na Perštýně 14, Prague 1
Tel: 2421 8600
Strossmayerovo nám. 10, Prague 7
Tel: 879992
Slezská 8, Prague 2
Tel: 2423 7258
The best sporting equipment,
including everything for hiking,
camping and climbing, is in this
excellent chain of stores, operated
by a professional rock-climber.

Children

Children's Activities

Most children will probably enjoy
exploring Prague's treasures as
much as their parents will. For more
child-orientated activities, consider
the Toy Museum at Prague Castle,
or the zoo (near Troja château,
Prague 7, tel: 688 0480; open daily
9am–6pm).

The **Mirror Maze** on Petřín Hill
might be frightening to very young
children, but those over the age of
eight or so will probably love it. **St.
Matthew's Fair**, held annually in
March and April at Prague 7's
Výstaviště fairgrounds, is always a
hit with its bumper cars, roller
coaster and special sweets.

Black-light theatre, puppetry and
mime performances (*see page 279*)
are good for all ages.

What's On

To keep abreast of current
sports and games, keep an eye
on the sports pages of the
weekly English-language
newspaper *The Prague Post*.

Wax Museums

Prague has not one, but two wax
museums. No threat to Madame
Tussaud's, they still provide good
kitschy entertainment for slightly
older children.
Wax Museum Prague
Ul. 28. října 13, Prague 1
(near Můstek).
Open daily 10am–8pm.
**Pražské panoptikum (Prague Wax
Museum)**
Národní třída 25, Prague 1 (in the
passage). Open daily 10am–8pm.

Sport

Spectator Sports

Football

Regular, first-division matches are
held at the following venues, and
tickets are very cheap. But in
recent years, the games have been
attracting a rowdy following in the
British style, and fights are
disturbingly common.
Sparta Stadium
Milady Horákové 98, Prague 7
Tel: 2057 0323
The SK Sparta team tends to
dominate Czech football. Their team
colours are red, yellow and blue.
Slavia Stadium
U Slavie, Prague 10-Vršovice
Tel: 6731 1102
The SK Slavia team colours are red
and white; they are arch rivals to
Sparta, above.
Viktoria Žižkov Stadium
Seifertova, Prague 3-Žižkov.
Tel: 272277
The FK Viktoria Žižkov team tends
to lose a lot but has an ardently
loyal following.
Bohemians Praha Stadium
Vršovická 31, Prague 10
Tel: 722180
TJ Bohemians play in green and white.

Ice Hockey

The Czech Republic can proudly
claim many world-class hockey
players. Ticket prices to the games
are extremely low, and the quality
will not disappoint; these players
aspire to the big leagues.
HC Sparta Praha
Za elektrárnou 419 (not on the
same site as the football stadium,
above), Prague 1
Tel: 2423 2185
HC Slavia Praha
Vladivostocká 1460, Prague 10
Tel: 6731 1417

Horse Racing
The main track in the Czech Republic is in Pardubice, 110 km (65 miles) east of Prague (tel: 04/030096). It has races about ten times a year and hosts the grand Velká Pardubická Steeplechase on the second Sunday of each October.

A track closer to the city centre is **Chuchle**, Radotínská 69, Prague 5-Chuchle (tel: 543 091). Racing on the flat is held here almost year-round: gallop races in warm months; trots in spring and fall.

Participant Sports

Golf
Golf Club Praha
Plzeňská 215
Prague 5-Motol
Tel: 651 2464
Founded in 1926. An 18-hole golf course open year round, weather permitting; adjacent to the appropriately named Hotel Golf.
Erpet Golf Centrum
Strakonická 510, Prague 5
Tel: 545264
An indoor driving range open year round; pitching course and putting green, plus tennis courts.

Bowling
Bowling Club
Bořivojova 83
Prague 3
Tel: 279395 or 697 5289
Bowling and billiards daily.
Vršovický Bowling
Ruská 946
Prague 10
Tel: 7173 2371
Bowling alley, open daily from 3pm–midnight, located in a converted cinema.

Swimming
The modern five-star hotels, as well as the simpler AXA Hotel, below, have swimming pools and saunas which are open to non-guests as well as residents.
Podolí Stadium
Podolská 74, Prague 4
Tel: 6121 4343
The king of public swimming pools, open daily year-round. Three huge pools, one indoor, two outdoor, all maintained at 26°C (78°F), with sauna, steam bath and massages available. The waterslide in summer is fun for children.
YMCA
Na Poříčí 12, Prague 1
Tel: 2487 2111
Open from early morning through late evening. School groups take over during the weekdays.
AXA Hotel
Na Poříčí 40, Prague 1
Tel: 2481 2580

Ice Skating
HC Sparta Praha Malá hala (Výstaviště)
Winter Stadium (Zimní stadión), Prague 7
Tel: 371141
Not to be confused with the hockey rink in the same area, this smaller stadium has public skating from November to March.
Winter Stadium HC Praha
Na rozdílu 1
Prague 6-Dejvice
Tel: 362759
Nice rink for public skating, but only open Sundays, November to March.

Tennis
For years now, Czech tennis players, both men and women, have found themselves right at the top of the world rankings. Martina Navratilova is the most famous example, and Steffi Graf certainly owes much of her success to her Czech trainer Pavel Složil.

The **Prague Tennis Arena** on the island of Štvanice, the venue for Davis Cup and Grand Prix tournaments, is considered one of the best complexes in Europe. The important events are usually announced on huge billboards around the city.

For public tennis courts see the list below, or ask at PIS or Čedok for current information (*see page 265*).
Český Lawn Tennis Club
Štvanice Island
Prague 7
Tel: 232 4601
Hilton Atrium Hotel
Pobřežní 1
Prague 1
Tel: 248 1111
Two tennis courts as part of an extensive sports complex.
Erpet Golf Centrum
Strakonická 510
Prague 5
Tel: 545264
More than golf here: indoor and outdoor tennis courts, too.

Hiking

The Czech Republic is criss-crossed with well-marked, well-maintained hiking trails, many of which link heritage sights such as natural formations and/or castles and châteaux. Hiking maps are on sale in all the bookshops in the city centre.

The most appealing hiking day-trips from Prague include the Český ráj (Czech Paradise) region of forests and sandstone formations one-and-a-half hours north of Prague, and around Mělník. Longer journeys should be arranged in the Šumava forest, or in the region known as České Švýcarsko (Czech Switzerland).

Fitness Clubs

The best fitness clubs in Prague are in hotels, and are open to non-guests for a fee. The following have swimming pools as well.
Hotel Intercontinental
Nám. Curieových 43
Prague 1 (off Pařížská)
Tel: 2488 1111
Considered Prague's best fitness club, with high-tech equipment.
Hotel AXA
Na Poříčí 40
Prague 1
Tel: 2481 2580
The Cardio fitness room upstairs at the hotel offers very good facilities at fair prices for serious weight lifters. Can be humid in summer, as there is no air-conditioning.
Corinthian Towers Hotel
Kongresová 1, Prague 4
Tel: 6119 1111
Excellent facilities on the 25th and 26th floors (what views!), plus squash court.

Language

In the Czech language stress is always given to the first syllable.

Vowels:
Long vowels are indicated by an accent (the long u by an accent or small circle): á, é, í, ó, ú or ů and ý.
I and r can be pronounced as half vowels: Plzeň = Pilsen
ý long "e".
ou pronounced as in "show"
ě pronounced as in "yea"

Consonants:
č pronounced as in "church"
ř pronounced with a sibilant
š pronounced "sh"
ž pronounced like a "s" as in "pleasure"

Understanding Menus

The menus in many restaurants are usually written in two or more languages, and most waiters in Prague speak a little German or English. Nevertheless, here is a short list of most of the food and drink you're likely to encounter on a standard Prague menu.

Beverages
vídeňská káva Viennese coffee
Becherovka bitter herb cordial
čaj tea
černý čaj black tea
káva coffee
černá káva (Turecká) Turkish coffee
káva s mlékem coffee with milk
limonáda lemonade
pivo beer
malé pivo small beer
černé pivo dark beer
světlé pivo lager

točené pivo draught beer
slivovice slivovitz
víno wine
bílé víno white wine
červené víno red wine
voda water

Meat
bažant pheasant
biftek steak
drůbež poultry
guláš goulash
hovězí beef
hovězí pečeně roast beef
hovězí vařeně boiled beef
husa goose
kachna duck
kančí wild boar
králík rabbit
krocan turkey
kuře chicken
kuře smažené roast chicken
ledvinky kidneys
párky sausages
pečené roast meat
polévka dršťková tripe soup
rostěnka roast meat
salám sausage, salami
sekaná meat loaf
šunka ham
telecí veal
uzenina smoked meat
vepřová roast pork
zajíc hare
zvěřina game

Fish
kapr pečený baked carp
kapr smažený fried carp
kapr vařený boiled carp
pstruh trout
ryba fish
sardinky sardines
štika pike

Fruit and Vegetables
bramborák potato fritter
brambory potatoes
fazole beans
houby mushrooms
hruška pear
jablka apple
kapusta savoy cabbage
kaše bramborová mashed potatoes
knedlíky bramborové potato dumplings
knedlíky knedlíky ovocné fruit dumplings

kyselé zelí sauerkraut
meruňky apricots
mrkev carrots
ovoce fruit
rajčata tomato
salát salad
třešně cherries
zelenina vegetables

Miscellaneous
buchty sweet cakes
chléb bread
bílý chléb white bread
černý chléb brown bread
cukr sugar
houska roll
houskové bread dumplings
máslo butter
ořechy nuts
palačinky thin pancakes
pečivo biscuits
polévka soup
rýže rice
sladký sweet
slaný salty
topinky toast
vejce na měkko soft boiled egg
vejce na tvrdo hard boiled egg
zmrzlina ice cream

Useful Vocabulary

dámy, ženy ladies, women
muži men
kavárna coffee house
restaurace restaurant
hostinec; pivnice; hospoda pub
vinárna wine bar
snídaně breakfast
oběd lunch
večeře supper
volno free
obsazeno occupied
stůl table
židle chair
nůž knife
vidlička fork
lžíce spoon
talíř plate
sklenice glass
číšník waiter
vrchní head waiter
servírka waitress
ubrousek serviette
jídelní lístek menu
specialita speciality
párátko toothpick

Further Reading

Franz Kafka

Amerika by Franz Kafka (translated by W. and E. Muir), Penguin Modern Classics. Kafka's tale of a young boy exiled from his European home and his misadventures on his own in the New World. It was originally entitled *The Man Who Disappeared*, but later renamed *Amerika* by his literary executor, Max Brod. The first chapter, "The Stoker", was first published as a short story – the only part of any of Kafka's three novels to make it into print during his lifetime. This early work has been compared to the novels of Charles Dickens, and Kafka himself admitted the influence.

The Trial by Franz Kafka (translated by W. and E. Muir), Penguin Modern Classics. Probably the best-known of Kafka's works (along with the novella *The Metamorphosis*), *The Trial* tells the story of Josef K. who is arrested, accused and tried – but no one will tell him the charge. The story of his long and ultimately futile struggle against an incomprehensible legal system no doubt was influenced by Kafka's own profession as a lawyer for a government insurance company of the Austro-Hungarian empire.

The Castle by Franz Kafka (translated by W. and E. Muir), Penguin Modern Classics. In Kafka's great unfinished, final novel the protagonist, simply called K., arrives in a strange town on page one, and spends the rest of the book attempting to gain entry into an impenetrable castle. His progress is blocked, not by armed guards, but by an endless tangle of red tape, inept bureaucrats and corrupt officials. Some interpret this tale as an allegory for man's search for enlightenment; but there isn't too much that is uplifting in this relentlessly frustrating story that ends, literally, in mid-sentence.

Description of a Struggle and other stories by Franz Kafka (translated by W. and E. Muir), Penguin Modern Classics. Kafka's early short stories show the flashes of genius that would be given its full measure in his novels. Of special interest are the descriptions of Prague, local references of a kind that do not appear in his later works.

Diaries by Franz Kafka (translated by W. and E. Muir), Penguin Modern Classics. This collection of Kafka's private musings, ideas for stories and recordings of daily events provides a rich insight into the author's life. However, as Kafka tended to turn to his diary when he was depressed, a good companion piece is *Letters to Friends, Family and Editors*, which shows the author as witty, ironic and charming.

Other Classic Literature

The Engineer of Human Souls by Josef Škvorecký (translated by Paul Wilson), Picador. Powerful fictional tirade against the Communist régime; it also explores expatriate life in Toronto, the destination of many Czech émigrés after the 1968 Warsaw Pact Invasion.

The Good Soldier Švejk by Jaroslav Hašek (translated by Sir C. Parrot), Heinemann. This irreverent and very funny classic of Czech literature relates the misadventures of Josef Švejk – an unwilling conscript into the Austrian army – and his efforts to avoid being sent to the front through smiling, servile sabotage.

Too Loud a Solitude by Bohumil Hrabal (translated by Michael Henry Heins), Harcourt Brace Jovanovich. The melancholy story of a paper-shredder who tries to save the books he loves but which he should be destroying in his job.

Prague Chronicles by Ludvík Vaculík (translated by G. Theiner), Readers International.

Selected Poetry by Jaroslav Seifert (translated by E. Osers), André Deutsch. Poems by a winner of the Nobel Prize for Literature.

Tales of the Little Quarter by Jan Neruda (translated by Michael Henry Heim), Central European University Press. Stories of people and places in Malá Strana.

Other Insight Guides

Apa Publications has assembled a matchless range of books designed to cater for the different needs of different types of traveller. The main series of 190 Insight Guides provides an in-depth cultural background to countries, cities and regions throughout the world, with incisive text paired with the world's top travel photography.

Insight Guide: Czech and Slovak Republics, a companion book to the present one, provides full coverage of both countries, with maps, full listings and stunning photography. Other titles include Hungary, Budapest, Berlin, Poland and Eastern Europe.

Insight Pocket Guides
Apa publishes more than 100 Insight Pocket Guides, each containing carefully selected personal recommendations for people with limited time to spare. Many titles in the series contain a full-size fold-out map.

Insight Pocket Guide: Prague contains three full-day itineraries, seven "pick and mix" shorter itineraries, four excursions to towns and sights outside the city, plus sections on nightlife, shopping, eating out and special events.

Compact Guides
Each of the books in this new series is designed to act as a handy mini-encyclopedia – portable yet comprehensive, and both readable and reliable.

Prague is also represented in the Compact series, as are two other popular destinations, **Budapest** and **Vienna**. Each book contains an easy-reference guide to the city plus more than 200 colour photographs.

ART & PHOTO CREDITS

INSIGHT GUIDE
PRAGUE

Cartographic Editor **Zoë Goodwin**
Production **Stuart A Everitt**
Design Consultants
Carlotta Junger, Graham Mitchener
Picture Research **Hilary Genin, Britta Jaschinsky**

Index

Numbers in italics refer to photographs

6 6 I was first drawn to the
Insight Guides by the
excellent "Nepal" volume.
I can think of no book
which so effectively
captures the essence of
a country. Out of these
pages leaped the Nepal
I know – the captivating
charm of a people and
their culture. I've since
discovered and enjoyed
the entire Insight Guide
series. Each volume deals
with a country in the
same sensitive depth,
which is nowhere more
evident than in the
superb photography. 9 9

Sir Edmund Hillary

The World of Insight Guides

400 books in three complementary series cover every major destination in every continent.

Insight Guides

Alaska
Alsace
Amazon Wildlife
American Southwest
Amsterdam
Argentina
Atlanta
Athens
Australia
Austria
Bahamas
Bali
Baltic States
Bangkok
Barbados
Barcelona
Bay of Naples
Beijing
Belgium
Belize
Berlin
Bermuda
Boston
Brazil
Brittany
Brussels
Budapest
Buenos Aires
Burgundy
Burma (Myanmar)
Cairo
Calcutta
California
Canada
Caribbean
Catalonia
Channel Islands
Chicago
Chile
China
Cologne
Continental Europe
Corsica
Costa Rica
Crete
Crossing America
Cuba
Cyprus
Czech & Slovak Republics
Delhi, Jaipur, Agra
Denmark
Dresden
Dublin
Düsseldorf
East African Wildlife
East Asia
Eastern Europe
Ecuador
Edinburgh
Egypt
Finland
Florence
Florida
France
Frankfurt
French Riviera
Gambia & Senegal
Germany
Glasgow

Gran Canaria
Great Barrier Reef
Great Britain
Greece
Greek Islands
Hamburg
Hawaii
Hong Kong
Hungary
Iceland
India
India's Western Himalaya
Indian Wildlife
Indonesia
Ireland
Israel
Istanbul
Italy
Jamaica
Japan
Java
Jerusalem
Jordan
Kathmandu
Kenya
Korea
Lisbon
Loire Valley
London
Los Angeles
Madeira
Madrid
Malaysia
Mallorca & Ibiza
Malta
Marine Life in the South
  China Sea
Melbourne
Mexico
Mexico City
Miami
Montreal
Morocco
Moscow
Munich
Namibia
Native America
Nepal
Netherlands
New England
New Orleans
New York City
New York State
New Zealand
Nile
Normandy
Northern California
Northern Spain
Norway
Oman & the UAE
Oxford
Old South
Pacific Northwest
Pakistan
Paris
Peru
Philadelphia
Philippines
Poland
Portugal
Prague

Provence
Puerto Rico
Rajasthan
Rhine
Rio de Janeiro
Rockies
Rome
Russia
St Petersburg
San Francisco
Sardinia
Scotland
Seattle
Sicily
Singapore
South Africa
South America
South Asia
South India
South Tyrol
Southeast Asia
Southeast Asia Wildlife
Southern California
Southern Spain
Spain
Sri Lanka
Sweden
Switzerland
Sydney
Taiwan
Tenerife
Texas
Thailand
Tokyo
Trinidad & Tobago
Tunisia
Turkey
Turkish Coast
Tuscany
Umbria
US National Parks East
US National Parks West
Vancouver
Venezuela
Venice
Vienna
Vietnam
Wales
Washington DC
Waterways of Europe
Wild West
Yemen

Insight Pocket Guides

Aegean Islands★
Algarve★
Alsace
Amsterdam★
Athens★
Atlanta★
Bahamas★
Baja Peninsula★
Bali★
Bali Bird Walks
Bangkok★
Barbados★
Barcelona★
Bavaria★
Beijing★
Berlin★

Bermuda★
Bhutan★
Boston★
British Columbia★
Brittany★
Brussels★
Budapest &
  Surroundings★
Canton★
Chiang Mai★
Chicago★
Corsica★
Costa Blanca★
Costa Brava★
Costa del Sol/Marbella★
Costa Rica★
Crete★
Denmark★
Fiji★
Florence★
Florida★
Florida Keys★
French Riviera★
Gran Canaria★
Hawaii★
Hong Kong★
Hungary
Ibiza★
Ireland★
Ireland's Southwest★
Israel★
Istanbul★
Jakarta★
Jamaica★
Kathmandu Bikes &
  Hikes★
Kenya★
Kuala Lumpur★
Lisbon★
Loire Valley★
London★
Macau★
Madrid★
Malacca
Maldives
Mallorca★
Malta★
Mexico City★
Miami★
Milan★
Montreal★
Morocco★
Moscow
Munich★
Nepal★
New Delhi
New Orleans★
New York City★
New Zealand★
Northern California★
Oslo/Bergen★
Paris★
Penang★
Phuket★
Prague★
Provence★
Puerto Rico★
Quebec★
Rhodes★
Rome★
Sabah★

St Petersburg★
San Francisco★
Sardinia
Scotland★
Seville★
Seychelles★
Sicily★
Sikkim
Singapore★
Southeast England
Southern California★
Southern Spain★
Sri Lanka★
Sydney★
Tenerife★
Thailand★
Tibet★
Toronto★
Tunisia★
Turkish Coast★
Tuscany★
Venice★
Vienna★
Vietnam★
Yogyakarta
Yucatan Peninsula★

**★ = Insight Pocket Guides
with Pull out Maps**

Insight Compact Guides

Algarve
Amsterdam
Bahamas
Bali
Bangkok
Barbados
Barcelona
Beijing
Belgium
Berlin
Brittany
Brussels
Budapest
Burgundy
Copenhagen
Costa Brava
Costa Rica
Crete
Cyprus
Czech Republic
Denmark
Dominican Republic
Dublin
Egypt
Finland
Florence
Gran Canaria
Greece
Holland
Hong Kong
Ireland
Israel
Italian Lakes
Italian Riviera
Jamaica
Jerusalem
Lisbon
Madeira
Mallorca
Malta

Milan
Moscow
Munich
Normandy
Norway
Paris
Poland
Portugal
Prague
Provence
Rhodes
Rome
St Petersburg
Salzburg
Singapore
Switzerland
Sydney
Tenerife
Thailand
Turkey
Turkish Coast
Tuscany
UK regional titles:
  Bath & Surroundings
  Cambridge & East
    Anglia
  Cornwall
  Cotswolds
  Devon & Exmoor
  Edinburgh
  Lake District
  London
  New Forest
  North York Moors
  Northumbria
  Oxford
  Peak District
  Scotland
  Scottish Highlands
  Shakespeare Country
  Snowdonia
  South Downs
  York
  Yorkshire Dales
USA regional titles:
  Boston
  Cape Cod
  Chicago
  Florida
  Florida Keys
  Hawaii: Maui
  Hawaii: Oahu
  Las Vegas
  Los Angeles
  Martha's Vineyard &
    Nantucket
  New York
  San Francisco
  Washington D.C.
  Venice
  Vienna
  West of Ireland